More praise for

A Family and Friend's Guide to Sexual Orientation

"This book is a delightful and poignant eye-opener and a much needed, frank discussion about the barriers many face before fully accepting gay and lesbian family members and friends. By talking to people about their attitudes toward gays and lesbians, Powers and Ellis pull out universal lessons about life, coping, understanding, compassion and acceptance. One day we won't need a book to remind us to 'keep an open mind and value diversity.' Powers and Ellis have made an important contribution in moving us to a more accepting, less judgmental future."
—Julianne Malveaux
Economist/Columnist
Pacific Radio

*"**A Family and Friend's Guide** will win over people's hearts and minds. Powers and Ellis present the lives of real people from a wide range of backgrounds, and give us a powerful look at the impact of sexual orientation on our families."*
—Helen Zia
Contributing Editor, MS. Magazine

*"Like panels of the AIDS Memorial Quilt, the personal histories described in **A Family and Friend's Guide** will soften hard hearts and open closed minds. In describing the experiences of a broad cross-section of the American public, Powers and Ellis' book offers effective tools and strategies for helping us all to fulfill our God-given responsibilities to nurture more caring relationships and embrace a new, more inclusive society."*
—Anthony Turney
Executive Director
The NAMES Project

A Family and Friend's Guide
to Sexual Orientation

A Family and Friend's Guide to Sexual Orientation

BOB POWERS
ALAN ELLIS

Routledge
New York and London

Published in 1996 by
Routledge
29 West 35th Street
New York, NY 10001

Published in Great Britain by
Routledge
11 New Fetter Lane
London EC4P 4EE

Library of Congress Cataloging-in-Publication Data

Powers, Bob, 1941—
A family and friend's guide to sexual orientation / Bob Powers
and Alan Ellis.
    p.   cm.
Includes bibliographical references.
ISBN 0–415-91275–X (alk. paper)   ISBN 0–415–91276–8 (pb.)
    1. Gays.   2. Lesbians.   3. Sexual orientation.   4. Attitudes.
5. Diversity.   6. Gays—Case studies.   7. Lesbians—Case studies.
8. Family issues.   I. Ellis, Alan, 1957— .   II. Title.

HD6285.P69   1995   95-23654
658.3'045—dc20   CIP

This book is dedicated to our respective friends,
Paul Edward Johnson and Eric Bean,
who have enriched our lives,
and to Courtney Powers,
whose youthful wisdom is
a lesson in acceptance
for all people.

Contents

Acknowledgments

There are many people we would like to thank for their support in developing this book, most especially the authors of the stories. Without their courage and remarkable portraits, this book would not exist.

In addition, we would like to thank Dennis De Biase for introducing us to our wonderful editor, Cecelia Cancellaro, Laurie Harper of the Sebastian Agency for her support and encouragement, and Robert Mitchell and Chris O'Sullivan for their editing suggestions. We would also like to thank the many staff at Routledge who have worked hard to support our books. Thank you Paul, Darren, Amy-Lynn, Adam, Rob, Kim, Vickie, Claudia, and Charles.

Getting Started
The Road from the Closet Door
to the Magic Line

THE HETEROSEXUAL CLOSET

While many of us are well aware of the proverbial closet door with which gays, lesbians, and bisexuals have contended, few people are conscious of the impact those closets have on heterosexuals and fewer still know that heterosexuals—families and friends of sexual minorities—face a heterosexual closet door.

> **Closet: a perceived place of hiding (one's sexual orientation or the sexual orientation of a loved one).**

This closet contains the same dark emotions—fear, terror, dread—that initially crippled and ultimately led lesbians and gays to fling their closet doors open in a quest for self-acceptance. For most heterosexuals, the closet is terrifying.

> When I told my mom I was gay, I realized that while that step was one step on my journey of self-acceptance, for my mom, it was one step into her own private hell—her closet. How can I possibly tell anybody, she asked? [I'm so ashamed.]

Family and friends, upon learning that a loved one is gay, lesbian or bisexual, are immediately thrown into a process of "coming out" as a parent, a child, a spouse, a friend—similar to the process gone through by any sexual minority.

> **Coming Out: the act of telling another person about your sexual orientation.**

It's not unlike the process that anybody faces when they are hiding—whether it be an addiction, a sick family member, or an abundant inheritance. Hiding takes its toll! And, heterosexuals need to learn how to fling open their closet doors. They too need to "come out"—to go through the steps of self-acceptance. Yet, when it comes to sexual orientation, most families have adopted a U.S. Military-like policy of "DON'T ASK, DON'T TELL." In other words, "I won't ask if you're gay and I don't want you to tell me if you are." This approach has a disastrous effect on family life for it completely destroys any chance of an intimate family relationship.

IN THE CLOSET: OUR TOP TEN FEARS

So why do so many families fall victim to such a situation that decreases the possibility of family intimacy? The answer lies in fear. A DON'T ASK, DON'T TELL family develops out of our fears. Here are ten fears that keep families closeted.

1) **Fear of personal shame.**
   Our culture and many of its institutions send negative messages about homosexuality, and, as a result, many gays and heterosexuals experience shame about either being gay or having a relative or friend who is gay. These feelings of shame come from our having internalized these negative messages.

2) **Fear of public embarrassment or social ostracism.**
   In light of the negative stereotypes and the shame that have been associated with homosexuality, gays and heterosexuals alike fear public ridicule or ostracism when one's homosexuality or that of a loved one is revealed.

3) **Fear of being labeled as "not normal."**
   In many ways this fear is the result of the personal shame and public embarrassment that lead us to feel that we do not "fit in." Many people tend to seek others' approval, which leads them to act in conforming ways so as to appear "normal." The fear of being labeled as "not normal" is very real.

4) **Fear of discussing unpleasant or sexual topics within the family.**
   Many families have difficulty communicating about serious matters and avoid discussion of all topics that create discomfort. Often, sexuality is one such topic. The hiding or ignoring of significant aspects of family members' lives, however, often leads to a complete breakdown in family communication.

5) **Fear of loss of family and friends.**
   One of the most predominate fears many people experience is that

talking about sexual orientation will lead family and friends to disown or abandon them. This fear of loss will cause many people to remain closeted.

6) **Fear of confusion about one's own sexuality.**
Any deviation from perceived norms can lead one to experience confusion about his or her own sexuality. This can be disturbing. Because of our culture's conflicting messages about sexuality, it is not surprising that all of us, at some time or another, find ourselves confused about our sexuality—it is part of normal psychological development.

7) **Fear of violence.**
Every day there are numerous attacks on gays and lesbians simply because of their sexual orientation. In some cases, these attacks are extended to heterosexuals who support and love gay people. Such attacks are often the result of another person's insecurities and confusion about his or her own sexuality. Whatever the cause, however, this is a fear that families face in coming out on this issue.

8) **Fear of being "hit upon."**
During the DON'T ASK, DON'T TELL military hearings, many soldiers expressed fear that, *if gays were allowed into the military* (they are already there in large numbers), they would be subject to sexual advances and morale would suffer. For most gays and lesbians, making a sexual advance towards a heterosexual is akin to going to a hardware store to buy a loaf of bread.

9) **Fear of economic or job discrimination.**
This fear can create tremendous challenges for gays and straights alike to come out at work about their own sexual orientation or that of a loved one. Discrimination occurs (as you will read in Lisa Busjahn's story) and the fear of losing one's job often means that coming out at work is one of the last stages in most people's road to acceptance. In several of the life histories, you will see how coming out at work actually led to greater security and financial success.

10) **Fear of AIDS.**
Because of misinformation about AIDS and the association of AIDS with the gay community, some people fear that contact with gays puts them at risk for contracting the disease. This is simply inaccurate. Unless one engages in intimate sexual contact, sharing needles, or some other activity that results in blood-to-blood contact, there is no possibility of contracting the disease. It is not transmitted through casual contact. The virus does not discriminate on the basis of sexual orientation—it hasn't a clue as to whether you are gay or straight.

The preceding ten fears represent some of the more obvious fears that keep people in the closet. Ultimately, we all have the opportunity to both acknowledge and face these fears and then to make choices that will help us move towards greater acceptance and a DO ASK, DO TELL family environment.

THE CHOICES GAY AND STRAIGHT PEOPLE FACE

In a DON'T ASK, DON'T TELL household, the gay or lesbian family member has no choice but to:

1) **Force the issue out into the open.**
2) **Distance him/herself from the family.**
3) **Hide her/his true self.**

Few children have the tools to effectively force the issue. So, most kids distance themselves from their family—often moving or running away to places where they can live openly. Others remain and keep their life hidden from their family members. Any of these alternatives can create huge rifts in family relationships. Forcing the issue often results in blow ups; distancing and hiding contribute to building a closet of self-hate and low self-worth. All three options result in a loss of intimacy among family members. So when family members question if the closet has any effect on heterosexuals, they can know that the answer is a *resounding* YES. The closet contributes to and ensures the destruction of intimate, loving family relationships.

> Peter's parents were ready to celebrate their fiftieth wedding anniversary. Peter's family operated in a DON'T ASK, DON'T TELL environment. They all *knew* that Peter was gay but...Peter's siblings met to plan a surprise anniversary celebration for their parents. Peter was not invited to the planning session. During the session they became worried that Peter might bring a lover. "What would people say?" one of the sisters asked, and they all concluded that it would be unfair to the parents to force them to deal with this issue on such a wonderful occasion as their fiftieth wedding anniversary. So, they canceled the celebration.

Variations of this scenario occur in every DON'T ASK, DON'T TELL family. Straight people face choices too. Families and friends have three basic choices they can make when it comes to the issue of a loved one's sexual orientation.

1) **They can fight it.**
2) **They can accept it.**
3) **They can prepare for it.**

Fighting and accepting are reactionary. Preparing for the possibility that someone in their family might be gay is visionary. Let's look at each of these options.

Denial is probably the most common form of fighting it. "Oh, John isn't gay, why, he dated Sally just last week." Or, "It's just a phase, she'll be through it in no time." Sometimes the denial is strong—"There's *never* been a homosexual in this family and I can guarantee you there never will be, not so long as I'm alive." Sometimes the fight is life-threatening.

Timmy lived in New Orleans. One afternoon, his parents took him to one of the city's finest restaurants. He was enjoying the lighthearted conversation when his father abruptly changed the subject and asked, "Are you a homosexual?"

Until then he had always lied to his parents about his homosexuality. He was tired of lying. He loved his parents and wanted desperately to include them in his life. He had wondered if maybe it was possible to tell them the truth. He concluded he had to tell them. So he did. He told them the truth.

"Yes, I am gay," he said in response to his father's query. With that pronouncement, his father began to pound on the table; his mother screamed. He felt as if he were in a dream. Before he was able to collect his thoughts, his parents had stood up and stormed out of the restaurant. He sat alone in silence, with dozens of disapproving strangers and the bill. He went home and cried.

Two days later, his doorbell rang. He opened the door to face his mother and father along with every other adult member of his family. Among them was a stranger. He started to welcome them when the stranger grabbed him and pinned him down. The stranger thrust forward at him with a hypodermic needle and injected him with something. Timmy lost consciousness. Three days later he woke in a drugged trance in what appeared to be a hospital room. Standing over him was a wildly ranting preacher demanding the devil leave the body and soul of this young man. Behind the preacher he could make out the outlines of each member of his family.

As he told this story, Timmy seemed nervous and forlorn. He said, "I'm telling you this because I'm afraid. You see, this happened several years ago and shortly after, I moved several thousand miles away. No one in my family has ever mentioned it and I have not seen my parents since." And then he added, "Tomorrow they are coming to visit me and I'm afraid they'll kidnap me again."

Timmy's story illustrates the extent to which some families fight rather than accept the sexual orientation of a loved one. While Timmy's story may not be common, unfortunately, it is not rare. Many families, out of ignorance, are conned into believing that sexual orientation is a choice that can be changed. Compare Timmy's story with the acceptance exhibited in the next story.

Carol first came to San Francisco in the late seventies, at the peak of the feminist movement. She was seventeen and a budding activist. With her best friend, Ruth, both of whom considered themselves heterosexuals, Carol became involved in fighting the anti-gay Briggs Initiative. "Since Ruth and I were both attracted to men we often said if we were men we'd want to be gay men," she says laughing. "Frankly, it never dawned on either of us that we might be lesbians." Over time, Carol received numerous letters from various family members living in Los Angeles concerned about her activities. Her mom constantly asked, "Are you a lesbian?" "No," replied Carol, "I'm not a lesbian." Her grandfather wrote, saying, "If any woman comes up to you, you just pull back, punch her in the face, then turn around and run like hell."

A few years later, Carol moved to Columbus, Ohio, to attend graduate school. She was as surprised as anyone to find herself attracted to a woman and after some time came to accept that she *was* a lesbian. She called her friend Ruth, who accepted her completely. She then wrote her mom. "You were right all along," she penned—assuming that her mother would easily accept her newly declared sexual orientation. It was several years later, in the midst of an argument, that she learned differently. Her mom yelled at her. "How dare you be judgmental when you're living the kind of deviant, bizarre lifestyle you live," she said. Carol was shaken.

As fate would have it, her mom's best friend of ten years announced that she too was a lesbian. "My mom stuck by her friend Vicki. They're still best friends today. My mom was even in her wedding to another woman, if you can imagine that. She's learned a lot. She's changed," Carol said.

Nothing depicts that change more than Carol's last visit to see her mom and Duane, her mom's longtime boyfriend. They sat Carol down and her mom said, "Honey, we're so proud of you" (Carol had been selected to speak at an international health care conference). Duane added, "We know, with your studies and all, you don't have much money." Her mom continued, "We gave both of your sisters money for their weddings and since you won't have a wedding..." She caught herself and quickly added, "unless, of course, you want to. Anyway, we want to give you the same money we gave to each of your sisters, to use for your trip to Spain or however you like. We love you," she concluded.

As you read through this book, you will see more stories of people who have come to acceptance through gay friends, then applied that acceptance to family members.

Finally, some families have prepared themselves for the possibility that a member of their family may be gay.

Dexter is a young, black man with five brothers. The middle child, he was eighteen when his mother said to him, "Honey, I had a dream about you. In the dream you were having relationships with men. I mentioned this to your dad and we think that you may be gay." She paused and added, "And, that's okay with us. We love you and will do whatever we can to support you." Dexter went into a state of shock. With his head reeling, he blurted out, "I'm not gay." His mom responded, "That's okay, we just want you to know that if you are gay, we'll be there for you."

Dexter did know he was gay, but he just couldn't bring himself to tell his family. He was simply too scared. A few days later Dexter was in the family room watching an episode of the Phil Donahue show that featured a panel of gays and lesbians talking about the film "Paris is Burning" (which is about gay men). During the show, Dexter's father walked into the room. Flushed with embarrassment (as if he had been caught in a lie) Dexter reached for the remote control to switch channels when the mother of one of the panelists said, "My son is gay; I love him and his being gay simply doesn't matter." At that, Dexter's father said, in a voice strong and proud, "That's right!" It took a moment before Dexter realized that his father wanted him to hear what he had just said. Dexter turned to look at him, but his father was already gone. "I sat and cried, not because I was gay, but because I was lying to the two people I love more than anyone else in the world and because, at the same time, I was happy that my being gay was okay with my dad."

Shortly afterwards, he told his family he was gay. They told him they loved him. "My brothers used to stand up to the kids that would make homophobic comments," he said. "They were ready and willing to fight for me. I can hardly believe how accepting my family has been. I'm twenty-two now and feel nothing but love for all of them and know, without a doubt, that they love me."

MY FAMILY—IN OR OUT OF THE CLOSET?

At this point you may wish to examine where you are as a family or as a friend. How honest do you feel you are with other family members? Are there things you would like to discuss but feel you cannot bring up because it would be uncomfortable? What might be the costs associated with your denying yourself the opportunity to discuss these issues. Could your family have a sane and healthy discussion about sexual orientation—including an honest appraisal of the fears and concerns each has about the topic? With these questions in mind we would now like to take you through the four stages of acceptance.

THE STAGES OF ACCEPTANCE

Just as the experience of the closet is similar for all, regardless of their sexual orientation, so are the stages of acceptance. It doesn't matter if you're gay, straight, bisexual or transgender, nor does it matter if you're talking about accepting yourself for who you are or accepting others for who they are—you will go through a similar process. That process begins with admitting to yourself; then admitting to others, first privately and then publicly; and finally, it includes taking action. Let's examine these four stages of acceptance.

1) **Admit to Yourself.**
   Admitting to yourself that a loved one is lesbian, gay or bisexual is the first stage on the path to acceptance. For many, especially those who have lived years in denial, this is a huge breakthrough. This breakthrough is often, initially, accompanied by confusion and uncertainty, but it is also the beginning of self-acceptance and empowerment. You'll see this breakthrough in most of the stories in this guide.

2) **Admit to Others Privately.**
   Admitting to others privately is the second stage of acceptance. This step usually involves telling close friends and loved ones. This stage, like many others, is often filled with fear. But it is also an act that leads to an improved sense of self-worth and awareness that being who one is, rather than what others think one should be, is the foundation of feeling empowered.

3) **Admit to Others Publicly.**
   Admitting to others publicly is the third stage of acceptance. In this stage, you begin to "out yourself" at work and in other public areas. For those concerned with their financial livelihood, coming out at work can be a terrifying step. At the same time, coming out publicly begins to give people a sense of the power of accepting themselves, a power you'll see depicted in all the stories in this guide.

4) **Take Action.**
   Taking action is the fourth stage of acceptance. Coming out is not something one does one time only. It's actually a process of coming

out over and over again. The more one "comes out" and takes action, the more one experiences self-acceptance as well as acceptance of others. You'll find a detailed list of actions you can take when you read "101 Steps on the Road to Acceptance" in Chapter 5.

You'll see each of these stages in most of the stories of gays, lesbians, bisexuals, transgenders and heterosexuals in this book—from the eighteen-year-old daughter of one of the authors who "comes out" to her boyfriend about having a gay father, to the southern, Latino, religious heterosexual dad who "comes out" as the father of a gay man in his hometown newspaper.

A *Family and Friend's Guide* will help you understand the process of coming out and ease you along this path to self acceptance.

THE MAGIC LINE

The early stages of the road to acceptance are riddled with dark emotions like fear, dread and terror. At some point along this road, you will cross a line where no longer do you fear telling people that you're gay or that you have a lesbian daughter, a bisexual spouse or a transgender friend. At that point, which we call the "magic line," you will experience joy, love, peace and serenity. You will realize how courageous, loving and compassionate you are and you'll experience a sense of pride and, perhaps, a kind of beautiful sadness or amusement for all the time it took you to get where you are. Finally, you will experience gratitude that you are there now. Your path has been irrevocably changed, and you will never look at another person with the same fear that you once experienced. Crossing the magic line will fill you with power and self-love.

As you read the stories in this book you'll see the magic line crossed over and over again. Whether the storyteller is gay, lesbian, straight, bisexual or transgender makes no difference. Accepting ourselves and others as we are is powerful and loving. The more you can learn about the lesbian, gay and bisexual community, the faster this road to acceptance will be. So, let's become familiar with this community.

GETTING FAMILIAR WITH THE LESBIAN, GAY, AND BISEXUAL COMMUNITY

Many gays and lesbians will tell you that they possess "gaydar," an intuitive ability to spot other gays and lesbians. Few heterosexuals claim this ability. So, how do you know if someone is gay? Frankly, you can't know unless they tell you or provide a clear signal. The lesbian, gay and bisexual community signal you in many ways.

Many gays, lesbians and bisexuals make it easy for you. They speak openly of their sexual identity and generally are quite willing to help you know more about them and the community. Others will do anything to cover up their sexual orientation, and it is almost impossible to get to know this group. A third and fairly large group will talk about their sexual orientation only if asked. If not asked, they generally remain mute (which requires considerable conscious effort and energy). However, this group often display signs or send signals that are intended to open the door to those who will ask. Understanding these signs and signals requires you to know more about the community.

To begin, the symbol of gay pride is the rainbow flag. This red, orange, yellow, green, blue and lavender striped flag symbolizes the diversity in the gay community. It flies from rooftops and is displayed on bumper stickers, lapel pins, and often in the office. (The next time you take a road trip, look for rainbow flags on car bumpers—you'll be surprised by how many you see).

When you see a rainbow flag you can safely assume that whoever is displaying the flag is gay or lesbian or a friend or relative of a gay person. Acknowledging that you recognize the flag is an excellent way to start conversation.

Another symbol is the pink triangle. The triangle represents the patch that gay men were forced to wear in Nazi concentration camps during World War II (lesbians were forced to wear a black triangle). This symbol has deep meaning to gays and lesbians around the world because it depicts the extreme oppression sexual minorities have faced. This symbol is worn today not only as a reminder of that oppression but as a statement that all oppression and hatred must end.

There are many other symbols. At some workplaces, many employees (gay and straight alike) post "Safe Place" stickers in visible spots in their offices. These stickers display the pink triangle in a green circle and communicate that this is a safe place to talk. The new DO ASK, DO TELL stickers, available from most bookstores or by calling 1–800 DO ASK DO, in effect, say the same thing. Ask your openly gay and lesbian relatives and friends about these and other symbols. It's another excellent way to open up dialogue in this area.

The gay and lesbian community sponsors a number of celebrations and rituals. For example, most sexual minorities celebrate "Gay Pride Day," usually held in the latter half of June. The week-long celebration culminates in Gay Pride parades and marches around the world in places from Sydney, Australia, to Boise, Idaho. For sexual minorities, it is a time to celebrate, not just their sexual orientation, but their courage at coming out despite the oppression they have experienced. These marches draw thousands of people in small towns across the continent and hundreds of thousands in major cities throughout the world. Gay Pride Day honors the Stonewall riots, which occurred in New York City in 1969. On June 25 of that year, sexual minorities (mostly drag queens and lesbians) fought off a police raid of a local bar in Greenwich Village. This rebellion brought people of all sexual orientations together. In honor of the twenty-fifth anniversary of Stonewall, over one million people marched down New York's Fifth Avenue in June of 1994. Also celebrated at the same time were the Gay Games— an event of Olympian proportion (the event at which Greg Louganis "came out" as a gay man). Over 22,000 athletes from around the world partic- ipated in these games.

There are hundreds of events like Australia's gay Mardi Gras that attract hundreds of thousands of people annually. These events create sizable business opportunities, as well as a wonderful celebration of freedom and liberation.

Gays and lesbians stay well connected to these and other events through their networks of gay newspapers (there is one or more in most cities around the world) and organizations. There are thousands of social, cultural, political and support groups like gay and lesbian choruses, gay returned Peace Corps volunteers, gay teachers groups, gay police associations and so on. These groups exist in our largest cities and smallest towns. In areas where sexual minorities worry about their safety, these groups often do not use the words "gay" or "lesbian" in their titles, substituting instead terms related to the community such as "pride," "triangle," "lambda" and so forth.

Additionally, there are hundreds of religious and spiritual groups which attend to the spiritual needs of lesbians and gays—groups such as Dignity (Catholic) and Affirmation (Mormons). There are also local and regional business groups like the Lesbian and Gay Network of the American Society of Training and Development (ASTD), and San Francisco's Golden Gate Business Association (see chapter 6 for a complete listing of these organizations).

Family and friends can attain vital information and insight on how to connect with family members by contacting the Gay Community Center or PFLAG (Parents and Friends of Lesbians and Gays) nearest you. You can find these organizations listed in chapter 6, Using Resources.

HOW THIS GUIDE WORKS

A Family and Friend's Guide to Sexual Orientation provides you with the knowledge, actions and resources you need to cross the magic line and find courageous acceptance of your gay family members, friends, and yourself.

So far in chapter 1 you have been introduced to the heterosexual closet faced by family and friends of gay and bisexual people, the choices that both gays and heterosexuals have in relating to sexual orientation issues, the stages of acceptance and "the magic line." In addition, you have become familiar with the symbols and celebrations of the lesbian, gay and bisexual community. This information is designed to prepare you for a deeper journey into the lives and experiences of people who have come to accept varying sexual orientations.

In chapter 2 you will read two sets of family stories (including the stories of a gay father, his heterosexual wife and teenage daughter) and several family and friends stories. As you read these stories you will gain a better understanding of the road to acceptance and the "coming out" process of family and friends. In chapter 3 you will discover the diverse community of sexual minorities, when you read the stories of eleven gay, bisexual and transgender persons. You'll learn more about the process of "coming out" and self-acceptance.

In chapter 4 you will look, specifically, at two important areas of life, work and spirituality. In this chapter you will read the stories of five heterosexuals and four gay individuals who speak directly to the impact that sexual orientation has had on their lives at work or in religious and spiritual settings. These stories will help you move further along your own road to acceptance.

The heartfelt stories in chapters 2, 3, and 4 will help prepare you to take action and, in chapter 5, you will find a list of 101 steps that you can take to become more accepting. You will also find lists of invaluable resources to help you on this journey. In all of the above, especially in reading the moving biographies, you'll be asked to open your hearts and your minds. If you do, we assure you that the time you spend with this guide will have a high payoff. You will develop skills to become more accepting and empowered.

2

Gaining Acceptance
Stories of Families and Friends

What impact does someone's being gay have on families and friends? You will find out in this chapter as you read the stories of one gay man, a lesbian and eight heterosexuals. Through understanding their courageous stories you will take a giant step towards acceptance.

We have chosen life stories as the primary means to help you along the road to acceptance because we believe that as you read these stories you will find a part of yourself in each one. The experiences that these individuals—whether gay, lesbian, bisexual, transgender or heterosexual—describe are those of people like you and me, who tell how their own sexual orientation or that of a loved one has helped them in their life's journey. In connecting to their joys, their challenges, their successes and their pain, we believe you will come to feel similarly about the role varying sexual orientations can play in helping us all to heal the wounded areas of our lives. Our sexual orientation is, for all of us, an important aspect of who we are—and we all have many facets to our beings. In these stories you will find joy and beauty and, as in life, you will also find some challenges and even experiences and descriptions that may make you uneasy or uncomfortable. We are aware that the open discussion of some of the issues and experiences described may make it appear to some readers that the experiences are unique to gays and lesbians (or those who support them). In reality, the difficult and painful experiences that are included are all too common in our society, and the difference here is not their occurrence in our storytellers' lives but in the open discussion of them. In an effort to be true to the philosophy of a DO ASK, DO TELL book we have not attempted to "sanitize" our storytellers' lives. We strongly believe that the open discussion of the important experiences of one's life is critical to one's journey along the road to acceptance.

In this chapter you'll begin and end by reading two sets of family stories.

The first is the story of Courtney Powers, an eighteen-year-old heterosexual and the daughter of Bob Powers, one of the authors of this guide. You'll then read the wife and mother's story (Terri Powers), followed by the author's story (Bob Powers). In reading, you'll discover the path of acceptance along which each of these individuals moved. You'll read Courtney's hilarious and touching tale of telling her boyfriend that her Dad is gay. You'll see how Terri overcame her anger and, as a heterosexual, became outspoken about rights and freedoms for gay people. You'll read of the author's progression from shame to self-acceptance and love.

Following these stories, you will read about Vince Patton, a high ranking military officer who is heterosexual and African American. Vince tells of growing up in the Black Bottom section of Detroit and the impact that "Homer the Homo Man" had on his life and successful military career. Vince's story is followed by stories of three family members—Lexie Johnson, Art Moreno and Mick Miller. Lexie, the daughter of a football coach, describes her relationship and friendship with her gay cousin. Art tells of his religious upbringing and his condemnation and ultimate and public acceptance of his gay son. And, Mick Miller tells his moving story of love for his gay brother.

Janice Mirikitani, president of Glide Foundation, speaks of her "extended family"—of gay street kids and the impact that these children have had on her life. To conclude this section, Wendy and Rabbi David Horowitz talk of their lives as lesbian daughter and straight dad. In these remarkable stories you will see the terrifying impact closets have on gays and heterosexuals *alike*. Yet, you'll also discover the joy, peace and love that each of these family members and friends found as they moved along the path of acceptance and crossed "the magic line."

LEARNING FROM LIFE STORIES

After reading each person's story we strongly recommend that you take time to *write* your thoughts and reactions to their life history. At which points in their lives do you see them passing through the various stages of acceptance, and what occurred as they did so? Record your emotional reactions—were there parts of the story to which you felt a strong connection or that seemed especially relevant? Were there moments when you felt uncomfortable, ill at ease, or possibly confused? We encourage you to explore those feelings, as they are often key to proceeding along the road to acceptance.

Courtney Elizabeth Powers

I believe all Americans who believe in freedom, tolerance and human rights have a responsibility to oppose bigotry and prejudice based on sexual orientation.

—Coretta Scott King

My name is Courtney Elizabeth Powers. I'm eighteen years of age, and I live in Saratoga, California. I was born at Alta Bates hospital in Berkeley, California. My parents are Bob and Terri Powers.

Since then, like many other parents, mine have divorced. The reason they divorced wasn't because either of them was unfaithful, or that they fought too much, or had financial difficulties. The reason was my dad is gay.

I don't really remember how I found out my dad was gay; it seems that I have known it my whole life. I think I was about four years old when my dad told me he was gay. He said that when he told me I understood the main point (people loving people of the same sex) he was trying to get across. He wanted to tell me when I was young because he didn't want me to grow up and hate him for being gay, or hate anyone for that matter. Well, I'm not prejudiced and I'm glad he told me when he did. I might have hated him if he hadn't told me— not for being gay but for not telling me the truth.

Since I was four, I spent every summer with my dad and his boyfriend (lover), Alan. This last summer was the first time I didn't go. I remember weekdays in New York at my dad's and Alan's apartment and weekends in New Jersey. Eventually, we spent every day in New Jersey.

I don't remember the first time I met Alan, but I do remember how badly my dad wanted me to like him. I think it took a little time for me to get used to Alan because I remember one time my dad asked me if I liked Alan. I said, "Yes, I like Alan, but I came here to see you."

I accepted Alan into my life rather quickly. I admired him. "He's funny, talented, and brilliant," I thought. We got along great. As far as

I was concerned, he was part of the family, like another dad or something.

When I was about eight, my dad enrolled me in horseback riding lessons to keep me busy during the day, while he worked. I rode every year and I still love riding.

When I was little, I remember being afraid to tell any of my friends that my dad was gay. It wasn't because I was ashamed—I wasn't. It was because I didn't want my friends to dislike me because my dad was gay. I didn't want them to tease me and hurt my feelings. I knew little kids could be cruel and, I wanted everyone to like me, so I generally never said a word. When I talked about my dad, I would only say that he lives in New Jersey and has his own business. I would refer to Alan as his roommate. I wouldn't say anything else about him.

As I got older the subject seemed to come up more often; I was still afraid how people might react. I remember the summer before eighth grade; I was thirteen. I leased a horse at Silver Bit and Spur, a horse farm in central New Jersey. I was sitting in the office talking with one of the owners. She asked about my family.

"Is your mom remarried?" she inquired.

"No, but she is seeing someone," I replied.

"What about your dad, he's not remarried, is he?" she asked.

I said, "No."

She proceeded to ask questions about my parents' divorce, like how old I was when they parted, did I remember it, and so on. Then, she asked, "Do you know why your parents divorced?" I thought to myself, "Well, of course I know why," but I answered the question by saying, "Not really. I guess they just didn't get along." I felt so stupid. But, I didn't want her to look down on me. I knew she knew I was lying.

During the next couple years I told many people. Each summer, I leased the same horse at the farm. I had developed several close friends and we rode together daily. I remember one particular day I had invited a couple of them to spend the night with me at my dad's house. I thought it would be a little strange if they came over and saw Alan living there with my dad, especially when they shared the same bedroom. So I decided I had to tell them. I told my friend Yve first. I was surprised as she didn't care at all. Next I told Andrea who said the same thing—"I don't care." I was further surprised when they came over; they instantly loved my dad and Alan. I was so relieved. Soon, everyone at Silver Bit knew and not one person said anything bad. Occasionally, they would ask questions as they were curious about it. The experience amazed me!

After that summer, I came home and began my sophomore year in high school. I told all of my close friends that my dad was gay. No one reacted badly. One day I was talking to a close male friend and we got on the subject of my dad and I told him that my dad was gay. He reacted by saying very sarcastically, "Why did you tell me that?"

I replied, "Because I thought you should know." He said nothing more. Even though he didn't say anything bad, his sarcastic reaction made me feel so insecure and stupid that I stopped telling people for a while. During my junior year, I started seeing this guy Mark, whom I had liked for months. We were best friends, yet I never told him about my dad. I had many opportunities, but my other male friend's sarcastic reaction bothered me so much that I just didn't want to deal with it. I remember one day Mark and I were sitting on my bed when, all of a sudden, I realized I had forgotten Alan's birthday. I thought, "My dad will kill me." I became upset and stressed out about what I should do. Mark asked me what was wrong and I told him I forgot my dad's friend's birthday. Mark didn't understand why this would make me so upset. He kept saying, "What's the big deal?" and asked why it was so important to remember my dad's friend's birthday. I told him I just had to remember it. I realized he couldn't understand why it was important and I dropped the subject.

A month or two later, Mark, one of his friends, Mike, and I went to San Francisco to see a car show. I wanted to show them the place my dad had there because it was so beautiful. My dad was away, but my mom had a set of keys, which I used to get in. Mark and Mike were in awe over it. They thought it was gorgeous. Mark sat down at the piano. I was standing behind him and Mike was looking through a rack of magazines. I remember thinking, "I hope there is no gay newspaper stuff," because neither of them knew about my dad. Just then Mike pulled out a newspaper, looked at it (of course, it was a gay one) and said, "Courtney, is your dad gay?" I said, "Yes." Just then Mark smiled or smirked, and I slapped him across the face. I thought he was laughing at my dad. It turned out he wasn't laughing at all. He was just shocked and, as I was standing behind him, I really couldn't tell that it was a shocked look on his face and not a mocking one. I was very embarrassed that I had slapped him. Once again, neither of them said anything bad. They asked lots of questions, like why he got married, whether he had a boyfriend, and so on. Mark did get mad at me, not because my dad was gay, but because I wasn't open with him about it, especially as I had many opportunities to tell him. Eventually, he got over being mad.

The last time I told someone my dad is gay was about a year ago. I told my current boyfriend, Geoffrey. I didn't want to do what I did with Mark. I wanted Geoff to hear it from me, not from anyone else, or for any other reason than because it was my wish to tell him. I told him within the first month of dating him. I had known Geoff since seventh grade, and before we started going out we talked on the phone for hours every night. I was very comfortable with Geoff. The night I told him, our conversation went something like this:

"Geoff?" I said.

"Yes," he replied.

"Well I have to tell you something kind of important about my life," I blurted.

"Go on, what is it?" he said curiously.

"Well, it's actually not about me; it's about my dad," I replied nervously.

"Uh-huh," he mumbled.

"Well, you see...uh...Well..." I stammered.

"Court, just tell me. What is it?" he said anxiously.

"Well, you see, my dad...umm...he's...uh..." I mumbled.

"C'mon, Court, wait a second, I think I know what you're trying to say," Geoff stated.

"Tell me what you think it is," I said, a little calmer now.

"No, what if I'm wrong? Then I'll feel stupid," he replied.

"C'mon, Geoff, I doubt you'll be wrong," I said, becoming more and more curious as to what he thought I wanted to tell him.

"No, Court, you tell me," he replied.

"Okay, my dad's gay," I said quickly.

"I thought it was either that or that he was in prison," Geoff replied.

Then, like everyone else, Geoff asked me a few questions and said he was fine with it. In retrospect, I don't know why I was so nervous about it. Geoff met my dad at my high school graduation, where he also met another gay couple. He loved meeting my dad, as well as the other couple. He said they were hilarious and had a great sense of humor.

Recently, Geoff and I went to see my dad, and the three of us went to Glide Memorial Methodist Church in San Francisco. It was Geoff's first experience seeing men hug and kiss one another. He said it didn't bother him at all. I think that Geoff has been great throughout this experience. He accepted it well.

Since telling Geoff, I'm not afraid to tell anyone. In the past, I didn't tell any of my other boyfriends, with the exception of the two I mentioned. And, it was really difficult telling people because I was so worried about their reactions. I look at it differently now. If I think I should tell someone, or if it comes up, I tell them. It's not a problem.

Now, for all the readers who are wondering about the effects my dad's being gay has had on me, I'll tell you. There are no effects, except that I have learned not to judge people. I have learned to accept people as they are, and to defend, say, and do what I believe in. Those are the effects. I don't think they're bad ones. The only bad thing is that my dad and Alan, after fourteen years together, broke up last year and I have to deal with that. And that makes me very sad. But I intend to stay close to both of them and I won't forget about Alan. To me, he's family and always will be.

For those of you curious about my sexuality, I'm heterosexual. And I'm still seeing Geoff. We have been going out for about a year now. Hopefully, I'll continue going out with him. So, having a gay parent does not mean the child will turn out to be gay. I'm living proof of that.

Gays are no different from anyone. They have good times and bad times, just like everyone else. We need to learn not to discriminate against gays or anyone. This is America, the land of opportunity and freedom. By discriminating we take away opportunities and by discriminating we ruin the freedom to choose. We need to support each other, instead of judging each other. Otherwise, we will never get anywhere in this world. As I end this, please keep these things in mind. Like I said before: stop judging and start supporting one another.

Courtney's story vividly depicts the heterosexual closet. Because she learned about her father's homosexuality at such an early age (four years), she wasn't exposed to the hate and bigotry that older children sometimes encounter. As a result, she moved right through the first step: admitting to yourself. Courtney accepted the fact that her father is gay. As she grew older she was faced with the choice to tell people and initially that posed her some conflict. Courageously, she chose to tell her friends and experienced support from almost everyone. She now speaks out about these experiences demonstrating that she has worked her way through acceptance. She and her father enjoy a wonderful loving relationship today.

Note your thoughts and reactions to Courtney's story. This will help you move along the road to acceptance.

Terri Powers

Since when do you have to agree with people to defend them from injustice?

—Lillian Hellman

In 1945 I was adopted by two people (Dan and Clio Cronin of San Francisco, California) who claimed to have waited nine years to find an all-Irish child. My parents said that they looked at many babies at the adoption agency before they chose me. Today that story sounds rather unrealistic, like a myth. I do know one thing for sure, and that is that my birth mother's last name was McKenna. I also know that I can't remember a time when I didn't know I was adopted, and the myth surrounding it made me feel very special.

Both of my parents were at least forty when I came into their lives. My mother never revealed her true age to me. It was only after her death that I found documentation proving she'd lied about her age in order to adopt me: forty was the cut-off age for qualifying for adoption.

There was something else happening in the late 1940's: Shirley Temple was growing older. And my mother decided that I would be a perfect replacement. I was taken, from the time I can remember, to drama, ballet, and singing lessons. I even had a drama coach (Miss Lolly!) and starred in a children's theater production before I was five. The play was *The Three Bears* and I was the mama bear. I can remember holding up a pan to shield my eyes from the stage lights so I could find my "boyfriend" in the audience. I allegedly said, "Robert, is that you in the front row?"

So a great deal of my early childhood was spent living out my mom's fantasy of having a child star for a daughter. All of this culminated in my becoming a regular on a local T.V. show called *Aunt Lolly and Her Kitty Cats*. I played "Miss Priss," the maiden aunt. I absolutely hated every minute of all of this—the lessons, the permanents for my hair, the make-up (thick), and, most of all, the fact that I couldn't play or do whatever other things kids at six did.

My father worked for the Santa Fe Railroad, and when I was in first grade, he was transferred to San Jose, California. My parents were able to buy their first (and only) home, but I had to attend a few schools before they finally settled in. I hated that also. I was also attending new dancing and drama classes that my mom had found for me in San Jose, and my dad (my mother didn't drive) drove us to San Francisco three times a week so I could continue being on the T.V. show. I really hated that and remember having angry outbursts with my mother and always losing them.

In the third grade I became very ill with a chronic disease called ulcerative colitis. It is rare in children and very debilitating. I believe that on a subconscious level I ordered my body to protest for me so that I wouldn't have to continue with the high pressures of performance.

The illness radically changed the course of my life. My parents were smart enough to stop all my performance-related lessons, but I missed at least half of every school year, had home teachers, and spent lots of time in bed or in the hospital. Periodically I would lose so much blood that I'd have to have transfusions. Because of the severity of the illness, I literally was unable to lead a normal childhood and adolescence.

My parents became prisoners of my illness also. I'm sure they felt very afraid and helpless. And while they doted on me, they also hid any information about my illness from me—one of the strongest rules in our house was not to talk about "unpleasant" things. So they used to trick me into going to see the doctor by saying we were "just going for a ride." I lived in terror of seeing my father walk into our home in mid-day—it usually meant I'd be taken to the doctor for yet another horrible and painful examination.

My father was a devout Catholic. He insisted that my mother convert to Catholicism before he would marry her. So while I was ill, I had visits from the parish priests. I clearly recall thinking how meaningless those visits were. I simply did not relate well to this church that seemed so full of guilt—about everything. Nevertheless, my parents decided to send me to Catholic school, beginning in the seventh grade. They said "I was too frail to attend public school." As a result, I really became sick. I didn't know anyone, and I was different in that I didn't have to take P.E. and could leave class at anytime to go to the bathroom. To top it off, the nuns in their enormous habits intimidated the hell out of me.

Needless to say, while I was growing up I didn't know any gay people. I didn't know any Jewish people, any Asian people, any Hispanic people, or any African American people. And as I also attended an all-girl, Catholic, private high school, I didn't know many boys, either. I was sheltered, protected, and indulged.

My early dating experiences were dreadful. Because I'd been so sheltered and because I was in school for just enough time to hear the Catholic interpretation of sexuality (and dating), I regarded most boys as devil incarnates. My dates, and they were very few, were always awkward and riddled with tension. I thought that the girls who had steady boyfriends were probably promiscuous and very sinful. I also envied them.

In college, my world widened a bit as I met more and more people. More importantly, I got to know boys. I still don't remember having any contact with or conversations about gays.

When I graduated from college I got a job with Bank of America (B of A) in San Francisco. I worked in a relatively creative department and through my co-workers I met filmmakers, writers, and just plain late-sixties-type semi-radicals (you couldn't be a true radical and work at B of A). I discovered that one of the men in our underground network of liberalism was gay. I heard of it through his girlfriend, who discovered Richard in bed with a man. I remember being very shocked, but pretended to have complete tolerance.

Later, I met Bob through a mutual friend and found him fascinating and worldly. He was also very funny. We enjoyed each other tremendously and within six months we married. I didn't have a clue that Bob was homosexual. If anything was different, it was that he seemed more liberal than my other friends, and I liked that. I loved being married to Bob. He was even-tempered, generous, a good cook, and he seemed to adore me. I adored him back. I thought I'd found my soul mate.

After we were married for three years or so, I became pregnant. Bob was ecstatic; I was terrified. I couldn't believe that anyone could possibly live through childbirth. But I did, and we had a daughter, Courtney. Bob seemed extraordinarily happy after her birth—he took an equal part in her care. I thought he was a perfect father, and we were a perfect family.

When Courtney was eight months old, Bob told me he believed he was gay. He writes that I was "devastated." I also felt angry, fearful, and absolutely hopeless. I wanted to die. Worst of all, I didn't tell anyone—not because I was ashamed, but because on some unconscious level I knew that I could not absorb any additional emotion, no matter how well-intentioned any advice or comfort might be. I could not bear to hear the most obvious of questions, "Why are you staying married?" To this day, that time remains the very worst of my life.

I was shattered, emotionally and physically. My colitis, which had been in remission for years, began to act up and I became very ill once again. I lost weight (I'm five feet, four inches tall and I weighed eighty-eight pounds). I cried all the time. I didn't know what to do with my grief. I clearly recall the one occasion I called Bob at work and asked him to come home because I was hysterical and was afraid I'd hurt Courtney. I could not find a way to release my anger. He came home, and I remember us standing in the front hall holding each other and sobbing. And I remember feeling such horrible despair. I saw no way out: I was completely dependent on Bob—emotionally and financially. He was my life and my lifeline.

To make things even worse, Bob consistently gave messages that were conflicting to me. He'd send me flowers, he'd write love poems to me, he'd buy me presents. He threw a very lavish surprise party for my thirtieth birthday. I remember thinking as I walked into the party, "He really does love me." And maybe he did. But Bob has a penchant for doing things in a grand style, and maybe this truly grand event was one more thing done in his "grand" style.

I have almost no memory of the year after Bob's "announcement." I do know that at one point Bob insisted that we go to therapy. I agreed only because he threatened to leave if I didn't. Unfortunately, we went to a couple who practiced quick, contract-type therapy—popular at the time. Their first response to my telling them of my situation was, "So what?" I fell even deeper into despair. I mean, if two mental health professionals, one of whom is a psychiatrist, don't seem to think that your husband telling you he's gay is all that significant, why should I be feeling so distraught? It was a terrible introduction to therapy for me: I felt my life slipping very quickly out of my grasp. And we still seemed to others to be a happy and prosperous couple.

The duplicity of it all was staggering. My closest friend was killed in an auto accident very recently and her death was easier for me to accept than was Bob's sexual orientation. Death is "unsolvable," but with our marriage I still had to live through the nightmare and find a solution.

During that first year after his announcement, Bob was offered a promotion to AT&T headquarters in New Jersey, which he accepted. I thought (and probably prayed) that the move and all the attending activities would distract him, or at least change things. I think now that I saw the move as a chance to start over: a new state, a new house, and a distance of two thousand five hundred miles from all the sadness and pain. There was a flurry of good-bye parties; we were flown to New Jersey a few times to look at homes and meet new people. It was exciting and exhilarating. I felt as if I'd been released from hell.

Hell doesn't freeze over, but New Jersey does. And our first winter there was one of the worst in history. After the moving hoopla died down, I died a little bit more. I was immersed in sadness and immobility. We had moved to "the country." I am a city person: I need what urban life offers. I found myself stranded and alone physically, financially and emotionally. Bob's job required him to travel, and while he was faithful when he was home, I knew he led a gay lifestyle when he was away (this was 1978—pre-AIDS). Knowing what he was doing was almost unbearable. We didn't talk about it and we didn't have sex. We eventually slept in separate rooms.

So while we were digging out from various snow storms, we were digging ourselves even more deeply into duplicity. I continued to see no way out. After a year or so, Bob forced my hand and said he thought we should separate. And so we did.

Courtney and I returned to California to live with a friend of mine, and Bob met and moved in with Alan. The year following our separation was a horrible struggle for me, and I still find myself having very bitter feelings about it. I had to create an entirely new life, and Bob was madly in love and living with Alan. I had to rely on my friends and eventually my parents for housing.

Courtney and I lived out of a big yellow suitcase for almost a year. I had a hot and heartbreaking affair and was extraordinarily vulnerable. I began to tell my closest friends about Bob: they were highly unsympathetic toward him and more interested in helping me get on with my life.

After nearly a year of job hunting, I found a job and Courtney's and my life became more structured and peaceful. I liked my job and was meeting new people. Courtney tells me I dated a lot, that there were always two or three men I saw concurrently. I don't recall having that degree of popularity, but I do know that I began telling my dates early in the relationship that Bob was gay and that was why we separated. I had come to accept homosexuality and it was important to me that anyone I might become serious with accept it as well. Bob, after all, was still Courtney's father and would be an important part of both of our lives, as he shared in raising Courtney. It was important not to abuse the relationship between Bob and Courtney or even between Bob and me, so if any of my dates expressed negativity on the subject or even showed me pity, I wouldn't see them again. I got a lot of pity.

Two years passed before I told my mom about Bob. She had loved him and couldn't understand anything about our separation or why I was very adamant about either of my parents saying anything negative regarding Bob—in front of me or especially Courtney. I remember how much she (my mom) cried: I'd never seen her cry before. She was not judgmental or condemning. Her only request was that I not tell my dad. I didn't and have no regrets: he was bigoted and uninformed and I'm quite sure he would have tried to take Courtney from me to prevent her from spending time with Bob and Alan.

In 1983 I met a man I found very appealing. He was from Pakistan, his name was Sheikh Ashar Majid (very exotic to me!), and he had been in the United States for fifteen years or so. When we met, he asked about my divorce, which was now final, and I told him the truth. He was empathetic and seemed to have no prejudice regarding gays. He was also very funny. Bob and Alan and Ashi and I became friends. Ashi and I spent a terrific week with them in New Jersey a few summers ago. They both came to our wedding in 1989. I still remember them getting out of their car—Bob grinning with his arms full of flowers and Alan carrying a huge present which he said was outrageously expensive, but he knew I'd love it. I did and I also loved the fact that they flew three thousand miles to be with us. Ashi's ex-wife was also there. Bob grabbed her and together they proposed the toast, "from the Exes to the Exes". I still smile when I remember that.

I worked for a very large, very macho, and very homophobic organization. I told only a few people about Bob, with the exception of members of my small work group. One of my closest friends was a man named Bruce. I enjoyed him immensely, and his sense of humor pulled me out of many funks. At one point, Bruce and I discovered that we would be attending seminars on the east coast during the same week. I had made plans to stop in New York City and stay with Bob and Alan. I asked Bruce if he wanted to come with me, which he did. Shortly after, Bruce answered a call from Bob to me at work. Bob explained to Bruce that there was only one large bed and a couch in his loft and asked Bruce if it was okay to share the couch with me. Bruce replied that there would be no problem—he too was gay. Bob asked if I knew. Bruce said he hadn't told me, but that he would before we arrived.

So Bob and Alan and Bruce and I are at dinner in famed Greenwich Village at some trendy place when Bob says to me, "What'd you think when Bruce told you he was gay?" I kicked Bob as hard as I could under the table—Bruce hadn't said a word to me. Instead of being quiet, Bob asked me why I kicked him. If I hadn't had a couple of drinks, I might have become a victim of death by embarrassment. I wanted to eject myself out of the chair. I gave Bob a deadly look and snuck a look at Alan, who stared right back at me. Finally, I turned to Bruce, who said, "Terri, I'm gay." I looked at him, then Bob, and, finally, Alan. Within seconds, the four of us broke into hysterical laughter. The evening was saved. Today, Bruce and his lover are good friends of mine, and Bruce and I still laugh about "that moment."

Ashi and Courtney and I have had some wonderful, warm times with Bob and Alan. When Bob told me they were splitting up I felt sad for days. I miss Alan.

There's a gay activist chant that goes, "We're here, we're queer, get used to it." Bob was my husband and is my daughter's father. I am not ashamed. I love and support him and I got used to it.

> Terri reacted with anger when she discovered that her husband was gay. That made sense as her marriage was threatened and, ultimately, ended. But Terri moved through her anger and eventually established a caring and friendly relationship with her ex-husband. This process took time, as she, like Courtney, chose who to tell and who not to tell. Initially she felt some shame, but as she became more accepting, the shame dissipated and Terri is now a heterosexual who is outspoken and supportive of the rights of lesbians and gays.

Note your thoughts and reactions to Terri's story.

Bob Powers

To love oneself is the beginning of a lifelong romance.

—Oscar Wilde

When I was little, I knew there was something different about me, but I didn't know what it was. Later, I discovered I was attracted to other boys, and that scared the hell out of me.

I was born in Hastings, Minnesota, in 1941, and soon experienced my fifteen minutes of fame when I was selected the most beautiful baby in Minneapolis, Minnesota. My father also enjoyed some small fame, as he was one of a handful of professional bowlers during that time. Consequently, we were frequently on the move. My mother tells me that she forced my dad to promise that we would settle down when I was big enough that I no longer fit into a hotel dresser drawer. When I was four, we settled in Stockton, California, where I was raised.

My father spent the rest of his career as a life insurance agent. He was moderately successful and was well-known and well-liked in the community. He was also an alcoholic and a gambling addict. These addictions were kept hidden from the children, as were "bad" news and all feelings, except "happy" ones.

My mother was a housewife and she was good at it. She took pride in having a neat and tidy home, as well as neat and tidy kids (I was probably the only kid in school with white polished tennis shoes). My mom had made a "death bed" promise to her father never to touch liquor and this was a promise she kept. She was a strong-willed and independent woman. Growing up, I liked my mom a lot more than I liked my Dad, who was seldom home. I tolerated my two sisters, who were seven and nine years younger than I was. Despite my childish judgments about members of my family, I am still described by my mother as having been an absolutely perfect child.

We were a typical American family, middle-class and very nice. We were also Catholic. My parents never used the word sex in all my growing up. As a result, my discoveries about my sexuality were racked with shame. I don't recall exactly when I realized I was different from other boys. I was probably eleven or twelve when I went to the library to look up the word homosexuality. I'll never forget what I read. It said "homosexuality: a perversion, a mental illness." I stood there and cried. I didn't feel perverted and I didn't think I was mentally ill. I did not know what to do, so I prayed to God to let me die.

I immediately stopped all activities that I thought were remotely feminine. This led to my denying myself a number of childhood passions. For example, I recall this wonderful old neighbor lady, Mrs. Noyer, who had a big garden, which I just loved. Every day, during the county fair, she would pack up all the neighborhood kids into her car and trek us to the fairgrounds, where we would enter flower arrangements. Over the years I won hundreds of ribbons in the "men's division." I was often written about or pictured, with my arrangements, in the Women's Section of the local newspaper. It was a big thrill for me. I loved this old lady and her garden. But when I came to realize that flowers were "for girls," I abandoned these activities. My fear of being called a pansy was far greater than my passion for growing them. Thirty-five years passed before this passion was rekindled. I was in New Jersey and bent over to smell a geranium. A volcano of feelings erupted and I was overwhelmed with reminiscences of my childhood, the county fair, beautiful flowers, and Mrs. Noyer. I realized there was no longer anything to stop me from gardening. I was queer, and everyone who knew me knew I was queer. I spent much of the next several years helping transform an overgrown island into seven acres of paradise.

Growing up, I had two models of a homosexual. One was of a limp-wristed "flaming faggot." I used to practice shaking hands (with myself) in an effort to develop a "manly grip," so that no one would suspect me of being a queer. I spent hours standing in front of a mirror practicing. It never occurred to me that the mirror couldn't help strengthen my grip. The other model, which I created in my imagination, was of a dirty old man in a trench coat. The first time I went into a gay bar, I actually thought I would walk into a room full of men in trench coats. Boy, was I surprised.

I did have some sexual experiences with boys when I was young. Not many. I felt hatred towards them after and lots of shame. I was popular in school and active in student government—I was a real "rah-rah" type. In college I lived for fraternities and parties, and I lived in fear that someone would find out I was really queer. I often went out with girls and prayed I would be attracted to them. And I was attracted to them, but emotionally, rather than physically. I was also selected by a national sorority as one of their "dream men." I was so moved by that gesture, which I thought affirmed my manhood, that I burst into tears in front of ninety young women. Even though I wasn't physically attracted to girls, I could usually be found with a girlfriend. Looking back, I imagine that was one of the ways I protected myself. Another was to gain so much weight that most people simply wouldn't find me attractive.

As my parents maintained a DON'T ASK, DON'T TELL family environment, I was totally uncomfortable talking about issues related to sex or sexual orientation. Like the rest of my family I was only comfortable talking about "happy things."

After graduate school, I went into the Peace Corps. To this day, I don't know where I got the courage to apply. This was a period of time in our country when there was great excitement, generated in large part by the Kennedys. The Peace Corps was newly established and a perfect place for an idealistic young kid like me. But to get in, volunteers went through a lengthy process of extensive FBI screens, numerous psychological tests, and periodic psychiatric and peer evaluations. For months I lived in terror that I'd be found out and that my life would be ruined. Somehow I managed to pass all the cuts. I concluded that I must have fooled everybody, even the experts. The next thing I knew, I was living in a remote village helping develop local business in Malawi, Africa. My Peace Corps experience was transforming. I lived a very simple, yet wonderfully satisfying existence. I rid myself of the weight I had gained and some of the superficial values (the importance of status, possessions, and so forth) I had adopted. I also began to value differences in people. Although I noticed that most Malawians didn't possess the same sexual taboos about homosexuality as Americans—few Malawians would have considered themselves homosexual, yet they freely participated in homosexuals acts—I did not move any closer to accepting my own sexual orientation.

Shortly after joining the Peace Corps, I met a woman and became engaged. As soon as I became engaged, I wanted to be unengaged. I didn't have the courage to be honest about it, so I went about convincing my fiancee that she didn't want to be married to me. I had a couple of other relationships with women, and as soon as they got serious, I ran away.

After my two-year Peace Corps stint was up, I travelled through the Middle East and across Europe before returning to the states where, for six months, I taught junior high school. I went back to Malawi on a dual Malawi government and United States Agency for International Development (USAID) contract, where I worked as a planning officer in the Ministry of Natural Resources. I continued to suppress my sexual identity.

In 1969, I returned to the states. My relationship with my parents was cordial, yet distant. I still couldn't bring myself to talk to my family about problems. When that became unbearable, as it sometimes did, I'd sit down with my favorite Aunt and Uncle and talk about my problems, unless it had to do with my confusion about my sexuality. That I kept hidden from everyone.

Shortly after my return, I went to work for Pacific Telephone, which at the time was a wholly owned subsidiary of AT&T, in San Jose, California. I was in their accelerated management program. I almost wasn't hired because I didn't fit the "management mold"; fortunately, my best friend had enough influence to get me hired anyway. Along with eighteen other over-achievers (all of us stated in orientation that we hoped to become CEO), I began a year-long program where I would gradually take on more and more responsibility. At the end of the program, I would either be promoted to middle management or let go. After about nine months, I was told that I had successfully completed the program. I moved into my new assignment, where I was responsible for managing sixty or so employees, all women, who handled customer service, order taking, billing and payments. Although I received little training, I had a knack for managing people. After a couple of years, I was given a job training other managers. I loved it and knew I had found my career niche. Three months later, I was promoted to head the company's management training effort and eventually moved to lead the company's internal management consulting group. These years represented tremendous and rapid professional and personal growth, except in sexual areas.

Early on in my career, I met a woman who constantly made me laugh, and I asked her to marry me. To my surprise, I didn't want to run away and I thought maybe I wasn't queer. I concluded that the only way to know was to get married. I was twenty-eight years old. I remember standing at the altar and saying "I do" and then skipping down the aisle and clicking my heels in the air because I was happy to be married. I thought that meant I wasn't a faggot.

I lived a fairly happy married life. I didn't fool around. We had a beautiful daughter. After about five years of marriage, I went back to New York on business and met an AT&T executive named Robert, a man who came to have a tremendous influence on my life. It turned out that his roommate had served with me in the Peace Corps. Robert invited me to their house for dinner and I enthusiastically accepted. I took the subway to Brooklyn Heights and rang their doorbell. I hardly knew either of them, yet when they answered the door, I looked at them and burst into tears. I knew they were gay. They were my new role models. They weren't limp-wristed faggots nor old men in overcoats. They were simply two nice-looking human beings. At that moment, I also knew beyond a shadow of a doubt I was gay.

I felt as if my life were over. Robert helped me sort through the pain and upheaval that was to come. A short while later, I told my wife I was gay. She was devastated. We stayed together for four more years. During this time, we relocated to New Jersey. Terri became very depressed, spending most of her time lying down, reading. I responded to the situation by trying to be a good husband when I was home. When I travelled, which I did fairly often, I would meet other men. At the time I thought I was doing a good job of balancing my role as a husband with my newly accepted sexual identity. I was wrong. Our marriage didn't work and when we came to accept that, we ended it. That was a godsend for both of us, though at the time it didn't seem that way for Terri. She became very angry, bitter. Without telling me, she told my mom I was gay. She felt victimized. For the first year, our relationship was very strained. The one thing that enabled each of us to keep any integrity was the fact that we had a daughter, Courtney, who we both loved very much. After a year, Terri had an experience that changed the way she viewed life and transformed our relationship.

Courtney was four when I left. Leaving her was the hardest thing I have ever done, for at the time I believed I was a better parent than my wife. Yet I still left and for many years felt a shame only equalled by the shame I felt being in the closet. Today, Terri is happily married and a champion of gay rights. Over the years, we have enjoyed a warm and friendly relationship.

Shortly after our breakup, I told my parents and my two sisters I was gay. I was stunned when my mom told me Terri had told her, though not surprised to find my mom didn't totally believe it. While my family shys away from discussion of everyday problems and dark feelings, they respond well when it comes to separation, divorce, or death. Both my sisters were very supportive, and I have been forever grateful, as I needed that support. My folks said all the right words, like, "We love you no matter who you are."

I met Alan (Ames) fourteen years ago in a Manhattan bar called Boots and Saddles, affectionately known in the gay community as "Bras and Girdles." Alan lived in Chelsea, just outside New York's famed Greenwich Village. I vividly recall our first date. I stood on the street, underneath his fourth-story window, flowers in one hand and a bottle of Jack Daniels in the other, waiting for him to throw me his key. I felt like a teenager, ready to fall in love. I did.

My daughter came to visit us on our first Christmas together. By then, I had gone through the (terrifying) process of telling my friends and family that I was gay. They were generally supportive. I told them that I was going to tell Courtney, who was still four. Nobody except Alan wanted me to tell her. "Wait until she grows up," they advised. I couldn't, for I knew that if I waited her head would become filled with hated notions about what it meant to be a homosexual, and we might never find a way to communicate.

I said to her, "Courtney, you know how people love one another."
And she said, "Yes."
"Well, some men love other men, like I love Alan." Then I added, "Men who love other men are called homosexuals."
She asked, "What are women who love other women called?"
And I said, "They're called lesbians."
It seemed like an eternity passed as I waited for this four-year-old

child to make some sort of pronouncement. She looked at me and said, "Daddy, why do they have such big words?"

Strangely, I knew she understood. She didn't understand the sexual part, but it wasn't about sex, it was about love, and she understood love. I also told her that some people didn't like gay people, that some people might tease her if she decided to tell them and that she had to make a choice to tell them or not. Courtney lived with Alan and me every summer for the next fourteen years. That communication was one of the highlights of my life with my daughter. It gave both of us the opportunity to talk about being gay, and we did, every summer.

I would ask, "Who do you tell?" She would say she told her friends, and I would ask, "What do they say?"

And she would say, "Nothing."

"Nothing"—the word rings in my ears—for it means no hatred, no prejudice, no thing. Today she is a wonderful young woman, unbiased, and quite happily heterosexual.

My parents, I learned, wrestled with having a gay son. Dad seemed to accept my homosexuality better than Mom, which surprised me, as Mom was the parent I always felt more comfortable talking to. But I think my Mom felt her own shame about having a gay son. At first she wanted to know if she had "done something" that caused me to be gay. As the years passed, she seemed more accepting, yet she has never been able to talk about it with anyone except me, my dad, and my two sisters. This is true even though I eventually told every aunt, uncle, and cousin in my family. Mom just likes to keep these kind of things "in the family" and that only included me, Dad, and my sisters, Jane and Maureen. Around 1985, Alan and I treated them to a two-week visit from California to our home in New Jersey. We set out to give them the time of their lives. The night they left, my father said that while my being gay was initially difficult for them to accept, he wanted us to know that he thought we were the most wonderful couple he had ever known. A short while later, we received a letter from my mother that said their visit was the best two weeks of her entire life. That experience helped me go onto the next step, which was to come out at work.

It was shortly after I met Robert that I moved to New Jersey, the result of a promotion to AT&T headquarters. I became in charge of corporate training. Robert introduced me to the gay underground within the corporation. This was a network of lesbians and gay men who communicated with one another about corporate policies, people, and events in an effort to survive a homophobic environment. I was amazed that such a group existed and awed by the ease with which it operated and the warm way I was welcomed.

The final motivation to come out at work came as a result of attending The Advocate Experience, a weekend workshop which focused on being gay. That experience, along with the realization that the fear of coming out was usually worse than the actual process of coming out, gave me the courage to take this terrifying step. Added to this were the more personal reasons of my desire to stop hiding and telling lies at work and Alan's encouragement to be true to myself. And it was terrifying. I was so scared that I would be fired that each day during this time period I tape recorded who I told, what I said, and how they responded. Thirteen years later, I listened to these tapes and was stunned by the frightened voice I heard. I was also surprised by how thoughtful, organized, and systematic I was in my approach.

I had decided not to make a big deal out of it. I made no public announcements. Instead, I told people, one by one, as an occasion presented itself, which was usually a one-on-one meeting. I described the training in which I had participated, the extent to which I hid my sexuality from the person I was telling, and the effect that had on me. For example, I described meeting Alan, falling in love, and how horrible it felt to keep one of the most joyful events in my life a secret because I was afraid. I described how much energy it took to answer everyday questions, like, "What did you do over the weekend?" or, "Are you dating anyone?" and how much conscious thought it took to constantly change the pronoun "he" to "she," so no one would suspect I was a queer. I also told how these little lies reinforced my feeling of shame. But most importantly, I said to each individual, the result was a distance between us that, for me, was simply unnatural.

Over a period of several weeks, I had told forty or fifty people, who probably told many, many more, that I was gay. It was a remarkable experience. One person after another responded positively. I was deeply moved. Only one event occurred that I'd truly classify as negative. A few weeks after my coming out, I received a phone call from a woman who said I had just ruined my career. She was a lesbian, who I believe was frightened by my coming out successfully.

I stayed at AT&T another four years. I consistently received outstanding performance appraisals, was generally ranked at or near the top of middle management performers, received healthy, often substantial pay raises, and was made ready for promotion to the next higher level of management.

I joined a professional society in the early seventies. The National Society for Performance & Instruction (NSPI) is a ten thousand-person international organization dedicated to improving human performance. About the same time I came out at work, I became very active in NSPI.

In some ways, coming out to my professional colleagues was easier than coming out at AT&T, as I often attended NSPI's annual conference with Alan and on many occasions hosted committee and board meetings at our home in New Jersey. In 1981, I was elected vice president of the organization. Three years later, I was elected president of NSPI. In 1992, as co-chair of the NSPI's Diversity Committee, I was successful in guiding the executive board to adopt a very inclusive diversity policy, one that reaches out to all people, including gays and lesbians, and stands up against any and all forms of bigotry.

NSPI has been an organization where I have been clearly visible and accepted as a gay man. As a result, I have made substantial contributions to NSPI and, I hope, to the profession.

After fourteen years in the Bell System, I left AT&T in 1982 and established my own consulting firm. I had been out in the workplace for four years; I wasn't about to go back into the corporate closet. Yet, in many ways, going out on my own was scarier than coming out at AT&T. Not only was I giving up my financial security, but I was also losing the sense of protection I felt I had in a large corporation. Again, AT&T was remarkably supportive. They gave me my first contract.

I will never forget the day I had my first meeting with a potential client. I was getting dressed when I became overwhelmed with a sense of panic. I thought I had made a huge mistake. In my mind I heard the voice of my self-doubt say, "Nobody wants a fag consultant. Who do you think you are, anyway? You're just ruining your life." Alan came into the dressing room and found me lying on the floor in a fetal position. I managed, through my tears, to tell him I had made a big mistake. Very softly, he said he knew that I would be great and he'd bet that I'd come home afterwards celebrating my first new client. He was right. It was the beginning of a booming, celebrating business. Four years later, I was making a million dollars, working with some of the world's finest corporations as an openly gay consultant.

During this time period, there were many occasions where I was confronted with the choice to tell the truth, and seemingly risk my business, or lie. One of the earliest occasions occurred when I was working with the vice president and treasurer of a large telecommunications company and his five directors, all of whom were straight white males. I was facilitating a two-day off-site meeting and we were discussing staff development. One of the directors turned to me and said, "We were talking at lunch and realized that all of us have the same problem. With all the hours we put into work these days, we hardly see our families anymore and our wives are complaining about it. How do you handle that with your wife?" My mind went nuts! Thoughts of my business folding surfaced like a tidal wave. I felt nauseated and wanted to throw up. Instead, I took a slow, deep breath, looked into the eyes of each of them and said, "My situation is somewhat different from yours in that I live with another man, but let me tell you how I handle the same problem." And I proceeded to tell them. As I spoke I noticed that, one by one, each of them slowly looked in the direction of the vice president (for a signal, I presume) and then back at me. The vice president kept his eyes on me the entire time. I knew he was okay with my sexual orientation, because not only had we discussed it on numerous occasions, but he, his wife, Alan, and I had socialized many times together and enjoyed a longstanding friendship. When I finished speaking there was a slight pause, and then one of the directors thanked me, and the conversation resumed as if nothing out of the ordinary had occurred. But it was clear that something extraordinary had just taken place, and all seven of us had our way of thinking altered as a result of that exchange. Over time, each of those five directors hired me to work with them and their organizations.

Despite my success, however, being out could still cause me fear. One occasion occurred when *Training Magazine* wanted to do a profile on me. During the interview, I spoke of being gay and the relevance I thought it had to my work. To speak out about being a gay man gave me the illusion that I had control over who knew. But for some reason, the idea of seeing my name in print as a gay man gave me no sense of control over who knew. That frightened me. The subject matter frightened the editorial board at *Training Magazine*, who had never before printed the word "gay." It was one of the first professional publications to recognize the relevance being gay has to the workplace. The profile, entitled, "Bob Powers: An Unconventional Success Story," was published in August, 1986. It did shock me when I saw my name written in conjunction with being gay, but I got over it and soon saw myself written up as a gay man in numerous publications.

By the mid-1980's my business was booming. I employed several people and co-owned a second consulting firm with offices in California and England. On any given day, I could be found in first class on TWA, British Airways, or the Concorde, flying between New York, London, and San Francisco. Or, if I wasn't on an airplane, I might be huddled with a group of high level executives or advising a cadre of newly hired Harvard and Stanford MBAs. I was becoming, I thought, a terribly important consultant and very impressive person.

I began to add to the property I already owned, namely, a rental unit in California and our home, an eight-bedroom converted grist mill on a seven-acre island in Three Bridges, New Jersey. I purchased a chic

Manhattan loft overlooking the Empire State Building, a four-bedroom San Francisco co-op overlooking the Golden Gate Bridge, and a small "villa" a few steps off the Mediterranean in Marbella, Spain. My life looked like a fairy tale. In reality, it was becoming a nightmare.

I let the glamour and excitement of my new success almost ruin my life. I was constantly away from home. While I had friends all over the world, I didn't have a single friend at home. I lost whatever humility I had and replaced it with self-importance and added weight. I became fat, mentally and physically. I was also destroying my relationship with the one person in the world I most loved, Alan.

In 1989, I began to make major life changes in an effort to simplify my life. I reduced both my workload and income substantially. I spent most of my time at home. I wrote and completed two books. I acted in community theater. And, as I mentioned, I played in my garden. I also began to do some hard physical, therapeutic, and spiritual work. That same year I became active in a twelve step program for people affected by another's alcoholism. I joined a gym and lost the weight I gained. And I sought therapy. In addition, I became active in what has to be America's most diverse and accepting spiritual community, Glide Memorial Methodist Church in San Francisco, where I now live. All of the above have helped me through a difficult set of years. After fourteen years together, Alan and I ended our relationship in 1992. I don't know how I would have survived the pain I experienced as a result of parting without having undergone the changes that have occurred in me over these past four years.

Today, the changes I have made have enabled me to live like a regular human being. The experiences of my past seem to make sense today.

My dad passed away. I think he was proud, not just of my accomplishment, but how I lived my life. I love my mom and see changes in her. When I told her that my writing books might one day land me on "Oprah," she said, "Oh, that would be nice." I said suspiciously, "Oh, would it?" She laughed easily and said, "Oh, I don't care anymore." And I believe that's true.

Although we live very different lives, my two sisters continue to be supportive, in both words and deeds.

Given the extent to which I used to hide my being gay, and given how openly I live my life today, I find great irony in the following tale, especially for what it says about who we fool when we hide. It was Halloween Day, 1971.

In keeping with the custom of the phone company, I decided to dress in costume. As if I hadn't a fear in the world, I donned a wig, a two-piece woman's suit, high heels, handbag, and pillbox hat. I added makeup, nail polish, and a few accessories. I was completely in drag. Since I wanted to surprise the sixty or so women who worked in the office, I sneaked through the building's back door and began to hobble my way down the long, sterile corridor. About midway to my desk, I started to feel dizzy and within seconds I passed out. Now, here I was, a total closet case, looking like a poor imitation of Bette Davis, spread-eagle on the cold, hard tile of Pacific Telephone's Santa Clara business office. I came to and looked up into the blurry but smiling faces of the twenty-five or thirty women hovering above me. And I thought I wasn't queer.

In Bob's story, you can easily see the strength of denial. Like many of the other gays and lesbians whose stories appear here, Bob experienced great shame. This shame gave way to a sense of empowerment as he moved through the four stages of acceptance. His "coming out," which took over thirty years, was the beginning of this new-found empowerment. Today Bob is grateful for his sexual orientation, an amazing fact considering the extent to which he would earlier do whatever was necessary to hide it. With years of hard personal work following his breakup, Bob crossed the magic line, where fear turned to courage and shame turned to joy. He's never been the same since!

Note your thoughts and reactions to Bob's story.

Vincent W. Patton III, Ed.D.

You shall not take vengeance or bear any grudge against your own people, but you shall love your neighbor as yourself.
                                                      —Leviticus 19:18

I was born in 1954 in Detroit, Michigan and raised in an all-black area of town that was situated between two affluent white sections. Folks referred to it as "Black Bottom," to denote you were at the bottom of the heap. My mother was a nurse, and my father was a career Army man. Surprisingly, I never experienced life as a "military brat," because we stayed in Detroit while my dad did the moving around. It was a somewhat strange but loving relationship between my parents. They got along fine with Dad's never-ending absences. I am the third boy, fifth child of ten children. My parents still joke that the number of children is directly related to the number of times my dad said good-bye when he was off to another assignment.

Because my dad spent a great deal of time away from home and my mother worked full-time, my maternal grandparents, who lived with us, served as surrogate parents. My mother loved her job as a nurse, and it always amazed me how quickly she would get back to work at Henry Ford Hospital after she had given birth to a child, usually within a few weeks. Having the support of her parents made it possible for her to continue her career—which was unusual for a black woman in the 1950's and 1960's, especially for one with a large family.

Growing up in the inner city was a challenge. During my childhood and adolescent years, I witnessed drug deals, violent crimes, and the Detroit riots of 1967. Yet I don't recall living constantly in fear. Back then, everyone knew everyone, and the neighborhoods were sort of an internal urban family. During this time, blacks usually stuck to themselves and seldom ventured outside of the "hood," as we called it, because that meant leaving our comfort zone, thus our security.

Although I never really considered my family poor or destitute, I knew that the dollar had to be stretched. Hand-me-downs were de rigueur. My biggest luxury was going out once a month to a fast food joint, White Castle, for those "itty-bitty," square twelve-cent hamburgers, which I could eat in one bite.

My mother and grandparents were God-fearing, church-going people. Ironically, each of them attended a different church. My mother is Catholic, my grandfather Baptist. My grandmother, who had an "avant garde" approach to religion (her expression), preferred the no-nonsense, no-frills, storefront churches and crusade tents that were so popular in the black community in the fifties and sixties.

With such diversified religious backgrounds, I got my fill of the battle between the Baptists, the Catholics, and the "Whatevers" my grandmother followed. After comparing notes, each of us kids decided that Grandmother's church was the liveliest, with deep-rooted black spiritual singing and dancing. Come Sunday morning, all of us wanted to go with Grandma. So as not to offend our mother and grandfather, we would hold a weekly lottery to see who would go where. I always lost and became a Catholic by default. It was twenty years later that I learned that my older siblings had rigged those lotteries so they could get to go with Grandma.

I was educated in the public school system. I was a very good student in elementary and junior high school, getting mostly A's and B's. My good grades got me into the city's only science and arts college prep high school, Cass Technical. Cass Tech is where big stars such as Diana Ross and Lily Tomlin graduated. Shortly after I started high school, my hormones kicked in and I began to chase girls. While my social life blossomed, my academic success diminished—I did just well enough to get by and keep Mom and Dad happy.

When I was eleven, I frequently ran "errands" for my grandmother. Later, I found these "errands" were actually numbers running (illegal lotteries), which at the time I didn't realize was against the law. It was in fact conducted so openly that even black police officers patrolling the neighborhood usually "played the numbers."

Just a few blocks from where I lived there was a man named Mr. Homer Sylvester. As long as I can remember, the kids and neighbors referred to him as "Homer the Homo Man." I was warned by my entire family never to go by his house and that if I didn't heed this advice, he would get me and do "nasty things" to me. Not fully understanding what those "nasty things" were at eleven years of age, I imagined them to be pretty dreadful. Thus, whenever Mr. Sylvester walked by, I would either walk to the other side of the street or look down or away. There were times I sneaked a glance at him. I thought he looked like a very sad and lonely man. I wanted to ask him why he was called "Homer the Homo Man," and ask him if he was in fact a homo.

One day, my grandmother asked me to run one of her "errands." My grandmother was adamantly against Mr. Sylvester living in the neighborhood, so I was very surprised when she asked me to take some numbers over to him. I later learned that Mr. Sylvester was the backup numbers man in the neighborhood. She gave me at least half a dozen warnings not to go into his house, and to take someone with me. Obliging, I stopped by my best friend Marty's and begged him to come along. After accepting my promise of a quarter if he joined me, Marty promptly "wimped out" when Mr. Sylvester came to the door. He tossed the quarter to me, saying, "See ya 'round, Vinnie, I ain't letting that fag get me!" Then he took off as if he had seen a ghost.

For the first time, I got a good look at Mr. Sylvester. Until then I had always been afraid to look at him. I had imagined a man with a face that was grotesque somehow, perhaps with makeup and lipstick like Little Richard, and with a feminine voice and mannerisms. As Mr. Sylvester opened the door, I saw a man who in his late forties looked no different from any other black man I'd ever seen. He smiled as he opened the screen door, and I heard his voice, which didn't sound remotely feminine. As if he knew I was scared, he kept a safe distance from me, saying, "Hello, Vincent, your grandmother told me that you'd stop by. Let me get those [number] sheets from you, so you can quickly be on your way." As I fumbled in my pocket for little sheets the size of laundry tickets, he could see how nervous I was. I was so scared that I couldn't talk. I handed him the sheets and in doing so noticed how badly my hands were shaking. As I turned to walk away, Mr. Sylvester said with a smile, "Have a nice day. I hope your father's doing well and is safe [my dad was in Vietnam]. I will keep him in my prayers for a safe return. Take care, young man."

As I walked home, my mind was reeling with thoughts of my encounter with Mr. Sylvester. Suddenly, I began to feel really sorry for him. "Imagine that, he's praying for my father," I said to myself. I began to feel bad. My dad was a well-known homophobe in the neighborhood. Whenever he was home, he'd say things like, "Is that queer still hanging around here?" Sometimes he'd say this loud enough for Mr. Sylvester to hear. I truly admired my Dad, so it hadn't taken long for me to emulate him. I had hated Mr. Sylvester, as I did all homosexuals. Hearing Mr. Sylvester say what he had about my father really made me think.

For some reason I couldn't explain, I suddenly turned around and went back to Mr. Sylvester's house. He was surprised to see me. I said, "Mr. Sylvester, I want you to know that I appreciated what you said about my dad. Thank you very much. I also want to tell you how sorry I am for the way I have treated you all these years." Mr. Sylvester seemed stunned. All he could manage to say was a whispered, "Thank you." I left for home. A few days later on my way home from school, I saw him walking down the opposite side of the street. This time, I ran across the street—and almost got hit by a car—just so I could walk past him and look him in the eye to say, "Good afternoon, Mr. Sylvester."

As weeks passed, our simple encounter blossomed into a friendship. Eventually, I asked him the ultimate question, "Are you gay?" He replied that he was, and asked me why I was being so nice to him. He said he was concerned for me because other people in the neighborhood, and my friends, might think that he was taking advantage of me. I explained how moved I was by what he had said to me about praying for my father and that I now realized that he, Mr. Sylvester, was no different from anyone else. Too, I told him that I was embarrassed that I had treated him as if he didn't exist and said I was wrong for having hated him for no reason at all. I was ashamed that I had stooped to the level of the racists I had seen on T.V. during the marches and demonstrations led by Dr. Martin Luther King and I hated myself for contributing to discrimination.

Later that evening, I wrote a letter to my father and told him about this experience. My older brother begged me not to do it, saying that Dad would "go nuts." He said Dad might even try to kill Mr. Sylvester if he found I was befriending him. Surprisingly, when I got my dad's letter a few weeks later he told me that, as a result of what I told him, he had written to Mr. Sylvester expressing his remorse for acting so badly and saying the many things he did about him. He said to Mr. Sylvester, "Now that I see death every day from people of different hues, it doesn't matter who or what you are. I have to keep reminding myself of that. I'm over here fighting to uphold the Constitution of the United States for all of the George Wallaces of the country. I'm over here ducking bullets to keep folks who call me a 'nigger' free. Somehow, [by the way I treated you] I began to feel that I was no better than the 'nigger' callers."

After that my mother and grandmother began to befriend Mr. Sylvester as well. I learned from my grandmother that Mr. Sylvester's lover was killed tragically in an accident at the Ford Motor plant. Shortly after the funeral, Mr. Sylvester became seriously ill with pneumonia. My mother, who worked twelve-hour shifts, stopped by his house and helped nurse him back to health. While the rest of the neighbors continued to turn their backs on him, my mother and grandparents became strong supporters for Mr. Sylvester's civil rights in the

"Black Bottom" section of Detroit. My grandfather, who came around to accepting Mr. Sylvester's lifestyle despite his Baptist background, stepped right into the middle of arguments in Mr. River's barber shop, avowing that Mr. Sylvester belonged in the neighborhood, "the same as everyone else."

A few years later, Mr. Sylvester died of cancer. I learned he had been a strong advocate for the underground black gay community in Detroit. Nearly one hundred people, mostly gay, turned out for his funeral. My entire family, with the exception of two brothers serving in the military, were also there. My grandmother read the eulogy. As a family, we all agreed that we had lost a dear and close friend. I remember my mom saying, "I feel like I lost my brother."

I was proud of my family, all of whom, in a short period of time, rallied behind Mr. Sylvester. And I was especially proud that I was the one who initiated it. That experience led me to accept and appreciate the differences in all people, and I have stood taller and stronger ever since.

At the age of seventeen, I finished high school and joined the Coast Guard. On the day I left for basic training, I said good-bye to all of my family, friends, and neighbors. Everyone seemed proud of me, especially dad, who told everyone he saw that I was joining an elite group. He also warned me that the Coast Guard didn't have many blacks in it. I didn't know just how true his words were until I arrived in Cape May, New Jersey, for training. The year was 1972. The only other blacks I saw were a couple of other recruits. I was in the Coast Guard for almost a year before I met my first black Coast Guard officer.

In most groups I was the only black and it was grueling. In my first day of training, the senior instructor told me, "The job of a marine radio operator is to be a quick thinker and clear speaker," adding that he didn't think these were qualities my ethnic group possessed. I became determined to get through the twenty-four-week course. Proudly, I graduated at the top of my class.

After radio operator school, I was assigned to a weather patrol ship out of New York City at the Coast Guard's largest base, Governor's Island. Unknown to me, just months before my arrival a very serious racial disturbance had taken place, and some black Coast Guardsmen were court-martialed for inciting a riot and other offenses. The incident, which stemmed from a fight between a black Coast Guardsman and a white one, turned into a violent outburst in which one white Coast Guard officer was severely beaten when several black members attempted to take over one of the ships. Needless to say, the racial tension was thick.

The blacks didn't get together socially for fear that someone would think we were "up to something." Determined to make the best out of my hitch, I withdrew into myself. To pass the time, I began to take college correspondence courses. After serving two years on board ship, I had earned over sixty college credits. I was on my way to earning a college degree—something I had thought was almost out of reach for me.

My next assignment was Detroit, my hometown. I was very enterprising in the way I carried out my work, switching shifts, working nights—in an effort to continue my college education. Before my four-year enlistment was up, I had earned my Bachelor of Arts degree from Shaw College in Detroit.

In 1976, I re-enlisted and was offered the opportunity to go to Chicago to become a Coast Guard recruiter. I accepted, knowing that I would now have the opportunity to increase the number of African Americans and other ethnic groups in the Coast Guard. My tour was exciting and I became the most productive recruiter in the Coast Guard. I enrolled in Loyola University's master's program in counseling and graduated in 1978. By now, my Coast Guard career was beginning to take off. I became widely known throughout the service, and my notoriety earned me some exciting opportunities.

I decided to pursue the goal of becoming Master Chief Petty Officer of the Coast Guard, the highest ranking enlisted person in the Coast Guard. My advocacy for civil rights and equal opportunity fuelled this goal. I began to pick and choose career assignments carefully. I said "good-bye" to my occupation in marine radio communications and "hello" to the world of human resource management and development.

I re-enlisted once again and became the equal opportunity specialist for all Coast Guard units in the Great Lakes region, based in Cleveland, Ohio. This was a highly visible and demanding job. I was responsible for providing sensitivity and human awareness training to over twenty-four hundred Coast Guard members and for responding to complaints regarding civil rights, fair treatment, and equal opportunity. My passion for people and my interest in diversity was growing.

It was during this assignment that I encountered my first problem with the way gays were treated in the military. Unlike the other military services, the Coast Guard's ban on homosexuals was somewhat loosely worded, which made it confusing to interpret accurately. I decided to put this regulation to the test when a young female Coast Guard member admitted that she was a lesbian to several of her shipmates. Her commander submitted paperwork to discharge her. The letter requesting her discharge indicated that he was "sorry to submit this because her performance was outstanding." As part of standard procedure, such discharge requests were forwarded to my office for review and comment. I surprised my superiors by recommending her retention, explaining that there was no basis for discharge simply because she made an admission. I added that the regulations were so obtuse that one could easily interpret them to mean that you had to observe someone perform an act of sodomy in order to effect a discharge. While I felt I was taking a risk, I just couldn't back off, especially since her performance record was exceptional. Also, in the back of my mind was Mr. Sylvester. The risk paid off. Once the case was reviewed by the legal officers, they essentially agreed with my findings. This young woman is still in the Coast Guard and is highly regarded.

Not too surprisingly, the regulation was soon rewritten to "tighten up" the loophole. This new version was dubbed "The Patton Amendment," for which I was not too happy to take credit. In the eyes of my superiors, I had done a great job of bringing the loophole to everyone's attention.

In 1981, I became the first enlisted person ever to be selected to complete a special work project while attending graduate school under paid sabbatical. After less than three years, I earned a Doctorate of Education from the American University in Washington, D.C., where I developed a new performance appraisal system. Upon graduation, I remained in Washington for another year in order to implement and evaluate the system. I received much national recognition and earned numerous military and civilian awards for this work. My "fruit salad" (ironically, the name given to the ribbons on my uniform) began to grow.

When I completed this work, I had a strong desire to return to sea, where my work in education and training had started. I wanted to slow down the pace of my life and get back to the mainstream of the Coast Guard, working on the humanitarian missions that interested me when I joined. I moved to Seattle, Washington, in 1986, and for two years I was stationed aboard the Coast Guard Cutter *Boutwell*, patrolling the Alaska waters. I was thirty-two. It was the best tour of my career.

I returned to Coast Guard Headquarters in Washington, D.C., in 1988 as a training and performance analyst. Five years later, I was promoted to Command Master Chief for the entire Atlantic area, which includes all units east of the Mississippi. I am one short step away from reaching my goal to become the Master Chief Petty Officer of the Coast Guard.

I know now that the more open and willing I am to find out about differences in people, the more tolerant and accepting I become. That's what happened to me and my family. I'm fortunate that I began to learn this lesson at an early age. I remember Mr. Sylvester saying to me, "It's not important what others think of you; what's important is what you think of yourself." As a black, heterosexual male, that's the message I'd like to leave with people, especially my colleagues in the service.

Vince's story points out how fear can support unfounded generalizations and how hate, bigotry, and homophobia is learned and can be unlearned. An entire neighborhood abused "Homer the Homo Man." A small act of kindness exhibited by Homer caused Vince to question all that he had been taught about homosexuals. What Vince had learned, he quickly let go of as his friendship with this gay man grew. Vince carried these childhood realizations with him into his workplace. Today he works hard for the rights of all people. As a result, Vince knows he is a caring and courageous human being, a fact that builds strong self-esteem.

Note your thoughts and reactions to Vince's story.

Lexie Johnson

I tell people when I go out to speak that no matter how people got this virus, we've got to open our arms up to everybody—not just to me because I'm heterosexual.

—Magic Johnson

I was born in the midst of a blizzard in the spring of 1943 at a Navy base hospital in Newport, Rhode Island. My dad, a Navy lieutenant and former professional football star, was a bit disappointed. He had hoped that his firstborn would be a boy. "I had big plans for him, too," he confessed to my mom in a letter he wrote to her a few hours after my birth. I can smile now when I read his letter because I know my dad a lot better than when I was a pre-teen and discovered the letter. He added, "Well, I guess we can't name her Michael." And they didn't. Nor did they name my brother Michael when he was born four years later.

My dad was the "man's man" and a product of his environment. He was born in 1915, the second of five sons, in an ethnically diverse neighborhood. Kids were raised to be tough, and as one of the toughest he became the town hero. A high school football star, he was awarded a scholarship to a large university. He continued onto the pro circuit, then the Navy, and finally coaching "boys" into "men."

Once discharged from the Navy, he began his career as a football coach. Mom, my brother, and I trekked with my dad from east coast to west coast and back any number of times. I attended eight schools in twelve years as we moved to wherever a football team needed a coach. My mother, who grew up in Santa Monica, California, reluctantly followed my dad's dream. A housewife for most of her life, my mom was the typical California girl of the 1930's—beautiful, with stars in her eyes, and a Hollywood view of the world. I was her Shirley Temple, a blonde, curly-haired charmer in pastel organdy. I could perform a perfect rendition of "The Good Ship Lollipop" on cue. Yet, I could also imitate my dad pacing the sidelines of a football field, aping all of his gestures of elation and despair. I was a good student who learned to adapt academically as well as socially. I made friends easily, yet I dreaded the time when I would have to say good-bye...usually after a two-year stay in one place.

At home, I watched my mom follow the stars. She loved Lana Turner, Betty Grable, Loretta Young, as well as most of the glamorous breed of Hollywood lovelies. My dad had his heroes, too, all "men," bruisers who could tough it out both on and off the turf, scoring points and bone fractures with maybe a grimace, but never a tear. When my brother cried, my dad would call him a sissy. I even have a letter that my dad wrote to me when we were visiting my mom's family in California that said, "Tell Tommy to be a good boy and not cry for any silly reason." My role models were limited to nuns, cheerleaders, and majorettes.

Although my parents entertained and accepted people of every race and religion, our guests could be defined in shades of only black and white. Even the academically elite, when Dad coached at a New England Ivy League college, reflected the brains and brawn type. As the various teams paraded in and out of our home throughout the years, only once did I observe the slightest human vulnerability in the men and their coach. That was a tragic day. I was twelve. One of my dad's football players had been missing for two or three days, when my dad found him hanging from the rafters of his fraternity house. My dad wept openly for this tormented player. It was the first time I saw my dad cry. I overheard him tell my mom how the whole team cried at the funeral. I remember thinking, "Real men do feel, and there are even times when it's okay for them to cry."

I learned, often the hard way, to make my own choices in life. At fifteen I ran away with a punk, who not only rejected any type of sports, but any other accepted role in society. He hated everyone, including himself. After six weeks of physical and mental abuse, I called home. My parents wired me an airline ticket and picked me up at the airport. Again I saw my dad cry, but his tears of relief were soon replaced by anger. As we approached our housing development, my mom ordered me to crouch down in the back seat until we pulled into the garage and closed the door. They were ashamed of me and didn't want the neighbors to see me. I was now the proverbial "bad girl."

My perception of the world changed. No longer the innocent kid who could easily adapt to the peers around me, I began to learn and to feel what it was like to be different. Some of my friends rejected me—their parents felt I would lead them astray. My teachers were insensitive, making remarks that embarrassed me in front of the class. Even the principal treated me as though I had disgraced the school. On the day I went to his office for my transcripts (we were moving again), the principal said, "Look, I know all about you. Don't think you can ever come back here, if you change your mind again." Returning to high school was the hardest thing I had ever done.

In retrospect, my impulsive flight from home taught me to judge outsiders differently than I had been taught. Ironically, my first encounter with a homosexual involved a relative, a second cousin, who paid my family a surprise visit when I was seventeen.

Robin arrived at our home in the spring of 1960. He had been my very first friend. As a toddler I used to visit my grandmom who lived next door to him. I remember snapshots of me sitting proudly in his wooden wagon, Robin at the helm, protective of his curly-haired charge.

Robin had just been discharged from the Army after confessing that he was a homosexual. My parents, of course, were told another story, something about his having "flat feet" (a supposedly honorable means of military discharge), as I recall. One night after everyone else went to bed, Robin and I stayed up and talked. He told me about his being gay and about the gay community. I was enthralled and was curious to know everything.

"Who else knew?" I wanted to know. "What was the community like?" I asked.

I asked a million questions. I listened to every word, absorbing each detail of information as he sat explaining his life to me in my dad's La-Z-Boy. We talked until the sun came up.

I felt that Robin was as brave as any of my dad's football players for acknowledging his homosexuality to me, as well as the army chaplain, army psychologist, and his immediate superiors. I loved him for sharing his secret with me and I accepted him completely.

The following day, my mom suggested that my dad take Robin on a tour of the university where he coached. My dad vehemently refused. While my parents didn't know for certain that Robin was a homosexual, my dad certainly suspected. It took a heated argument, some manipulation, and much coaxing by my mom before the coach reluctantly agreed to take Robin on campus. But Dad arranged the excursion so that Robin never approached the athletic building. He dropped him off at the library and told him he would pick him up at an arranged time. The coach complained to me, "Your mother doesn't understand what people would think if I introduced her cousin to the athletic department." I must confess, I secretly enjoyed my dad's dilemma.

Robin moved back to Los Angeles, where he eventually came out to his family and friends. I have always felt a special bond with Robin, for he was the first to share such an intimate part of himself with me. While I empathized with my dad's (narrow) field of vision, I didn't agree. I knew in my heart that he was wrong about Robin.

Shortly after Robin's visit, I entered dental school, hated it, and quit. In 1963, I married Bill Johnson and over the years brought two children into the world, a daughter and a son. For a while, I worked as a dental receptionist. In the mid-seventies, I returned to college and began a long quest to attain a degree in English Literature, which I did in 1981. Following college I worked for a while as an editor. Today I am a freelance writer and real estate agent. We are settled in Media, Pennsylvania.

I'm no longer that organdy clad little girl who could mimic Shirley or the coach on cue. Nor am I the "bad girl" who was shunned and teased after returning from my runaway journey to womanhood. After almost fifty years, I am the sum of these experiences and more. I sing my own songs, some torch songs, some ballads of joy. And through them all there is a refrain of self-acceptance, sometimes barely audible, and other times loud and clear. Self-acceptance, the never ending process. Without it I fear I would miss the hugs of love and acceptance from others, as well as those dreaded jeers from the sidelines.

Sometimes that acceptance has been difficult, like when Dad died six years ago. My brother and I discovered that my dad had written to his football players telling them he loved them. Neither my brother nor I ever received such a letter, even though I wanted one. To know that Dad was capable of expressing love helps me to understand him.

Over the years, my exposure both to the arts and the workplace has brought me a diverse network of friends and clients, both homosexual and heterosexual. Bill and I, who celebrated our thirtieth wedding anniversary in 1993, have always judged our friends and co-workers on the merits of their spirituality and integrity as human beings. I feel that we are fortunate to have close friends who have helped us, teaching us lessons in self-acceptance and diversity, in ways that are unique when compared to our family backgrounds. My dad and many others of his generation were raised with the heroes of the John Wayne and Knute Rockne era. I suppose they served a purpose, teaching men to be tough and face the world with a strong-armed conviction of manhood. It was a simple lesson in the much more simple world where tunnel vision helped them to focus on the light at the end of a narrow, yet safe passageway of life.

Last year, when I lost a first cousin to AIDS, I realized that even that passageway is no longer safe in dealing with life or death. My uncle and aunt had learned of my cousin's (and their son's) gay lifestyle over two decades ago. In fact, I was visiting them when my cousin, Gab, first came out. My aunt's twin brother from Kansas was also there. My aunt knew he would not handle the news well, and she kept putting off telling him. She confided in me how hard it would be to explain his nephew was gay. She was right. His reaction was shock, disbelief, and anger. But the harder and more painful ordeal was yet to come.

Gab, who gradually cut himself off from the rest of our family, met Bill and me for dinner on many occasions. Early on, he confided to me that he knew of three other cousins in our immediate family who were gay. I still believe him today, even if they have yet to come out. Gab moved to Palm Springs around 1983. He asked his parents not to divulge his whereabouts to his aunts, uncles, and cousins who lived nearby. I'm not sure why he chose to cut himself off from the family. I can only guess that he wasn't able to cope with reactions from uncles from Kansas or those who didn't give personal tours of campuses where they worked. Yet what Gab missed, I later found out, was accepting family members who loved him and would have liked the opportunity to tell him so.

I wrote to him a few weeks before he died. I told him how much his kinship had meant to me and recalled fondly memories we shared growing up. I told him I loved him.

My aunt (Gab's mother) called my mom and told her that she was upset that I had written to him. She asked my mom to tell me and the other members of the family not to contact him again. She insisted he was fine, that he was misdiagnosed and had, in fact, just attended a party the night before. This was confusing since she and my uncle had told the family that Gab had been HIV positive for over a year before I mailed my letter. I can only guess that her action was part of a pretense of denying the inevitable. I will probably never know.

Last month I had dinner with my aunt and uncle. They told me about disposing of Gab's estate. "Only an antique chandelier was left," they explained. They didn't know how to place a value on it, so they hadn't sold it and, at this point, they didn't care. I was struck by the fact that they didn't talk about Gab's last days, or the day that they and Gab's brother and sister rented a boat so that they could scatter his ashes across the San Francisco Bay. Maybe, in time, they will share this moment with me.

I know that Gab struggled with the parent/son relationship, as many sons do. I also know that in the last years of his life he created a new family, finding acceptance and respect from the many friends he made in Palm Springs. Gab owned a complex of garden apartments, where he lived. His tenants, as well as his parents and sisters, helped care for him during his long illness and his death.

I will always remember Gab. I'll remember the trip we took to Disneyland when he was twelve and I was seventeen. We rode the Matterhorn, thinking it was the scariest and most fun ride we'd ever taken. I'll remember how we giggled and carried on at the family gatherings when we were delegated to the "kid" table in the kitchen.

Throughout the years, the table expanded as our family grew to twenty-three cousins. I've always thought of my cousins as an intimate barometer of society—each member of our family circle reflecting, in some way, society at large. There are divorces, of course, and a single father raising a daughter. There is Patti Ann, the youngest girl cousin who is a dentist and new mother. My brother, the CEO of a major publishing company. Bobby the sportswriter and comedian, who lives in Fairbanks. There are interracial marriages with beautiful second cousins who light up a room.

Most of us have remained close and visit each other even though we live in the far corners of the continent. We share secrets and discover the secrets our parents shared. We laugh at how transparent they are in attempting to cover up what they don't think we should know even though we've reached middle age. We compare discrepancies in the stories of our parents' childhoods. We are proud of our Italian heritage and marvel at the fact that our grandmother, Nicholena, came to this country all alone at the age of fourteen, never to see her parents again.

Fifteen cousins attended a reunion last April where my aunt and uncle celebrated their fiftieth wedding anniversary. As we gathered from all across the continent, many of us remembered Gab and reminisced about him, the first of us to pass from this earth. He was our most handsome cousin and one of the most caring. He was the cousin that none of us had the opportunity to embrace before he left us.

Like many kids, Lexie was perplexed by the messages she received from her father, an ex-Navy man and current football coach, and her experience with young gay people. Not knowing how to deal with these conflicts she chose to run away. Eventually, she came to rely on her experience rather than her father's advice which helped her move along the path of acceptance.

Lexie's story also depicts how views of homosexuality have changed over the generations. Her parents and her aunt and uncle found it almost impossible to speak about homosexuals and when they did it was often accompanied by disparaging remarks. Lexie and her cousins experienced much greater freedom when it came to talking about homosexuality as evidenced by their easy reminiscences of her cousin Gab who died of AIDS.

Note your thoughts and reactions to Lexie's story.

Art Moreno

...[T]ime will change and even reverse many of your present opinions. Refrain, therefore, awhile from setting yourself up as a judge of the highest matters.

—Plato

I was born on March 16, 1934, and experienced what I believe to have been a very normal childhood. I was the middle of five children. I had two older brothers and two younger sisters (one of whom died of a diabetes-related condition a few years back). My family was Catholic and I was raised with Catholic beliefs.

My father worked for a photographic services company in El Paso, Texas. Beginning in grammar school and throughout my schooling I spent evenings and Saturdays working with him. My father taught me in order to prepare me for a career. In high school, I worked in a photography studio, and although I was somewhat envious of my friends who did not have to work on Saturdays, I enjoyed the money. In addition, I learned a great deal from the owner of the studio. He had worked in the carnival and really knew how to "work" people, how to promote himself. It was a fascinating education. I was the school photographer at my high school and I won awards for my photography.

In the (Catholic) environment in which I was raised sex was never discussed at home. So homosexuality was never mentioned. Sex was something I learned about through my friends and life experiences. At the time, all I knew about homosexuality was that it was a sin and was wrong.

Homosexuality simply didn't concern me. My only contact with homosexuality was through movies. Whenever my friends and I saw obviously gay people in the movies we would make negative comments between ourselves. We never made such comments directly toward an actual gay person because we didn't have the chance—we didn't know any.

During my teenage years and my early twenties, I subscribed to the notion that homosexuals were bad. I don't know why really. Certainly I was not that great. I mean, I had many flaws, being something of a womanizer and a partier. At the time, I thought the worst thing a father could have happen to him was to have a homosexual son. There was no logic or reason for believing this, but I just felt that way. I felt that if God ever wanted to punish someone that that would be the way he would do it.

Well, God punished me (although he really blessed me) by giving me a son who is gay. Mark Steven is my fourth son, and when I first found out he was gay I was devastated. Once I found out, I planned to dis-own him unless he sought help and found a woman to marry so he could be in a heterosexual relationship.

I felt shame, guilt, and concern about what my friends and others would think. I was determined to get help for my son. I was very hurt. But I see now that I hurt him more by the lack of acceptance and the rigid stance I took. My relationship with Mark was strained. I couldn't deal with it, much less accept it, and I told him so. I was so unaccept-ing that he moved to Phoenix where two of his brothers lived. In the midst of all this, I met an openly gay, celibate Catholic priest, who I hired to work for me while he was on sabbatical.

If it wasn't for this priest's help and my three older sons, who were very accepting of Mark—and for that I am now very grateful—I don't know if I would have been able to get to the point where I am now. The priest told me about Parents and Friends of Lesbians and Gays, commonly known as PFLAG. I began to attend meetings and they were very revealing and very rewarding. The meetings offered me the chance to share my pent-up feelings and let me know that there are a lot of parents in varying stages of acceptance when it comes to their gay children.

As time went by, I continued to attend PFLAG meetings. I read all that I could get my hands on and I came to realize that homosexuality is not a choice and that only God knows why some people turn out to be gay. Soon, communications with my son increased, and our relation-ship and love blossomed. I no longer think of Mark as my homosex-ual son but as a warm, loving, friendly, thoughtful, considerate creature of God, who now knows my heart. I became accepting of my son.

Time passed. Soon Mark brought his lover home for Christmas. I knew his cousins (my nephews) whom he grew up with would be at the house and I wasn't sure if they knew if he was gay or not. So, I got them all together before Mark arrived to let them know that he was gay. I simply wanted to prepare them in the event that they did not know and that he would be coming with his lover. I also wanted to see if there would be any negative reactions. Their response floored me. They said, "So, what's the big deal? He's our cousin and we love him." That was the extent of it.

I became very active in PFLAG. One day, one of our local county commissioners made a very disgusting comment publicly that to contain AIDS all homosexuals should be castrated. Until then, I had been closeted about my son's homosexuality. Only family members and friends who needed to know were told my son is gay. "I didn't make an issue of his sexuality," I thought. I was simply trying to deal with it, understand it, and accept it. But when the county commissioner spoke so ignorantly, so hatefully, I just didn't feel right in doing nothing about it. I spoke with my wife and all of my sons and told them that I planned to go public and stand up for what I believed was right and, perhaps, to try to make up to my gay son for all the hurt that I caused him as well as to stand and speak as a heterosexual to defend the gay community.

I was given 100 percent support from my sons and wife. This was a big step for me to take—to go public and come out of the closet about my son. I just knew in my heart that I had to do it.

I told a priest friend of mine (not the one mentioned earlier) that I was planning to go to commissioners' court and make a statement admonishing the commissioner. My friend, the priest, accompanied me. This is the essence of the statement I made:

> I am here to address the AIDS issue and to respond to Mr. Fonseca's recent statement. I come first as a concerned father of a gay son who resides out of El Paso and whom I love very much.... I represent PFLAG, a support group of parents and friends of lesbians and gays, and on their behalf I wish to respond to the recent insensitive and bigoted remarks made by Commissioner Fonseca concerning AIDS and the gay community.
>
> It is particularly distressing to witness an elected official display in public such ignorance and prejudice about a subject so serious. His attempt to explain away his intolerant comments by saying he was only making a joke shows not only bad judgment, but callous disrespect for us all. In addition, to try to explain his prejudice by referring to his religious beliefs is equally deplorable. All the religions we know teach understanding and compassion, not ridicule and intolerance.
>
> If Mr. Fonseca is truly concerned about AIDS in our city and the potential high cost of care for those afflicted with this dreaded virus, then we suggest he spearhead a concerted city-county effort

to provide the necessary funds to educate our community about the virus and how it can be avoided—because the affected population is everyone. Every dollar spent now for such education will surely save hundreds, maybe thousands of dollars later.

We ask all locally elected officials to fully inform themselves about this serious problem and take a leadership role in helping to solve it rather than stooping to, as Mr. Fonseca has, making unproductive crude comments in public which vilify those unfortunate persons afflicted by the virus.

Mr. Fonseca has embarrassed all fair-minded El Pascans by his recent actions. We can only hope the voters in his district remember this embarrassment when they next have the opportunity to vote.

My comments made the television news, and, surprisingly, of some twenty-five or thirty telephone calls and comments made by customers and friends coming into my photography store, all but one came to express their support for me and my position. The one that didn't was a little old lady who wanted to read scripture to me. It was a great feeling to know that I had done the right thing, and I was reassured by the positive comments that were made.

My wife and I are actively involved in PFLAG, helping parents to understand and love their children, and we are also involved with the Southwestern AIDS Committee as advocates. I have been blessed or fortunate to be the advocate for two young men, one heterosexual and one homosexual, who have since passed away from AIDS. Both were very angry young men when I began as their advocate, but as time passed our bonding and friendship grew. I feel that I was instrumental in helping each to re-establish a relationship with God.

As St. Francis of Assisi said:

> Oh divine master grant that I may not so much seek to be consoled as to console. To be understood as to understand. To be loved as to love. For it is in giving that we receive.

I am blessed with a gay son without whom these wonderful life experiences would never have been possible.

Art's cultural and religious background led him to initially feel that having a gay son was punishment from God. Today, no longer judgmental, Art speaks out about his son and the gay community. In order to move so far, Art had to overcome his religious (Catholic), cultural (Latino), and geographic (Southern) backgrounds, all of which sent messages that homosexuality was, in some way, evil. Along his path to acceptance, Art was helped by a Catholic priest, members of PFLAG, and his own family. It is critical that people find support from others to effectively deal with these issues. The support Art received helped him to move to a place of acceptance, a place where he now enjoys an intimate, loving relationship with his son.

Note your thoughts and reactions to Art's story.

Mick Miller

The ultimate lesson all of us have to learn is unconditional love, which includes not only others but ourselves as well.
—Elizabeth Kübler-Ross

My name is Mick Miller, and I am a forty-one-year-old white heterosexual male. My story involves my early experiences and attitudes with homosexuality, people I have known, my own growth, sexuality (both heterosexual and homosexual), and the evolution of my values and beliefs.

My upbringing is important to my story. I've lived all my life in a rural area of New Jersey. I am the second son of Catholic parents, lower-middle-class. I have three brothers, one older and two younger, and one younger sister. My mother died when I had just turned fourteen. My father died when I was twenty-seven. I also had another younger brother. He died two years ago, six days after his thirty-second birthday. The cause of his death was starvation; I'll tell you about that in a moment. My family has a long history of alcoholism. My father was alcoholic, my mother co-alcoholic. I can't speak for my siblings, but I am an alcoholic in recovery, as is my youngest brother. Our heritage is Irish-German.

Ours was a family that had strict unwritten rules: don't talk, don't trust, don't feel. We were expected to obey blindly, have unwavering loyalty, not question the authority of our elders, rise above the standard of living my parents had, and never make mistakes. We never said, "I love you." There was no need to—it was simply understood. When we were punished we were told, "This hurts us more than it hurts you. We're only doing it because we love you." That was when we were told we were loved. Irish-German Catholics: stiff, authoritative, fearful of the wrath of God—unless you were drunk, then you might loosen up a bit.

As a child I was not very happy. There were fun days and events, but basically I was miserable. I had to follow my older brother's footsteps, and he had big feet and a long stride. I never lived up to my parents' expectations. I was told that anything I wanted to do was foolish, that I was a dreamer and dreamers never make it. I was also a daily bed wetter until age eighteen. That had a profound effect on my sexuality due to the abuse my mother forced on me. She would humiliate me, diaper me, threaten me, right up until her death.

In recent therapy, I have remembered having thoughts of wanting to be castrated as early as age eight. I thought, "If I didn't have a penis maybe I wouldn't wet my bed." Nice thoughts for an eight-year-old. It later caused me trouble in my relations with women; for years I preferred masturbating to direct sexual encounters. This I learned was due to my unconscious hate of my own sexuality. If I hated my penis, how could a woman possibly enjoy it? My mother, being so strict and severe, left me with a feeling that I could not be safe with a female. Having had no homosexual desires, I was better off alone. A very non-threatening decision. My attainment of puberty and years of sexuality were fairly typical. I had crushes on girls since early childhood. I modeled myself after what I saw in the world around me. Mom and dad, lovers in movies and on TV, everything was heterosexual.

My first awareness of homosexuality came in the seventh grade. A friend of mine would come from school and pretend he was gay. What fun we had. Swishing, lisping, holding our wrists limp. He told me that was how queers acted. I had no idea what homosexuality was, but I thought I was learning all about "them."

Puberty gave rise to experimentation, both heterosexual and homosexual. School chums and I would gather in the woods with a stolen Playboy magazine. We would look at the pictures of naked women. We had a new mission in life, masturbating in mass and wondering what it was like to actually have sex with a woman. We weren't quite sure what we were supposed to do, but we knew it definitely involved someone of the opposite sex. We would constantly check to see whose erection was the biggest. We would have contests to see who could ejaculate first. There was little shame, just experimentation with and curiosity about our newfound toys.

When I was about thirteen-and-a-half, I had a direct homosexual encounter with another boy whom I now believe to be heterosexual. I never was his friend after that, avoiding him in school and on the streets. I also knew that I wasn't a queer and didn't want to be one.

I had another negative experience a few years later. Living in a rural community, it was common practice to hitchhike. School was fifteen miles away and if you missed the bus home, you would simply thumb a ride. The fears of today were just not prevalent twenty-five years ago. Crime was virtually nonexistent in our area.

One day I had to hitch a ride home, something I had done many times. Within five minutes I had a ride. The driver told me he had to stop at his house to let the dogs out. It sounded okay to me. His house was many miles away in territory I was not familiar with. He let the dogs out and asked if I would like to come in his house for a soda. I agreed. While in the house he took out some pornography and asked me if I had ever fucked a woman. I told him no. He came up in back of me, reached around me, and started to rub my penis. He asked me if I had ever had a man suck my cock and told me that he would, if I wanted him to. I pushed him away and said, "No." I told him that he had better take me home right away. On the way to my house he told me not to tell anyone what had happened. He said he meant no harm, that he would like to be friends. I was paralyzed with fear.

After he dropped me off I realized that he knew where I lived. I was terrified he would come back. That night I lay in my bed unable to sleep, just knowing he was coming back to get me. I woke my father and told him what had happened. The end result was that the police were contacted, and I showed them where the man lived. They arrested him and charged him with impairing the morals of a minor. He pleaded guilty and I have no idea what happened to him after that. I definitely had some strong feelings about "queers" by now. But it was more fear than hate. I'm sure that if I hadn't had future contact with homosexuals, my fears could have developed into the homophobic hate that is so prevalent in our society today.

At age eighteen I was working in a restaurant in a nearby town that had a large homosexual population. Many of the waiters and clients were gay. I was intrigued by them. They would act very campy in the kitchen, calling each other "Mary" and referring to a he as a she. It reminded me of what my friend had taught me back in the seventh grade. The hitchhike driver was a child molester. These men were not. At first I was fearful, but no one ever approached me. Eventually, feeling safer with them, I began to trust them. To me they were just a bunch of wild guys who loved to swish and lisp. I came to love being with them. They were clever and funny, qualities I admired.

Doug, a cook there, was about ten years my senior. He was a large man, about six-foot-three and 290 pounds. In his youth he was much slimmer and had worked as a female impersonator. In his later years he did parodies, Ethel Merman and the like. We became close friends. I would go to his house for dinner and got to know his parents quite well (they were aware of his sexual orientation). I felt at ease with him. He would take me to gay clubs and cabarets to see the impersonators and would introduce me to all the stars. Different jobs eventually separated us and we lost touch with each other. I would occasionally talk to someone who had seen him and they would tell me how he was doing. About six years ago I read in the paper that he was murdered. I was deeply saddened. Doug had helped turn my fears into acceptance. He was someone who lived life as I did, but was sexually attracted to people of the same sex. Nothing more, nothing less. He influenced my beliefs and attitudes, and for that I will always be grateful. But the true test was yet to come.

My brother, Thom, would help me grow in ways I never dreamed possible. Thom was the "oddball" of the family. At birth, he had blond hair. No one in the family had blond hair. He was always frail as a child and even my youngest brother, one year younger than Thom, soon assumed a higher position in the pecking order. We used to tease Thom unmercifully as siblings do, since he was the weakest. He was my mom's pet. "Midgeon," she used to call him as an infant, combination of midget and pigeon, because he was so small and would make little cooing noises.

Thom excelled in school. He was a veritable genius and popular with everyone. He had poor athletic skills, a quality that ranked high with my father, and instead he developed his artistic abilities by going into theater. I admired Thom for this because I also was not up to snuff in the athletic field, at least by my father's standards. I quit the basketball team in my junior year in order to be in the class play. What disappointments we were. My other brothers were wrestling stars (one a state champion), a basketball star, and a track star (with school records). Thom and I were nothings. Actors. Actors were dreamers. Actors were sissies, not "real men." So I could identify with Thom.

In our later years I pursued cooking (I was the only male in my home economics class) and photography, while Thom remained in theater. To our family, these were definitely artistic professions, and being artistic was equal to being unmanly. Thom, because he was slight and had absolutely no athletic demeanor about him, had an even harder time breaking out of the family mold, but break out he did. For years I suspected Thom was gay. For years he didn't tell me. Being aware of the homosexual stereotype, I observed that Thom had many girlfriends, but none that was steady. In addition, he was slight, artistic, and sensitive. Actually, it was more of a gut feeling than a stereotype that made me wonder about Thom's sexual orientation.

About five years ago Thom came out of the closet to me. We talked about what it was like for him to grow up being gay, how tortured he felt by Dad. He didn't remember Mom well, as she died when he was still very young. Had I been homophobic, I might have rejected Thom as our father did. I am grateful I didn't reject him. I believe we helped each other reach out for intimacy in a way neither of us had ever experienced. That leap of faith has helped me a great deal as I continue to strive for trust and meaning in close relationships.

In one of our conversations I asked if he was practicing safe sex. He said he was, but sex was not all that frequent. He simply could not find a lover. He had never been in a relationship. Any lover he ever did have had been casual or just someone he met in a club. Six months later, Thom came down with a cold that lingered on and on. When he finally went to a doctor, he was told it had developed into pneumonia. Upon hospitalization, it was discovered he had AIDS. He said he probably contracted it about seven years earlier while in college. He had no idea who gave it to him, or who he may have given it to. All this happened during the time AIDS was new and not much was known about its transmission.

I was devastated by the news, but what shocked me most was my first reaction, anger. My first thought was "that's what you get for being queer." I was disappointed and surprised at myself. I thought I was beyond an attitude like that, but there it was—a value judgment directed at my brother. It only lasted a few seconds. I truly do not know if it was just a defense mechanism, because my brother had just told me he was going to die soon, or if I still had, or have, prejudices against homosexuals. I want to believe the former.

During the next two years, Thom kept having bouts of pneumonia, each one lasting longer and weakening him further. For all the years he spent in the theater, he was never financially successful. He lived hand-to-mouth. The year before his diagnosis he finally quit the circuit and accepted a job as assistant professor of Theater Arts at a small university. He was finally earning a decent wage. After he learned he had AIDS, he quit his job and formed another theater company. He wanted to spend his remaining time doing the things he truly loved even if it meant living hand-to-mouth again. He decided he wasn't dying with AIDS, but rather, he was going to live with AIDS.

He moved to Seattle, Washington, formed another company, and applied for and received grants to produce plays to be performed in the rural interior of the state for a summer cultural program. He was truly living. He even met a lover and had his first committed relationship. Just as the troupe hit the road for its first performance, Thom's lungs collapsed. He was driven 250 miles back to Seattle to be admitted to the hospital again. I received a call from my youngest brother, who lived in Baton Rouge. He said he was going to move to Seattle, to take care of Thom. He did and he ended up marrying a woman who was Thom's close friend.

A month later, Thom was back in the hospital. His lungs would not stay inflated. The doctors told him that they could operate by literally removing his lungs and abrade the outside to build scar tissue. The hope was that it would keep the air from escaping. He agreed to the operation. I called to talk to him the morning of the operation. I told him that I loved him very much and that if he died during the operation, that I would miss him very much. It was very hard for me to tell him that, but I didn't want him to die without having said how I felt. Remember that love was not spoken about in our house, it was assumed. God, how we needed to hear the words. Thom told me he loved me too and would wait for me if he died. I got a call later that night that he survived, but was in guarded condition. He was released several weeks later.

Upon returning home with my youngest brother, Thom's health deteriorated rapidly. He was so weak and short of breath he could barely walk. He was admitted to the hospital again within a few weeks, this time fighting respiratory infections. It was at that point Thom decided to refuse any more treatment. He no longer wished to fight the inevitable. It was October when he told me about his decision. I flew out to see him one last time. When I got there he was emaciated, but in good spirits. He was refusing food and medication; all he had was saline drip and morphine for the pain.

We spent the week talking. I had remembered in therapy about my abuse and came to understand my sexual dysfunctions. I could identify with him all too well. Mom tortured me. Dad tortured him. We had both suffered shame and humiliation that affected our sexuality. I had trouble in relationships with women, he had trouble in relationships with men. We both had trouble dealing with intimacy and sexuality. We established a bond, a deeper understanding of ourselves and each other. He told me how he never felt "right." He always wanted to come out, but was afraid. He told me he so desperately wanted to be loved by our father, to be able to say, "Dad, I'm gay, I'm everything you find repugnant, but I'm still your son. Can you tell me you love me? Can you love me for who I am unconditionally, not for what I do or what I don't do?" I found I could identify with his longing to be loved for who he was regardless of whether his lifestyle was acceptable to society or any individual.

I went home and called frequently. As the weeks passed he grew weaker and weaker. We began to use humor to lighten our moods. I would call and announce that I was "just seeing if you've died." He would respond, "Not yet, but I'll call you as soon as I do." I told him I had an airplane reservation to come out during the Christmas season and asked if he thought he would live until then. He said he didn't think so. As the time grew near, I urged him to hold on until I got there so I could see him in person one last time. It was out of his hands now, he said, just as he always believed it had been.

He lived until I was able to get there during the holidays. On December 21, 1990 he celebrated his thirty-second birthday. He was not to have another. In the two months that had passed since I had seen him last, he had not eaten enough to keep a mouse alive. He looked like a person I had seen in a photo from the concentration camps in Nazi Germany. And yet he was full of life and spirit. We talked about spiritual things. About dying in peace. We talked so there would be no regrets. I said things to him so that after he died I would not be plagued by the thought, "I wish I had told him that before he died." I told him, again, how much I loved him and would miss him. He told me, again, that he would wait for me, that we would see each other again. It was a beautiful thought to me that the God we were taught to fear was going to accept us both. We both truly believed that the God who created us would not refuse our love. The God of our youth, we felt, had prejudiced men write the rules by which we were expected to abide. Our new God loves us just as we are, for we are only men and suffer the frailties of being human.

Every day when I left the hospital, I would kiss Thom good-bye. I was no longer ashamed. I had not kissed another man since I was a child. I stopped the day I decided I was too old to kiss my father. I was not afraid to catch AIDS, I was not afraid of what others might think. To love is to give and to give is to be humble. In our society I think there is nothing as threatening or possibly humiliating for most heterosexual men as kissing another man. Most would die first.

I left Seattle on December 26, 1990. When I left the hospital room that day I kissed Thom one last time. I knew I would never see him again in this life. It was so hard. We both knew it was the end. In the hallway I saw one of Thom's friends. I embraced him and I cried. He held me and cried too. Two men, one gay, one straight, suffering the loss of another human being, found comfort and strength in each other that morning.

In our society Thom would not be accepted by the majority because he was gay. But to me he was one of the bravest, strongest men I have ever known. He overcame his fears and accepted himself for who he was, unconditionally. He gave his love freely to all regardless of sexual orientation, sex, race, age, or any other characteristic that our society uses to differentiate us and assign value and judgment.

Two days after I left, Bob, the man by whom I was comforted in the hospital, called to tell me Thom had died. He had taken his last curtain call.

Looking back I find it symbolic that Thom, who had been starved of love all his life, died of physical starvation. In the end he finally found the love he had longed for all his life. He loved himself, and many others loved him too, unconditionally, and they told him so. He died a peaceful man.

I am now working on that same task. I am trying to truly love myself. I know what they mean now, when they say you need to love yourself before you can truly love another. There were many things I was taught as a child that I am now trying to unlearn. I recognize today that it is important to respect all people, regardless of how different they are from me. I believe that people are like snowflakes, unique in their own right, and created by a loving God. I want to love unconditionally, the way Thom did. Since I can't change society, I am learning to act out my beliefs about the beauty of diversity with my many friends and acquaintances. As a restaurant owner, I have employed gays and lesbians. I find that my attitude towards them is a model for my employees. My concern is that they do the work I've hired them to do, just like everyone else. I seek out people who are loving and caring, regardless of their sexual orientation. As a result, I have made friends with exceptional people, gay and straight.

I still struggle with the prejudices I learned growing up. Today, I try to be aware of them, and challenge myself to change my thinking. I am finding that I have become intolerant of bigoted, small-minded people. Once an employee made a comment about "niggers." I told him to keep his thoughts to himself if he wanted to keep his job. Last year I saw an offensive bumper sticker on a motorcycle that was owned by an acquaintance. It said, "AIDS CURES FAGS." I was furious. I fantasized ways to hurt him. It is as if my prejudice now is about people who are prejudiced.

Even though my goal is acceptance of others unconditionally, I am afraid of not being accepted myself. I still have fears. I know what I am sexually and yet I would, at times, be very frightened to display any type of affection or behavior that might label me as homosexual. Still, there is a lot of hatred and fear in our society and, at times, I am not sure I want to put myself in a position that could quite threaten my life. It's as if I live in a paradox of fear that I'll be seen as less than a "real" man, and yet a real man would be sure enough of himself to express how he feels. I admire those who do have that courage. I am sure enough of myself, though, to write this story.

I am grateful that I am still alive and growing as a human being. I believe that children are not born homophobic, or with any other prejudice. Those traits are taught and can be unlearned if one's desire is strong enough. I have that desire. Just as I have had to unlearn my lessons about homosexuality, I have to continue to unlearn my lessons about my other prejudices. For those are the lessons that, in my opinion, are the most dangerous.

In my primary relationship today, I am able to share openly about my life experiences, and I continue to learn through the sharing. The woman I am involved with knows this story I have written. She was also an abused child and has had homosexual experiences. It is difficult to describe how freeing it is to be open, unashamed, and accepting. I couldn't have achieved this had it not been for all the people in my life, most especially my brother Thom. Through his death I have experienced a rebirth.

Mick's story speaks volumes about why it is important to become accepting. Without that acceptance, Mick would never have been able to tell his brother how much he loved him. Because Mick was accepting, he was able to focus on what was truly important—showing his brother he loved him and finding peace with him before he died. Unfortunately, when it comes to illnesses like AIDS—that are charged with issues around sexual orientation—many family members are either too ill-equipped to cope or so estranged that they never get past their judgments or homophobia to come to peace with their loved ones or friends before they pass away. Mick's beautiful story is a model for all family members to emulate.

Note your thoughts and reactions to Mick's story.

Janice Mirikitani

The freedom we should seek is not the right to oppress others, but the right to live as we choose and think as we choose, where our doing so does not prevent others from doing likewise.
—Bertrand Russell

I was born into a community overwhelmed by a sense of humiliation, vulnerability, and injustice. The year was 1942. My parents were first-generation Americans of Japanese descent.

For Japanese-American families, it was a time marked by fear. Our homes were raided, curfews were imposed on us, and our men were often picked up and arrested without cause. In a futile effort to stave off internment, Japanese-American families destroyed many of the remnants of our heritage and anything written in our language.

I spent my earliest years in a concentration camp. Not in Germany or Poland, but in the United States of America. Although I do not remember much about the camp, it does provide my earliest memories of life—the swelled numbers of Japanese, the sweltering heat of the desert, and the bugs. We were interned for three and a half years.

Shortly after we were released, we relocated to Chicago. My family made this move because of the strong anti-Japanese sentiment that existed in California, where I was born. We lived in the south side of Chicago, an area of extreme poverty. Like other Japanese children, I was often beaten by whites in the neighborhood. The blacks generally left me alone, perhaps out of a sense of empathy with our oppression.

These events of life were simply too much for my parents and they divorced. My father left my mother for another woman. I could not understand why my father would leave my mother as I believed she was the most beautiful woman in the world. I concluded that I had done something to drive my father away.

In order to support us, my mother worked at several jobs, including, ironically, one in which she made papier-mache flowers for the American Legion. She remarried when I was about five, and we returned to California, to a farm in Petaluma, a rural town that proclaims itself "The Chicken Capital of the World." We lived in a chicken house, and soon my half brother was born. As we had no refrigeration, all of the available milk was given to my brother. I look back and realize that this was only the beginning of preferential treatment for the male members of the family. In my culture, women "took a back seat."

My stepfather worked for the U.S. Army as a code breaker during the war. He was full of rage. As a child, I did not understand his rage. Now, I can comprehend the terrible conflict he must have felt working for the United States at the same time his family was interned. And I imagine this internal conflict translated to rage, much of which was directed at me. My stepfather abused me verbally and physically for much of my young life.

Abuse has been a large part of my life. At the age of five or six, a male relative began to abuse me sexually. It began with his fondling and touching me under my pants and proceeded from there. So-called friends of the family and other relatives soon joined in this abuse. I tried to tell my mother about it, but she simply wouldn't listen. She must have known about it; I can only imagine that she didn't know what to do about it.

My grandmother, who lived on an adjoining farm, was the only one who offered me unconditional love and support. However, she was unable to speak English, and I never learned to speak Japanese, as we had been prohibited from speaking it during the internment. We did find ways, other than words, in which to communicate, and she let me know that she could not do anything about the abuse, that I must find a way to take control of things. As we lived a fairly isolated existence, there was no one else to turn to. My options were limited: I concluded they were to live or to die. "The best revenge would be for me to live," I thought.

I developed a rich fantasy life. If the stars appeared, in a certain way, I believed that it meant "he" would not come into my room that night. I had out-of-body experiences in which I observed the abuse as it occurred, and I developed an ongoing fantasy where I was a beautiful white girl. This helped protect me against the realization that, as a Japanese, I was not accepted in American culture. These are the ways I survived my abuse.

My mother often told me not to call attention to myself, not to make waves. So, I lived quietly. I made no waves and I did not call attention to myself. But others did call attention to me. As there were only fifteen or so Japanese families in all of Petaluma, we stood out. I was often called "Jap" and "slant eyes." I became outspoken and determined to not let the abusers and the whites do me in. I learned how to rebel against and to be bitchy toward my parents. Even so, the sexual abuse continued almost daily.

I was a second-class citizen; that message rang out loud and clear. In my family, I was second-class simply because I was a woman. I loathed the men who abused me and was full of contempt for the women who allowed it. I knew no one who was being or ever had been abused. However, I did know that my family had a history of madness among a few of the women and I identified with them—those who had been rejected, who took the crooked path. These were the women, aunts in my larger family thought to be mad, who sought to break "the cycle" of madness, and I gained strength and insight from them.

Through it all, my grandmother remained my greatest source of support. I felt that she was a gift, given to me to help me survive. I spent much time with her. We made paper flowers and raised all kinds of animals. I remember we had a hen that mothered all these kittens— these little furry things would follow this hen wherever she went. There was all sorts of strange "imprinting" going on in our home. This time spent with the animals was nurturing and one of my few respites from abuse.

Another refuge was school. I concluded that school was my only ticket out. So, I worked hard and I did very well. My need to study for an exam or work on a class project was the only time my mother protected me from my abusers. There were about a dozen or so Japanese-Americans in class. We were a model minority, too few in numbers to be a threat, yet numerous enough to have some protection. There was only one black girl in our school. She was constantly harassed. There were no openly gay kids. In Petaluma, in those days, that would have been cause for lynching.

For someone who had isolated herself so, I became surprisingly popular in high school. I made the cheerleader squad and put a great deal of time and effort into cheerleading and social activities.

Surprisingly, too, given my history, I eagerly joined in the abuse aimed at the slightly masculine girls in our class, the athletes who played basketball and soccer. The other cheerleaders and I would giggle in front of them and say jokingly, "Well, I guess she won't be at the dance this Saturday," or something equally cruel. I was so self-absorbed by this point in my life that it never occurred to me that what I was doing was abusive. Nor did I notice any gay boys in class.

I had first heard about homosexuality from my abusers. They made derisive and abusive remarks about a Chinese worker on the farm. He was effeminate, and I was told never to go near him. One of my aunts befriended him and was beaten by her husband for playing mah-jongg with the Chinese man. I stayed away from him, as I did all the men around me.

I graduated from high school at the age of sixteen. I moved to Southern California, where I attended the University of California at Los Angeles (UCLA). Soon, I had my first direct experience with a lesbian. As a part of my teaching curriculum, I attended a two-week intensive physical education and dance camp, where I met Noreen, who told me that she was very attracted to me. I was embarrassed by her attraction. I told her that I wasn't sexually attracted to her. In some way, both of us knew that she could have attempted to exploit me sexually had she wanted to. Instead she befriended me, taking me under her wing and nurturing me. Soon I told this loving woman all of my "secrets." She realized that I was a "very sick puppy," and told me frankly that I needed help. "Without help, you may not make it," she said, knowing how deeply eleven years of abuse had affected me. Soon after, I entered therapy and began my process of recovery.

Noreen also told me about the discrimination she experienced as a lesbian, and we shared a common bond based, in part, on our pain. Contradicting every stereotype I held about gays and lesbians, Noreen was my best friend for almost four years. She helped me establish my first boundaries and she didn't violate them. Nor did she play games or care that I was a heterosexual. In fact, as I look back, she helped me to affirm my own heterosexuality.

After a short teaching stint, I took a job at Glide Memorial Methodist Church, in the gritty Tenderloin district of San Francisco. It was 1968. I worked with Glide's Vanguard Program, created by young, gay street kids. My job was to transcribe tapes of interviews talking about violence against gays and lesbians as part of the Citizen's Alert program. I learned an enormous amount.

The kids of Vanguard were extreme; they were flamboyant and absolutely queer, in the finest sense. They were cross-dressers, hustlers, and transsexuals. And they were a complete affirmation of who they were. They had nothing to hide anymore and nothing they could lose. They had "lost it all." Rejected by virtually everyone, these gay kids were brutally real, honest, bold-faced, up front, and frank. I learned what it was like to be gay. And I learned how similar our lives were.

Glide was a hotbed of activities during the sixties and seventies. Embroiled in the hippie movement, the civil rights movement, the feminist movement, Glide has consistently been at the forefront of change. By the time the eighties rolled around, Cecil (Glide's Reverend Cecil Williams) and I had become good friends. Five years after his wife and he divorced, we married. That was over ten years ago.

Throughout my twenty-five years at Glide and my life with Cecil, my eyes have been opened by many gays and lesbians in addition to the street kids—Sally Gearhart, Del Martin, Phyllis Lyon, to name but a few. These women, who have spoken eloquently of their sexuality and their suffering, have broken their silence (around these issues), much the way those of us who have suffered sexual abuse are now breaking our silence. I believe that when we break free from that which holds us back—whether it be abuse, homophobia, racism, or even our own fears—and speak out, we find acceptance. And as we do, we experience a profound sense of peace and joy. We experience love.

> While the nature of her abuse changed over time, it was still abuse whether in a concentration camp or in a bedroom. Perhaps Jan's own experiences contributed to her easy acceptance of lesbians and gays. We know from her story that her first lesbian friend was one of the few people who did not abuse her. We also know that as Jan began to work with gay and lesbian youth, her affinity for the rights of gays and children grew stronger. Her ease in working with these groups, which are two group from which many adults feel disconnected, sets a sterling example of how relationships can be developed and the value of coming to terms with these issues.

Note your thoughts and reactions to Jan's story.

Wendy Horowitz

...but it is wisdom to believe the heart.

—George Santayana

When I was growing up, all that I learned about homosexuality came from a book called *Everything You Always Wanted to Know About Sex But Were Afraid to Ask.* My parents probably don't know this. I took the book off their bookshelf when I was around twelve years old. I read the part about homosexuality over and over. I also read about prostitutes, because that section was the only one that mentioned "female homosexuals." I knew I wasn't a man, so I couldn't be one of those disgusting homosexual men that the book said were unhappy and lonely. And I wasn't a prostitute, so it didn't seem likely that I was a lesbian.

My family moved to Akron, Ohio, from a small town in Indiana when I was fifteen. A lot changed in my life when we moved. I made some new friends...good friends...friends for whom I would have done anything. But I had trouble maintaining these friendships. Most of the people close to me were girls and I was always somehow disappointed in my "girl friends." I always wanted more from them. I just couldn't get enough attention from them, nor could I do enough for them. I thought we should be more important to each other than anyone else, but it was never a mutual feeling. I lost one friend after another because my expectations were not met. As a result I bonded with men, and dated many of them. I received special approval for dating "nice Jewish boys." During my last two years of high school I had a boyfriend. We broke up when I went to Ohio State University, where I immediately found another boyfriend. I acknowledged to both of these men that I had an interest in women. They didn't seem to think it was anything to be "concerned" about.

I was very lonely. I couldn't talk to anyone, and everything in my life that was even slightly painful hurt me terribly. I wasn't able to deal with a lot of what was going on in my life. It's hard to explain what set me into such a state. I started trying to hurt myself. I didn't want to die. Well, I did want to, but I was too afraid to try to commit suicide. I still have the scars. I thought that being more sexual with boys would make me feel better about myself. Needless to say, it didn't work that way.

When I was going into my senior year in college, I met Brian, who was and is a wonderful friend. Although I was dating someone at the time, Brian and I became close friends. Eventually, we started doing just about everything together. He was my best friend. We talked a lot about some of my feelings about sex, which weren't all that great. Sometimes, when I got really upset, I would ask him why I felt so differently from the way everyone else did. He would say he had some ideas, but he wouldn't tell me. He said I had to figure it out for myself. Brian and I began dating. During this time, I met a couple of people who were involved in the Gay and Lesbian Alliance (GALA) on campus. With them, I went to some meetings. It seemed very natural for me to get involved in gay rights activism as a straight person. I was even described in a newspaper article once as someone who "didn't identify as a lesbian." It was at one of the meetings that I met Jill, whom I later saw at a lesbian bar (on "straight night," of course). We exchanged phone numbers. We went to dinner one night with some of her roommates, and made a date for New Year's Eve. That was the beginning of 1990. I was twenty-one.

After a while, Jill and I started dating. I continued to date Brian. I told both of them about each other. It was very stressful for me to date two people at the same time. I thought, "Maybe I'm bisexual," but I also sensed that my relationship with Brian would be the last one I would have with a man.

Actually coming out wasn't particularly confusing for me. Having been involved in a gay group made my transition to identifying as a lesbian easy. I think a turning point for me was when Jill gave me a labrys (lesbian symbol) for my twenty-second birthday. At one point I was really stressed out from trying to maintain relationships with two people, so I called my brother. I called him a lot when I needed someone to listen, as I knew he wouldn't talk to our parents. I remember that particular conversation *very, very* well. I told him I wasn't sure what to do about these two relationships I was having. He knew about Brian, and asked, "Do I know this other guy?" I said, "Sort of..." (he had met Jill) and added, "It's Jill." He said, "That's what I thought." And we continued with the conversation. Just like that. He was the first person in my family I came out to. He gave me his usual advice (just listen to Simon and Garfunkel and you'll feel better), and that was that.

In June, my family (mother, father, and grandmother) was coming to visit for my graduation from college. I told my brother that I was going to "come out" to them. He encouraged me. In retrospect, college graduation wasn't the best time to come out to my parents but that's when I did it: I came out the night before I graduated. My family will never let me forget it! I don't remember my father's reaction (he does), but I watched my mom slip easily into denial. She said, "Let's go shopping for furniture!" We talked for another few hours, went to dinner with Brian, and they took me home. On graduation day they didn't seem to want to talk to me. I was preoccupied with what I was supposed to do that day. Jill joined us for the ceremonies and for lunch afterwards. To say it was tense is an understatement! My mother and I ended up in the car, crying. Jill, my dad, and my grandmother ate lunch in silence. My mom tried to convince me that I just had bad experiences with men, and that I shouldn't give up on them. I think she said just about everything my friends told me she'd say. One thing I'll remember more than anything is that they said they loved me. Especially my grandma.

When they left, I lost it. I was on the phone to Jill's mother, crying. I didn't think my parents would talk to me again. I thought the situation was hopeless, that I had just lost the most important people in my life. The people I thought I could count on; I thought they hated me. Jill's mom, who had accepted her daughter as a lesbian, assured me that it would take some time, that they didn't hate me, and that they'd learn, just as she had when Jill came out to her. And over time, they did.

Upon graduating, I went on vacation in Canada and then returned home to spend a week with my family. I had found some "coming out" books for them. I think they actually read them all. I know I did. Next, I wrote to my friends and came out to them. I never heard back from some of them, but I was prepared for that. The true friends—the ones who loved me for who I am—are still my friends. They appreciated my honesty and, as a result, we have gotten to be even closer, because I have been honest with them.

In July 1990, I moved to Dayton and started working for a large company. At first, I thought I'd stay closeted. I figured people wouldn't want to work with me if I came out. However, I soon came out to a man at work who had constantly asked me for a date. It was the only way I thought I could shut him up! He urged me not to tell anyone else. He said he thought people hated him because he was Jewish, and he thought it would be worse for me, being Jewish and gay. That conversation didn't stop me. In some ways, it furthered my resolve to come out at work. The next person I came out to inadvertently. She asked what I was going to do for the weekend, and I told her I had plans with friends to go to out dancing. She wanted to know where, and, assuming she had never heard of the place, I gave her the name of the gay bar I was going to. Well, she knew what it was, asked if I did, and that was that. I was out to her. It was such a relief! I now had someone I could talk to about Jill and me. The next couple of people figured it out on their own. I talked about Jill at work (she was moving in with me), and some perceptive people knew she was more than just a roommate. Eventually I stopped pretending at all, and, though I didn't say, "I'm a lesbian," I talked about Jill in the same way everyone else talked about their opposite-sex significant others.

At one point, Jill was quite sick. She had to have her tonsils out, and she didn't have health insurance. I decided to request spousal equivalency benefits for her from my company. I knew they'd say no, but "It couldn't hurt to ask," I thought. The first reply I got was a polite, "No." I then wrote to someone one level higher. That reply was rude and inappropriate, comparing my request to that of someone asking for benefits for their "illegitimate" grandchild. I couldn't believe it (he actually used the word illegitimate). I put together a lot of information I had seen about gay issues in the workplace. I went to my manager. I told him I was a lesbian. He already knew that. I told him about the letter, and that I wanted to continue to pursue it. He asked for permission to discuss it with his management, to elevate it as far as it needed to go. Soon after that, I transferred (voluntarily) to another department to assist in the merger of two companies. I soon found out that I had already been outed to the people in that department. It ended up not being a big deal. I was just out to everyone.

When my relationship with Jill was ending, I needed all the support I could get. I don't know how I would have handled the stress if I hadn't been able to count on my family. In fact, my parents have come a long way since I came out to them. They have become true activists for lesbian, gay and bisexual civil rights. They are active in Parents and Friends of Lesbians and Gays (PFLAG), they march in pride parades (with or without me) and they attended the 1993 March on Washington for Gay, Lesbian and Bi Civil Rights with me.

In my latest job transfer, I was outed before the initial interview, and without my knowledge. I was talking to a former co-worker about an article that was going to be in the newspaper that was about gay issues in the workplace and found out that my picture was to appear with that article. This person told me that I shouldn't worry about having to come out to everyone. They already knew! I sat down with my director to let her know that I was going to be pictured on the front page in an article about being gay in the workplace. She indicated that she didn't think it would be a problem, and wanted me to let her know if I received any negative feedback. She also offered to discuss it with our division assistant vice president, so he wouldn't be taken by surprise. I accepted her offer.

The company I was working for was bought out by a company that had a solidly established lesbian, gay, and bisexual employee group. One of the best things about being out in my workplace was that I was able to get hooked into their network quickly. I got more involved in workplace issues; I networked with people across the country. More importantly, this is how I met my current girlfriend, Ilane. It was a comfortable place for me to be. I was motivated to try to make a change in my workplace environment. I joined the Diversity Team at my company (which, in many ways, remained independent from the company that purchased it) as an open lesbian. I have had meetings with the Equal Employment Opportunity office, and was able to provide some education about gay issues, especially how they relate to the workplace. They expressed their support for making the workplace a safe place for lesbian, gay, and bisexual employees. I attended the lesbian, gay, and bisexual employee group's second annual conference with the support (financial and otherwise) of my management. I learned more about how I can make a difference in those three days than I had in years! It was empowering to me. It was wonderful to be in an environment full of openness and affirmation.

I am out to everyone at work and everyone who is a part of my life. I have been able to discuss the conference I attended with my co-workers. I think the rewards of being out are many. I don't spend a lot of energy censoring what I say and do, though I still do some of that. I know that my co-workers know I'm a lesbian, and our work relationship has not been harmed. In fact, I think I have a better relationship with them. I feel more a part of the department. I don't feel like an outcast. They have all met Ilane—it makes me feel good that they have accepted her as a part of my life, just as I have accepted the people who are a part of their lives. I can't imagine being in an atmosphere where I feel uncomfortable or unwelcome. Being an activist for lesbian, gay, and bisexual civil rights is very important to me. If I could not share that with people I see every day, and with my family, a lot of people would simply not know me at all. I can't imagine not being out to everyone in my life and having to live with the fear and the loneliness of being in the closet.

The one thing that Wendy will remember more than anything after telling her parents that she was a lesbian is that they told her they loved her. Knowing that her parents loved her helped Wendy give them the time they needed to work through their issues. And work through them they did. In April 1993, they walked with Wendy in the March on Washington for Gay, Lesbian, and Bisexual Civil Rights.

Wendy's experiences with her loving family have made it easier for her to come out at work and to let others see her for who she is. She knows that because of her family's acceptance she can be out everywhere in her life and still maintain a loving relationship with her family.

Note your thoughts and reactions to Wendy's story.

Rabbi
David Horowitz

Great Spirit, help me never to judge another until I have walked in his (her) moccasins.

—Sioux Indian Prayer

Three years ago I never dreamed that I would be writing this story. Go figure.

I was born in New York in 1942 but, within two weeks, moved to Connecticut with my parents. At the age of five, I was diagnosed with rheumatic fever. As a result, my father gave up his toy jobbing business and we moved to Miami, where the doctors said I would have a better quality of life. My father worked as a travelling salesman in the toy industry, and my mother was a homemaker. My father covered thirteen states and was often out six weeks at a time and then home for one. I was raised by my mother and my grandmother, who lived with us until her death. My relationship with my father was cordial but not close. He was away much of the time. His efforts allowed us to lead a reasonably comfortable life as a middle- to lower-middle-class family. Our house was small. For a long time I shared a room with my grandmother. Later I occupied a carport that had been enclosed. I was shielded and rarely knew when things were financially difficult for my family.

In elementary school I was a well-behaved, somewhat better than average student. Fat from age seven onward, I was often picked on by the school bullies. Though I had friends, I continued to be picked on through junior high and high school. I was an honor student. I was a top-notch public speaker and debater, skills which were widely recognized. At the age of sixteen, I had my own car, was president of my B'nai, B'rith Youth Organization chapter, and had a girl friend.

My family was very conscious of its Jewish identification, but only moderately religious. We celebrated Jewish holidays, had special Sabbath dinners most weeks, but did not regularly attend the synagogue. I had a typical Jewish education and celebrated becoming a barmitzvah at age thirteen. I was always interested in Jewish causes and the Jewish youth group dominated my life. As a child, I thought that becoming a rabbi would be wonderful, but abandoned that to the more popular notion of becoming a physician. My father really wanted to say, "My son, the doctor."

I have few early memories of being aware of or concerned about homosexuality during those days in my parents' home. I recall my parents referring to people as "faigalas" (Yiddish for fairies) and some jokes here and there, but nothing of note. As a teenager I didn't know anybody who I knew was gay.

I obtained a wonderful scholarship to Tulane University in New Orleans. There I quickly realized that physicians had to have a knack for science, and since I didn't have it, I majored in English with a minor in philosophy. My goal was now seminary and ordination as a rabbi. Breaking this news to my father was met with his anger and disappointment with me. It was my "coming out." His disappointment was evident until the day he died. My academic progress had been good enough to keep my scholarship. Now that I knew what I really wanted, it dramatically improved.

As an English major, I assumed that a number of my professors were gay. I laughed a bit about it but, in general, thought very little of it. My interaction with the gay community was confined to celebrating Mardi-Gras amid cross-dressers and going to a bar whose fame was showing off female impersonators. The bar employed stereotypically gay wait-ers who made me uncomfortable. By accident, I wandered into a gay bar or two in the French Quarter—I always left quickly. Again, in col-lege, I didn't know anybody who I knew was gay.

In 1963, during my senior year in college, I married Toby, a sociology major at Tulane. She recalls her mother's warnings about marrying me because I was, "a man who might be weak having been raised primar-ily by women." In June of 1964, Toby and I graduated from Tulane and we moved to Cincinnati, where I had been accepted by the Hebrew Union College-Jewish Institute of Religion (HUC-JIR) in their rabbinic program. In Cincinnati, I began my studies and Toby worked, first as a social worker and later as a teacher. I recall her advice to one gay client. It was "move to New Orleans or San Francisco." She was ever the liberal.

At HUC-JIR, I regained my honor student status and even taught some Hebrew courses. While a rabbinic student, I was quite aware that the college used psychological tests to screen out homosexuals. Once again, as a seminarian, I didn't know anybody who I knew was gay. I was ordained in 1969. Later, I learned that one of my Hebrew students came out after his ordination. He was the first to do so in the Reform rabbinate. I remember thinking that it was a brave act that would probably adversely affect his career. I had no other reaction.

I served first as an assistant rabbi in Indianapolis, Indiana, and, three years later, as rabbi of my own congregation in Hammond, Indiana. In 1968, my daughter Wendy was born. In 1970, my son Daniel joined the family. We were the perfect family: mom, dad, two children, and later, a dog. I recall being approached once around this time by a gay man about his membership in the congregation. He talked of "marry-ing" his lover. Since his lover was not Jewish, the question became moot for me and I never had to face my religious feelings about homo-sexuality. Tragically, the young man died of cancer within the year. During the first twelve years of my rabbinate, he and his lover were the only people who I knew were gay. During my stay in Hammond, a close friend and colleague shared with me that his sister was a lesbian. Being a liberal person, I thought it not a bit shameful. I later learned that his sister-in-law was also gay. No big deal.

In 1983, I accepted the congregation in Akron, Ohio, and my family and I became Buckeyes. Wendy went off to Ohio State University (OSU) in 1986, and Daniel to Miami of Ohio in 1988.

If love is truly blind and deaf, then so is parenthood. For about six months, Wendy, who was then a senior at OSU, had been dropping hints regarding the exploration of her sexual identity. I had not picked up on any of those hints. I knew she had many gay friends. One, a lesbian, came to Akron to visit with her. That was "okay" as long as Wendy, being straight, was not "leading her on." I told anyone who would listen, "Wendy has had boyfriends since she was three years old. She's the most heterosexual person I know." My wife and I attributed her membership in the Gay and Lesbian Alliance (GALA) as a wonderful way for her to support her gay friends. When she told us she would wear a pink triangle on her cap at graduation, we had no idea what it meant. My wife proclaimed, "Wendy, you hate pink!" But Wendy was truly championing her friends' cause. During that year, a close friend, a psychologist, had been sensitizing me to the gay civil rights struggle and the horror of AIDS. I was proud of Wendy.

The day before her college graduation, Toby, my seventy-three-year-old mother, and I sat in Wendy's apartment. Wendy said, "I have something to tell you." She told us she was gay. She told her tale well. She was organized, concise, and had much material for us to read. She talked about Parents and Friends of Lesbians and Gays (PFLAG) and had the phone number of somebody in Akron to call. Her presentation was true to her nature. Wendy is an accountant.

We stayed up all night. We had been called on our liberal stance and platitudes. Our dreams had been shattered. We went through all the stages of mourning. We denied it (it's a phase), we were angry (how could she do this to us?), sad (her life is ruined). We cried (gay people are okay unless it's our daughter). The next day was worse. We went through the motions of graduation, but all we could think of was our own tragedy. Lunch with her gay "friend" was awkward at best.

We needed to talk, yet, there was no time. I had to return to my congregation that day. Once at home, we began to read. We were on a roller-coaster of emotions, mostly down. Wendy came home a week later and became our teacher, our guide, and our coach. She pushed, prodded, and educated us towards acceptance. She was the same as before, only gay. Nothing had changed, and everything had changed. No wedding, no grandchildren.

Who could we tell? Toby was accustomed to being open and intimate with her feelings, so she embarked on a mission. One by one, she made dates for lunch with her friends and came out as the mother of a lesbian to them. Each encounter was nerve-wracking. All were accepting, curious, and eager to learn. I could tell my psychologist friend and my colleague with a gay sister. We denied that we were ashamed, but we were. No need for the congregation to know. Perhaps just a few. What would they think? How would we look as parents? Would it endanger my position? Would people talk behind my back? These were some of the worries we had.

Ironically, shortly after Wendy came out, the Central Conference of American Rabbis voted to knowingly ordain gay and lesbian rabbis. I proudly spoke in favor of the motion and voted with the majority. PFLAG gave me a safe place to talk and to practice saying the phrase, "My name is David and my daughter is a lesbian." I realized that Wendy had changed my life. Slowly, Toby and I became more involved in the gay community. We continued to read all that we could. We began to feel good about ourselves and understand more about homosexuality. As a part of PFLAG, we began to speak to groups of gay college students. A year after Wendy came out, we went to our first gay pride march in Columbus, Ohio. It was exciting. We felt a part of the movement. We were embraced by gay and lesbian young people as we proudly marched in our "PFLAG" shirts. I looked up into the sky and saw a plane circling above with a trailing sign that said, "Sodomites go to Hell." I knew we were safe. There was nobody from Sodom in that march. I had come to grips with the religious question and homophobia and bigotry. Most of those who lined the streets with signs proclaiming religious warnings were bigots, not people of God. I knew as a religious person and as a clergy, I had to raise my voice to protest those who used religion to justify hatred and discrimination.

We have since done just that. Toby and I have worked together at the State Fair as PFLAG representatives and we have met with parents whose children have come out. We have been where they are and are eager to help parents share their children's lives. We have shared our religious beliefs with those plagued with guilt because of their beliefs and have tried to make those who will listen understand that their hatred leads our children to internalized homophobia and suicide.

Three years later my life is truly different. We have become, much to my delight, true advocates of gay and lesbian civil rights. We are out to the entire community. When somebody says, "How's your daughter? Is she dating anybody special?" I answer, "She's fine. She's a lesbian and is dating a very nice woman." There have been no negative repercussions in my congregation, thought I am quite vocal and public about my feelings. Toby and I still spend a great deal of time with parents and gay children. I speak about the "coming out" process whenever I can and about religion and about homosexuality. Most of the gay people I know are nice, wholesome, bright, dedicated people. Some are not. Hey, gay people and straight people are very much alike! I now know a lot of people who are gay, including three cousins. Three years ago, I knew nobody in my congregation who was gay, had gay children, siblings, or friends. I now know over eighty.

When we returned from the April 25, 1993, March on Washington for Gay, Lesbian, and Bi Equal Rights, Toby wrote of her feelings. Her words express my own. She wrote:

> Twenty-five years ago, as I looked on my newborn daughter, Wendy, I never dreamed that I would celebrate her twenty-fifth birthday in Washington, D.C., at a march for Gay, Lesbian, and Bi equal rights.
>
> Hopes and dreams can be wonderful, but I learned that reality is better. Dreams are ephemeral goals; reality is concrete. When I had dreams for my daughter, they were my dreams, not hers. Being able to join with her in pursuit of her dreams became our shared reality as we marched.
>
> I have never felt safer than when I rode an eight-car-long subway train that was crammed to "standing room only" with marchers and supporters.
>
> I have never felt more proud than I did as a part of a crush of diverse humanity that filled the wide sun-drenched boulevards of our capitol for a seven-hour-long parade.
>
> From birthday celebration and sunshine, I awoke on Monday, April 26 to overcast skies that produced a chilling rain. Nature set the tone for the day—death.
>
> Experiencing the Holocaust Museum as a parent of a gay child added a new dimension and fear to the experience. As I was introduced to those classified as killers, victims, and bystanders, I also realized that humanity changes little and learns less from past atrocities; note AIDS and Bosnia. Not only does "Silence = Death," but "Knowing (does not equal) Helping."

So where is the hope? It is found among the people who were caught up in the Holocaust and are described as Rescuers. These few people actively (openly and secretly) chose to help save lives.

We are all given a choice when faced with injustice and horror. We can choose good or evil. We can choose life or death. For me, the hope is with those who choose life.

I am proud of my lesbian daughter. Go figure.

> David didn't confront his feelings about homosexuality until his daughter, Wendy, announced—the day before her college graduation—that she was gay. Despite many hints provided on numerous occasions, David was stunned and totally unpre-

pared to hear this news.

At first, he denied it, then when he admitted it was true, he, first, became angry, then sad. These strong emotions are typical of what people experience when learning an unexpected truth. Slowly, David began to tell people his daughter was a lesbian but he couldn't imagine telling his congregation. He had a million worries and an equal number of questions. With the help of PFLAG, David and his family came to accept his daughter's sexual orientation. A year after she came out, David and his wife marched in their first gay pride parade. Three years before telling his congregation he had a lesbian daughter, he did not know of a single gay person among his church members. Today, he know upwards of eighty. David's story vividly depicts how denial and lack of information can color one's perceptions of reality and how living in and accepting reality can be a source of abundant pride.

Note your thoughts and reactions to David's story.

3

Gaining Knowledge
Stories of A Diverse Community

In Chapter 2, you witnessed the road to acceptance of ten ordinary (yet remarkable) human beings. You read how their coming out, regardless of their sexual orientation, fueled this acceptance. You'll learn more about the coming out process in this chapter as you read through the stories of gays, lesbians, bisexuals, and transgender people. In choosing our storytellers in this diverse community, we sought to include everyone. So, we have storytellers of differing races, classes, geographic locations, genders, abilities, and ages. We have done this because, just like the world, the gay, lesbian, bisexual, and transgender community is diverse and, as a result, confronts our common stereotypes.

Many of the heterosexual storytellers in the preceding section spoke of their contact and involvement with gay children, siblings, relatives, or friends, and told how these experiences increased their acceptance and positive feelings toward people who were different from them. This contact and involvement also decreased feelings of prejudice learned as children. The overwhelming majority of research also shows that simply knowing gays and lesbians reduces prejudice and discriminatory behavior. There is little doubt that greater awareness, understanding, and contact with gay and bisexual individuals can help improve attitudes toward them, a finding that holds for other minority groups as well.

Like all of us, our storytellers' lives are not simply defined by one characteristic but by many. In some cases, these individuals speak of the challenge of integrating multiple identities—ethnicity, sexual orientation, physical ability, and gender issues. In some cases, they speak of painful experiences—experiences that are often kept hidden and secret. In many cultures, speaking of issues such as sexual, psychological, or physical abuse is discouraged, in part because of the discomfort and pain it ignites in many of us, in part because many of us have been conditioned to deny aspects of ourselves that don't fit what is considered by society as "normal" or "desirable." Yet, "being oneself" is normal and desirable and to accept others as they are is healthy human behavior, so we've asked our storytellers to "bare all."

In this section, our attempt to foster greater acceptance of gays, lesbians, and bisexuals is coupled with a desire to heal some of the hidden wounds people have experienced in our culture through the guarding of their secrets. "We're only as sick as our secrets" is a common refrain among people in recovery. We believe that most people are ready to hear the truth, including these secrets. The truth will help set us free and moves us along the path of acceptance.

The truth will also alter the way we hold broad stereotypes and overgeneralizations. The experiences described by our storytellers will call into question many theories you may hold, especially those that claim to provide overly simplistic explanations of sexual orientation.

You will find that one's knowledge and beliefs relate to one's attitudes. For example, surveys looking at this relation find that those who believe that homosexuality is innate, inborn, or beyond conscious control of the individual are more accepting of gay men and women than those who believe it is simply a choice. Recent studies provide strong evidence that homosexuality is either innate or determined within the first two or three years of life and show that, regardless of the cause of homosexuality, the probability of significantly altering one's sexual orientation is virtually nil, a view held by both the American Psychiatric Association and the American Psychological Association.

As you read these stories you will see that it is literally impossible to use one theory to explain each of our storytellers' experience with her or his sexual orientation. However, one thing is clear, and that is that gay, lesbian, bisexual, and transgender people exist, and we have the choice of either working to foster acceptance or creating disharmony and pain. And, as evidenced by our heterosexual storytellers, that disharmony and pain is not limited to the sexual minority community but involve us all.

This chapter begins with the story of Tom Metz, a gay male with a disability and a "Horrible Secret." It ends with Frank Wong, a Chinese American born in Vietnam, raised in Hong Kong, Canada, and the eastern United States, who tells the story of integrating his multiple identities. Along the way, you will meet Jana, a young African American lesbian; Randy, a self-described "queer hillbilly"; Jillaine, a bisexual; Susan, a deaf Latina; Dean, a Native American Indian and recovering drug user; Zoe, a feminist and member of the Sado-Masochism community; Eric, a white male with AIDS; Mitch, a transsexual; and Lynn, entertainer and abuse victim. These stories will open your heart.

Tom Metz

Courage faces fear and thereby masters it.

—Martin Luther King, Jr.

Okay. My Gay Story. What can I say? It's like every other Gay Story. Funny how a lifetime of gothic dread and drama seems pretty ho-hum when everyone you know has gone through the same thing.

I was born in Durham, North Carolina, in 1960. Dad was in medical school there, at Duke. Mom taught school. Yes, I knew I was different even then. In kindergarten I played with the girls at recess. Score one for the stereotypes. Kelly Brown was my "girlfriend," and we scandalized the other kids by kissing on the lips.

I was a little too well-behaved for a boy. My parents actually began to make jokes about my amiable "okay" to every request at chore time. But it wasn't always so amiable. For one thing, I sang like a girl—Julie Andrews, specifically, because I listened to *The Sound of Music,* and memorized every song. I fashioned a skirt from an old Army blanket and twirled around the living room like Leslie Anne Warren in *Cinderella.* Both of these were the focus of parental opprobrium and they stopped by the time I entered first grade, by which time I was making a concerted effort to be "normal," unlike my classmate Rickie, whom everyone knew to be a sissy. When Dad corrected the girlish way I held my hands when I walked, I studied how boys were supposed to walk. When my brother sneered at the way I put on a jacket (over my shoulder rather than under my elbow to find the sleeve), I didn't get angry, just paid attention and tried to do better next time. I was a good student. By the time I was eight, in Ohio, you could have mistaken me for a normal kid.

But I knew I wasn't. For one thing, I was physically aroused in the fifth grade when Steven and Roger whispered in math class about how they ran naked through Roger's mother's attic. But when they invited me to join them, I knew better than to accept. When the whole sixth grade went to camp, I came back with a bad case of weeping fits. Dad quickly put a stop to that. I couldn't explain why I was crying. It had something to do with seeing for the first time the other boys and girls begin the rituals of flirt and parry. Something in me knew even then that this was important, normal, and good, and I couldn't have it.

But if I couldn't learn to flirt, I could learn other social skills, and in the seventh grade I asserted myself and formed a social clique of the brightest kids in my math class that did everything together: went to the football games, the swimming pool, the Dairy Queen. These diversions had the important effect of putting a face of normalcy on the unspoken perversions I felt in my heart. I was surely the horniest kid in the seventh grade, and my heart and groin were full of dark thoughts about the other boys on the track team, especially the eighth-graders, who were more developed and full of the irresistible arrogance of adolescents who had discovered their own sex appeal.

Then I was seventeen. I wanted to die. I prayed for God to change me. I prayed a lot. I was an acolyte in my church (Lutheran). I was a lay reader on Sundays. I was treasurer of the Junior Youth Fellowship. I borrowed books on religion from Pastor Trump. *Mere Christianity*, by C.S. Lewis. I wanted to figure it out: Being homosexual was a sin, and yet when I prayed to be changed, God wouldn't help me. I even got my friend Linda to pray with me—although I didn't tell her what we were praying for (it was a silent prayer)—because I read in the Bible that whenever two or three of you are gathered in My name, there am I also. *And your prayers will be answered.* So He had to hear me then, right?

Then I gave up on God. He made me a sinner, but He wouldn't let me change. Screw Him.

I tried to date girls. Madhu Rustagi. I'm sorry, Madhu. I really liked you. Jeanine Howe. Liz Witiak. Sorry. Can we just be friends? I liked kissing anyway...

This was all in Ohio. It's no good trying to describe it here. I can't go back and bring you a picture of what it was like. It was like a nineteenth-century novel—anguishing over the moral aspect. Why don't gay people ever get credit for that? We wrestle with God just like Jacob and that angel of his. How I wished that angel would visit me. I'd give him the fight of his life. I was living a lie, living in disguise, trying to act masculine enough that no one would find out my Secret, My Horrible Secret. Would I get beat up? Shamed? I was ashamed. Would my parents still love me if they knew? There was a special tone of contempt and disgust in his voice that Dad saved for when he talked about the "queer" at work, or male ballet dancers, or the dancer Tommy Tune, whom I idolized. I learned to keep Tommy Tune a secret. I met him once when I was an usher for a summer stock show. I wanted to sing and dance. "What I don't understand is why you would want to be involved in a line of work that attracts people who are like that?" What would happen when I grew up? What would happen when everyone else got married and I didn't? How would I explain?

I read books about Jews a lot. Anne Frank. Elie Weisel. Hiding out. It was comforting somehow. God, don't let them find me out. Please, O Lord, save me. Help me to hide.

Driving Dad's Camaro over Wilson Bridge, back and forth, back and forth. One of these days I'll take a right-hand turn, just before the spot where the cement part of the guardrail begins...

My best friend (I'll call him "Adam"). Turns out his dad is...gay! He comes out to the family just as eleventh-grade Adam is discovering girls. Adam is in a really bad kind of adolescent pain. I'm good-looking and popular, so Adam assumes I'll have some answers to the girl stuff. He wants advice. He presses me. What should he do to make Barb Turner like him? How should he handle the embarrassment of a gay dad? You're my friend, Tom, level with me. He just keeps asking me all these questions...I drop him as a friend, my best friend. He's getting too close...to my horrible secret.

Sorry, Adam.

Then I was in college at Ohio State, too depressed to get out of bed for class. I got A's on my tests, then I got F's, depending on the cycle of my mood swings. I would hold out as long as I could, then withdraw from a class when it looked like an "F" was imminent, accepting the stigmatizing "W" on my record since it was better than an "F." Finally, I was in danger of just plain flunking, in my senior year, and one day I showed up in Dad's office at the hospital, begging his help. Stammering and flushed, I finally blurted it out: "I'm queer!"

Dad was not convinced. I didn't act queer. I confessed to a drunken attempt at sex with a former roommate. (Dad warned me not to tell him anything I would regret later.) Did I ever have sex with a girl? No. Then how did I know for sure? I was just young. Confused. Undeveloped. I had the wrong kinds of friendships with girls. My friendships with them were too "serious." I needed to relax about this. I wasn't really queer at all; the thing to do was just remember that. Would Dad please help me find a shrink? Well, that was a difficulty. Shrinks couldn't be trusted. A shrink would probably just try to help me come to terms with being gay, and we didn't want that. I agreed. Well, could I at least talk to you about this? I need to talk. It's eating me up inside. Sure, we'll talk. You'll feel better. Just remember, you are a good person, whom God and I love. Everything will be fine.

I could have walked on air. I wasn't really queer. Dad said so. Dad's a doctor. I passed the next several days and weeks in a euphoric haze. I told my friend Mabel, the first of my three confidantes in this matter, that I wasn't really gay after all. False alarm! Ha, ha! Gosh, what a relief. I was a regular guy after all. Mabel was a little confused by this turnabout, following so quickly upon my first tortured confession, but she seemed to take it in good spirits considering the fact that she had recently made the same dark confession to me.

It turns out Dad doesn't have time after all to talk me through my sexual confusion, but it doesn't seem so important now. I returned to my studies with renewed vigor. I could do anything. In fact, I could even get accepted into a master's degree program at the University of Chicago, a fancy brand-name university with Nobel laureates and ivy-covered archways. I couldn't wait to start school there next fall.

But first there was one other minor inconvenience to deal with—my right hand. After typing, it fatigued quickly and the fingers wouldn't flex open far enough to strike the keys. I began to see neurologists and neurosurgeons at Dad's hospital and I was confident that under his direction this problem would be dispatched as efficiently as the other had been. Hell, this thing with the hand was nothing. I knew what *real* trouble was, and I had survived that. A stupid neuron ailment in one of my extremities was a day at the beach.

By the time autumn rolled around, the motor neuron thing was in my legs as well, so I postponed grad school till the following spring. No sense in courting academic disaster by trying to gimp it through one of those fabled Chicago winters. I stayed with Mom and Dad and went to the library a lot to prep for grad school. Then, only two brief quarters behind schedule, I matriculated the following spring.

It was complicated. The silly little motor neuron thing had accumulated several names by now. Peripheral motor neuropathy. Spinal muscular atrophy. Atypical motor neuron disease. It's like amyotrophic lateral sclerosis, only it moves more slowly. And it's not so silly anymore. My body is wasting away. I've lost the function of my right hand and I've learned to write with my left. I'm wearing braces on both my legs, walking with a cane. Two hundred and fifty milligrams of Prednisone every other day. I think I'm going to die. And so, I learn years later, does my neurologist. But I have learned one sure-fire defense mechanism: *Denial*. I just pretend it's not happening and somehow I earn a master's degree, and I'm even accepted into the Ph.D. program. God, am I proud. But I'm becoming weaker with every passing month.

At the University of Chicago I meet Jonathan and Irwin. They are perfect and they run the Gay and Lesbian Alliance. They are smart, cute, Jewish, intellectual, and they have something I lack: integrity. They never lie about their sexual orientation. In the face of precipitous decline, things like integrity are the straws of dignity I can still cling to. It doesn't stop the slide down, but somehow it is important. I have no God, I have no hope, and I am going to die. I want a clear conscience. No more lies.

I go home for Labor Day. It's a busy weekend. I attend my high school reunion, and I systematically come out to every member of my immediate family except my little brother, whom Dad convinces me is too young and impressionable to hear about such a thing. This weekend is one of the hardest memories. My mother, sister, and older brother hear the news with poker faces, not really surprised, not really sure what to say. I act out the Phil Donahue show in my older brother's living room, explaining to him and my sister what "gay" means. Mom and Dad are another story. They wouldn't even show up at my brother's for the discussion.

When I talked to Dad, he closed the door behind him so no one would hear, then shouted a diatribe on rimming and child molesters. "What's rimming?" I asked. And I pointed out that most child molesters are straight men. By now I'd done some reading on the subject. Fact: You take a hundred gay men and a hundred straight men, and the child molesters are almost all straight. That's a fact. I'm trying to stick to the facts. I'm trying to stick to the truth. I need the truth. I'm in trouble. I need support. I'm slipping, and I'm trying to reach out for support. Dad says I will never be accepted this way. How many people have you told? I am ruining my life and he will never "accept" this. Don't even use that word. And there's another word he doesn't understand. "Support." What do I mean by that? He literally does not understand the word. And although I am in a master's degree program for language and literature, this is a word I can't define. It doesn't matter what you mean, Dad says, the only way to deal with this is to keep it a secret. Forget "support."

I was so afraid of the hate I saw in my father's face. I didn't know what he might do. There was something that sounded like a veiled threat: "If you tell your little brother, I just don't know what I'll do with you." That night I crept into the kitchen to retrieve my cane and slept with it at my side. Just in case.

The weekend ends and I am back at school, but it isn't over, because the motor neuron thing marches on through my body. I know there will come a time when I am dependent on these people who are so ashamed of me. Who will feed me? Who will dress me? How will I blow my nose and wipe my ass?

Home from school the following summer. I'm driving over Wilson Bridge again. This time I'm driving closer to the guardrail.

Back at school, briefly, then the worst happens. That winter I am back living in their house. It's for good this time. They try. I can't tell you how hard they try. They build an addition to the house, downstairs because I can't do stairs. This is where I will live. They do things for me. Dad, who has an especially gentle touch, clips my toenails for me. My sister takes me to the grocery store with her, so I get out of the house. My older brother takes me to a movie. My little brother pours my coffee. Mom makes my meals, washes my clothes, takes me to doctors. She finds clothes for me that have elastic and velcro. No buttons, no snaps, no zippers, no ties. She helps me put on my ankle braces each morning. She fills out stacks of paperwork for a Social Security nightmare. She does all this for me and once a month she drives three hundred miles to do the same for her dying father. Maybe it's true what they say about gay men, that they have strong mothers.

I honored Dad's fiat for a year. I didn't tell my little brother. The following year, when he graduated from high school, I considered the terms of that injunction to be over, and I did come out to him. He told me that he had in fact known all along—ever since my fight with Dad, which apparently everyone in the house heard. But nobody has said anything. At all. Nothing. We're that kind of family. We don't talk about unpleasant things. I have become an unpleasant thing.

I try not to make anyone mad. I'm funny. I'm charming. I'm a good conversationalist. I am a guest in their house. I am not grateful. I am ashamed. I am twenty-five. I want a life.

I live in my parents' house from December 1984 till September 1987. I'm turned down for Social Security. Because of the progressive nature of my illness, I can't prove I was disabled back on my "eligibility date," which is officially determined to be June of 1982. Ronald Reagan is in office and this is happening to everyone who applies. His administration gets more judicial reprimands than any other administration in history. Half of the people who are ultimately found eligible are turned down as a matter of course, to wear them down through the appeals process. It's not even a secret. It makes one news column in the New York Times. These are the 1980's and no one gives a shit. I do get Supplemental Security Income, SSI, it's $124 per month. I try the ALS Society, Easter Seals, MS. Nobody can help me. I have the wrong disease. It doesn't even have a name, for Christ's sake. But I don't complain. What have I got to complain about? I know I'm lucky to have a roof over my head, and my folks have a showcase house. I have one other thing: access. Because Dad is a professor of medicine, I try some very expensive experimental drugs. He comes home from the hospital with exotic treatments, and I sign on. Medicine is a calling, and Dad's a believer. So I believe, too. He's more than a doctor, he's a disciple. He's gentle, he's kind, he's generous, he's smart as hell, and he takes all the time in the world to explain exactly what's going on and how this drug might help you. When you see my father on the floor of the University Hospital, you understand that sometimes there's a reason why a doctor is beatified by his patients. It's because he's a saint.

I am so fucking desperate. I stay up late. I have not had a full night's sleep since I started Prednisone in 1982. One night on late-night TV, in spring of '85, I hear a pop psychologist talk about his self-hypnosis technique for quitting cigarettes. It's simple. Just tell yourself over and over that you are quitting. You don't even have to really believe it; your unconscious will hear the words and believe for you.

I try it. I walk around the backyard, repeating the words in my head, "My nerves are recovering." I make it once around the yard, sticking to the fence so I can hoist myself back up when I fall. I do this for a year, every single day. It's an exercise in delusion and I know it. But I am so angry and scared I don't care. I have no hope, but I have reached a place beyond hope where you try because there's nothing else. I get to the point where I can't walk from the family room to the kitchen without hearing my own voice in my head: "I am getting stronger." A year goes by. My stamina improves, and I'm walking twice around the yard. Then twice around the yard, twice a day, and, finally, onto the flood plain behind the house. But I'm as weak as before. Dad is still clipping my toenails. I keep walking, mumbling miracles under my breath.

Then in the spring of 1986 something happens.

I tilt the coffee pot.

Bracing the lip of the pot against the coffee cup.

Holding it at arm's length, the way I always do.

Grasping the handle with both hands.

Steadying the pot with my left.

Tilting it with my right hand.

And my right arm lifts the pot. It lifts the pot. My right arm lifts the pot. Something has changed.

I don't tell a soul. I keep walking around the backyard. At some point, my legs get stronger, too, and by autumn I can move my right leg from where the gas would be to where the brake would be, then back to where the gas would be. I think I can drive. I try it once in my sister's car in front of the house, and that's all I need. I begin to apply for jobs.

I typed up a resume on my computer. I think at this point I was typing the way I do now—by using my left thumb and wedging a ballpoint pen (the kind with an eraser on the end) between the fingers of my right hand. I filled out job applications by holding a pen in my teeth. I did this only when I wanted the writing to be legible and when I was pretty sure no one could see me. When I thought someone could see me, I used the more laborious method of holding the pen in my left hand. I could also write by wedging the pen in my right hand if I wore a hand brace, but then all the movement had to come from the elbow, and I wrote in letters that were too big to fit on an employment application. Life was complicated, you see. Complicated and full of all this infuriating adaptation.

So there's this guy, Vijay. This is where I hear Barbra Streisand humming in the background. Vijay loved me, in all my needy excess. He was beautiful—is beautiful—we're still friends. How did I deserve to be held and loved by such a beauty? It's strange, when you're disabled, you don't carry much currency in the meet market. Gay bars: going there for love is like going to the Praise-The-Lord Club for religion. I mean, they talk about it, and it looks like they're going through something like what you were after, but they've got another agenda. I never felt love in a gay bar, mostly just rejected by hot-looking guys who went to the gym a lot. Vijay loved me. I loved him. That's all I want to say about that. It was special.

I did find love in the Columbus gay community, but it was at the AIDS task force. This was real community—a couple hundred volunteers, 150 people with AIDS, a handful of staff—amateurs mostly, trying to do something about a really terrible disease that seemed to select as its victims only the most outcast. Learning as you go. Hugging everyone. Sharing your milkshake with someone you know is HIV-positive, and knowing enough about transmission to know that it's not a problem. At some point getting angry enough to stop using the term "AIDS victim." At some point getting angry enough not to care if your employer finds out what you do on your time off. This is where I count the beginning of being gay and being happy. Being proud to count among your friends drag queens and S/M dykes. Proud to kiss your friends hello when they show up on your front stoop and the hell with what the neighbors think. Proud you survived and found all those other people who listen so rapturously every time they hear "Over The Rainbow."

I'll never forget the first time I saw two guys kiss, friends, just saying hello. I'll never forget the time I held a friend's hand as he died, my AIDS task force "Buddy." I was such an inept volunteer. I'll never forget my gay uncle inviting me to his home on Long Island and showing me off as his "intellectual" nephew to all his queenie friends. I'll never forget reciting names during the opening ceremony of the Columbus display of the NAMES Project AIDS Memorial Quilt. I remember adding my uncle's name at the end of the preprinted list, and I remember that that was the only funeral he ever had. I remember that it was my AIDS task force friends, gay and straight, who held my hand that evening.

So things change. The impossible happens. I'm thirty-three years old now, and I'm writing my gay story. I'm not sure I like the tone that all of this has taken. It carries too much of the tenor of those bad old days—I can't think about them even now without getting angry, defensive, hurt, and scared. But life is different now. My life is a nice place to be. It's not always easy, and not always happy, but it's rich. And mostly it is happy. I have learned to forgive and move beyond that hard place. My family has never uttered Vijay's name, and that hurts, but I love them anyway, with some limits. They seem to love me, sometimes lavishly. We've all tried so hard. And I've worked at finding my own courage, my own acceptance, my own sources of "support," that word my father had so much difficulty with. I can take a broader view of things now because I have a job and I am independent and I don't need anyone's help. It was harder during the enforced dependency of my illness, when I was all grown up but not quite a grown-up. The people who loved me and cared for me hated who I was; they were ashamed of me. That's the picture that sticks: they loved me and they hated me, and I needed their help and they helped, with a generosity that was seemingly endless. And in a very complicated way, I am finally grateful for their help.

Support. Let me tell you about my friends. My friends are also my family. These stories here are a part of my family history, as much as Aunt Annie's spaetzle or Grandpa's collie dog named Watch. Gay people are making a new kind of family, and this is where I have found joy. There are a thousand networks of friends and lovers and ex-lovers who care for each other and take care of each other. At its best it's like the Columbus AIDS Task Force. My family can be as big as I care to make it. Mabel does Thanksgiving, Bob does Christmas, we all do Halloween. Linda reads my stories, Carol takes out my stitches, Doug lets me cry on the phone. Michael explains love, Ron explains astrophysics, and I boss Mabel about her flossing habits. It's a circle. We share holidays, we share jokes, we share ways of looking at the world. We share our lives. There are a lot of us out here and when we come together that makes a community, but each of us came here a different way, and we were only able to come together because each of us indi-vidually, one day, by ourselves, after long silence and fear, decided to tell the truth.

> At an early age, Tom was aware that there was something different about him and that it was something to be concealed, hidden, covered up. He called this difference his Horrible Secret. In an effort to become normal, Tom studied how other boys walked, practiced putting on his jacket so that he would appear to be a "normal boy." Such actions like Bob's practicing a manly handshake are typical of almost all of our gay, lesbian, bisexual, and transgender storytellers who realized at an early age that they were different. Each exerted considerable energy in an attempt to be what they were not. Tom's allusion to suicide points to the severe cost of having to hide who one is. The suicide rate for gay and lesbian adolescents is three times that of their straight counterparts. Perhaps, if as a society we learn to make it okay to talk about this "secret," we can make it safer for all teenagers to talk about their fears, their secrets, as all people can relate to trying to hide some aspect of ourself, of trying to be like others, especially as teenagers.
>
> Tom's story also focuses on his neurological disorder—a potentially life-threatening illness. His initial response to his illness was similar to this initial response to his sexual orientation—DENIAL. Once Tom began to accept his illness and his sexual orientation, he began to live an enjoyable and productive life.

Note your thoughts and reactions to Tom's story.

Jana Rickerson

People are lonely because they build walls instead of bridges.
—Joseph Fort Newton

I hadn't a clue what "lesbian" or "gay" was all about. I never had a thought of being homosexual, gay, lesbian, whatever you want to call it. No such things were talked about in my family. Then again, why would they? I remember seeing sissies who mostly did hair. No one ever seemed to talk bad about them or make fun of them. The women were always complimenting them about how they loved the way they did their hairdo! I also remember seeing women that people pointed out, made fun of and called names like bulldagger, diesel dyke, mannish, lezzie, queer, and funny, like Fred Sanford on *Sanford and Son*. It never seemed fair to me that, in a strange way, gay men seemed to be more accepted than lesbian women.

At about age eighteen I saw my first real "lezzie" up close. She looked like a man to me. I was in junior college and had heard there were some of "those kinds of folks" on campus, but I had never seen one up close. I was working at the local J.C. Penney store and this person that I thought was a man handed me a bedspread she wanted to buy. She wrote a check for the purchase and had to show ID. It wasn't until I looked at the driver's license that I noticed that he was a she. The shock was so big that my mouth dropped open wide enough to capture a troop of flies. I looked at the picture, the name, and then at her. I was scared. I didn't understand the fear at the time. All I knew was I wanted the sale to be over and for her to leave my station. As soon as she left I called the other sales clerks so they could see her too. I then ran into the employee lounge with a few of my peers and we all had a good laugh. And yet I felt ashamed of my behavior because she was another black woman.

A year later my fiance and I transferred from Southern California to San Francisco to continue our educations. At that time in my life, I considered myself young and gifted, ready to show the world what a powerful black woman I was becoming. Once again I began hearing talk of gay this and lesbian that. I was certain at that point that there were no other black women who did the unmentionable. I knew it was a white thing and that the woman at J.C. Penney was just an oddity.

In my final year of undergraduate college, my fiance remained at home and I returned to San Francisco on my own to complete my student teaching. I lived in the dorm and had a single room that semester. I met a woman, Sheridan, who lived around the corner from me, and we became good friends. We did everything together. We ate breakfast and dinner together every day. We talked about our day's activities, things that happened in class, and we complained about homework assignments. We were best friends. One night as we waited for the elevator to go down to the dining hall, she told me she had something important to tell me. She informed me that she was a lesbian and was just coming out. At that very moment the elevator door opened. I just stood there with my mouth on the floor in disbelief. How could my new best friend be a lesbian? The elevator doors shut and I just stared at her, trying to regroup. I stepped away from her, looked at her in the eyes and told her that it was okay. "She was my friend and that was her choice," I thought. I said, "Just don't touch me." I can still see the hurt on her face as we both stood there in an awkward silence. My appetite was gone and my heart felt heavy. Something had been sucked out of me and something else was instilled. I felt confused. I cared for and loved this woman as a best friend. I wasn't talking to my fiance as much anymore and knew I didn't want to return home to marry him. I knew all I wanted was to stay in San Francisco, experience being on my own, and hang out with my best friend from college. A best friend who was a "lezzie." Something wasn't quite right with this picture.

As the semester ended, Sheridan and I parted ways. She returned home and I set out looking for a teaching job and a new home. I missed her terribly. Slowly I began to realize that I had fallen in love with her. If anyone had approached me the year before and told me that I would fall in love with a woman, I would have taken them outside and whipped them up one side of the street and then down the other. No way was I a lesbian. At the same time my heart ached for her. All I needed was to see her or just hear her voice and I would be soothed inside my soul.

My parents hadn't said much about my decisions to stay up north and not get married. I'm sure they must have wondered what I was up to, but they gave me the space to find my life. I had been raised to be independent, self-sufficient, honest, and fair. I was a hard worker and had enough survival skills to take care of myself. I tried to forget about the confusing love I held for my college friend.

Later that summer I joined a women's softball team. I loved sports. I grew up with ten male cousins and they taught me to play early on so that I could play with them. I didn't have many friends in my first year of being in the city. The softball team was the perfect way to meet new people. It never crossed my mind that there would be no men to meet. When I showed up for my first practice, I noticed how they were all very good athletes, and I thought nothing negative about their ability to throw, slide, and slap the ball all over the field. It never crossed my mind that these women might be lesbians. After the practice they invited me back to Mother G's, a local bar. I didn't drink and had only been inside a bar once. I decided to take them up on their offer. I was half way through my ginger-ale when I realized that my teammates were hugging and kissing and laughing with one another. I sat in amazement feeling like I was watching a movie or something.

The jukebox came on and they began dancing with one another. I tried very hard to keep my mouth from catching another troop of flies. I looked on in confusion and amazement. I remember thinking back to junior high school where the girls always danced with each other, practicing steps, holding hands, etc. in preparation for when a boy asked one to dance. Here I was in a lesbian bar, watching a similar scene, but these women were not practicing for any boy.

As the summer progressed I found myself more and more comfortable in the company of my new friends. They weren't quite sure what to make of me. I always came into the bar alone and left alone. I danced with them, laughed, had a good time, played ball, and minded my own business. Being a new teacher in the time of Anita Bryant and playing on a dyke softball team was quite a juggling act for me.

By this time, my straight roommate noticed that not very many men called the house asking for me. When one did she seemed quite anxious for me to respond immediately. Finally she asked me if I was "contemplating my sexuality." I had never brought anyone home. I hadn't dated anyone nor had I slept with another woman. As far as I was concerned, I hung out with softball playing women who just happened to be lesbians and I said, "No."

One Saturday morning after a night of partying, I couldn't hide the truth from myself any longer. I sat on the edge of my twin bed with its J.C. Penney sheets, looked out the window and thought...Jana you don't know any men anymore, you don't even know many straight people anymore, and all of your friends are lesbians. What does that say? Are you a lesbian? I softly said out loud to an empty room, "I guess so." From that point on I stopped looking for Mr. Right and began my search for the first Ms. Right.

I ended my relationship with my fiancee and began to date women. After a year or so, I entered my first live-in relationship with a woman. I decided it was time to let others back home know about the love and joy I had found with Lori. My best friend in the whole world was Sheryl. We met in the tenth grade. She was like a second sister, same age, same grade, same interests. It was hard leaving her to go away to school and a new life, but we stayed in close contact, talking at least once a week on the phone.

One day I wrote her a letter telling her about Lori, our living situation, and my newly found lifestyle. I wasn't sure how Sheryl would react because I was dropping two bombs at once—I was a lesbian and Lori was white—and I knew that many African Americans weren't too keen on the idea of alternative lifestyles, nor interracial relationships. I was black and female in a white society. Why would I want to add another level of oppression to a life already dealing with two barriers to get over and to sleep with the enemy?

I was a wreck waiting for Sheryl's response. I calculated how many days it would take for my letter to reach her and added a week for Sheryl to recover from the shock. In the meantime, I was afraid to open my mailbox. Every time I saw the green blinking light on my answering machine I froze. I kept picturing my worst fear—Sheryl telling me I was sick and to never call her again. Lori tried her best to ease my stress. However, I had knots in my stomach for weeks. I had not told my family. Sheryl was the testing ground. I knew she loved me. We had grown up together and she was more open-minded than my family, so I decided if Sheryl rejected me, I would reconsider my decision to be a lesbian. It took her a little over a month to respond. When we finally talked, her first words were, "I got your letter [a long silence]. You know, you're my friend and I love you no matter who you choose to love. I just want you to be happy," she said. I silently cried. "God has answered my prayers," I thought. Sheryl was a mirror for me and I wanted her acceptance because she was my "bestest" friend and she was another black woman.

The first time Sheryl came to visit after my coming out was quite amusing...to her, not me. After picking her up at the airport I was trying to figure out how to bring up the issue of sleeping arrangements. There was only one bed—mine—and the floor (I had decided not to sleep with Lori while Sheryl was visiting). When nightfall came Sheryl asked what side of the bed I slept on. I told her and climbed in on my side. It was the most uncomfortable night of my life. I had been more comfortable sleeping with a new lover than with my best friend of many years. I spent the night clinging to the end of the mattress and hanging onto the side of the bed so as to be sure to stay on my side of the bed. Each time Sheryl shifted or changed her position, I jumped and almost fell out of the bed. The next morning she spoke of her wonderful night of sleep, while I nursed the circles and bags under my eyes created by a sleepless night. When I told her how nervous I was, she looked at me like I had lost my mind and then told me I had done so.

Sheryl didn't behave in any of the ways I thought she might. She was wonderful and has been consistent in her love and actions towards me for over twenty-three years. We continue to talk on the phone with regularity, and she visits when I celebrate special events in my life. On my thirtieth birthday, I held a travelling party in a limousine and she flew up and partied with me and my lesbian family of friends. When I left my job after six years, she flew up to join me at my good-bye party. Over the years, she has been a loving, listening ear for many of my trials and tribulations. She encourages my dreams and comforts me during disappointing times. She has never let our different choices of whom we choose to sleep with get in our way of a frienship blessed by God.

I don't hide who I am and who I chose to be with in life so much anymore. I don't wear "lesbian" on my shirt sleeve and yet I don't deny it. When confronted with the "why" of my choice, I always take it back to my place of truth...my heart. I still have to take that extra deep breath when I'm asked about my sexuality from someone in the African American community.

I fear being rejected or judged. In this society where I feel I have little respite from all the "isms," it is crucial to me that my own community (in whatever way it can) accept me, support me, welcome me, and shelter me. Sometimes I hold back because of my fear of rejection. Perhaps if I can cross that bridge I might meet other Sheryls who will support me following my heart.

Jana expected that she would face prejudice in the African-American community as a lesbian and as part of an interracial relationship. Perhaps she provides a possible reason for such prejudice from an already oppressed group when she notes that her family and friends were likely to wonder why she would "want to add another level of oppression to a life already dealing with two barriers (Black and female)." The more levels of oppression and the more identities one must integrate, the more likely it is—at least initially—that coming out is difficult. Jana's story illustrates the fear many feel when "coming out" to a best friend and the richer and deeper friendship that often develops when one does come out.

> Note your thoughts and reactions to Jana's story.

Johnny Randall Huff

Look within!... The secret is inside you.

—Hui-Neng

Hollow, pronounced "holler," is the land between two mountains. It is an area with very little flatland. The term originated because people would have to holler from one house to the next (before phones).

My name is Johnny Randall Huff; I go by Randy and mine is the story of a holler queer. I was born December the third, 1959, at Mount Mary Hospital in Hazard, Kentucky. Hazard is a small town in eastern Kentucky. Home to thousands of coal miners over the years, Hazard is a town that has never had much going on except coal, unless you count the on-going feuds between local families or the floods that have nearly washed it away. At one time, coal from this area was shipped by train all over the country. When the coal industry began to die in the mid-eighties, so did Hazard. Now, most of the tracks lie rusting and abandoned.

Hazard and the surrounding countryside were my world for many years. Separated by the mountains from the rest of the state, Hazard has maintained its old mountain ways and ideas. My family settled in the area over one hundred years ago—we have always been mountain people.

The place where I grew up, just outside of Hazard, was a spot called Campbell's Creek, pronounced "Camel's Creek." My grandmother's house, at the intersection of two dirt roads, was built by my great-grandfather in the early 1900's. It did not stand straight. Both the floor and walls were crooked. There was no running water, no indoor toilet. We did have electricity, and even a phone.

My grandmother raised four children in this house. Basically, she did it alone, as her first husband died in World War II, and she divorced her second, a drunk and a deadbeat. She was quite a woman. I got my temper from her.

My father was in the Navy. I don't really remember him being around when I was little. He was stationed aboard ships for periods of what seemed like years. I loved him a great deal when I was little and spent much of my time waiting for him to come home. My mother stayed at home. Not to say she didn't work—she did. She and my grandmother worked for people doing canning, or hanging wallpaper, or working in the garden. They always seemed to be doing something.

I've spent most of my first twenty years in and around Hazard, although for a while we lived in both Florida and Virginia—the result of my father's service stint. When I was little, my mother and grandmother used to take me to Hazard every Saturday. We rode the bus. I thought Hazard was such a big city. I knew someday I wanted to get away to a big city.

As a child, I knew very little about sex. My parents never discussed it or anything else outside of those items related to our daily existence. Unlike many hill people, my parents didn't teach me to hate people who were different. Perhaps this is because my parents had worked with people of other races—my mother, in her youth, worked with an African American woman and had only positive things to say about her, and my father worked with people from many different racial groups when he served on ships. I came to realize that my parents were atypical in this regard, because other relatives were quite prejudiced: against blacks, city people, anyone who was different. There was a lot of hate in the hills.

For the most part, my play was just like that of kids anywhere. My friends and I did thrilling things like filling our shorts with sand and letting it fall out as we walked around. We climbed the hills and made tents out of leaves and sticks. We explored the mountain cliffs, built fires by the creek that ran in front of my grandmother's house where we roasted hot dogs and marshmallows, and played softball in the middle of the road—our favorite place to play. I always liked playing with the boys best.

When I was about ten, we began to call everybody a creep or a queer. These were terms we freely tossed about without any of us actually knowing a queer or what the terms even meant. Up to then, my sexual fantasies were of men and women together—I realize now that I probably focused more on the men than I cared to admit then. In the holler, it was common for boys my age to play sexually with other boys, just as it was to play with girls. No one really thought much about it.

Not until junior high anyway, when the kids turned mean. I remember one day on the bus everyone was saying that these two guys were queer. They were taunting them. I thought the guys were just friends and I was disturbed that everyone was so intentionally mean to them.

This meanness wasn't limited to kids. I remember my father and uncle talking about ships docking in the navy and how there were shops (bars?) nearby where they saw guys with "their little faces plastered to the windows" looking at the sailors. My uncle said that some guy once touched him lightly and that he took the guy's fingers and bent them back as far as they would go. I remember feeling a very strange, very weird, very creepy feeling come over me as the story was told, but I didn't know why I felt that way.

In high school, I had a real big crush on my best friend, and I really wanted to have sex with him. But I never did; in fact, the only sex that I had during this time was with a male cousin. He later married and had kids. I dated girls, but I wasn't interested in having sex with them. Oh, I thought about it. I dated one girl for three years—she became a wonderful friend of mine, who I am close with and love today. We kissed, and caressed, but I never wanted more. Later, when I told her I was gay, she asked, "Did I cause it?" I laughed and said, "No."

It was in high school that I began to think that the word queer might apply to me. Of course, I never even imagined dating a guy then. When I graduated from high school at seventeen and entered Eastern Kentucky University, I had my first sexual experience with a guy who lived on my dorm floor. He was older and purported to be "only experimenting." For me however, it was more than an experiment. He was the first man I fell for and I felt some pretty strong emotion for him. He was also the first to break my heart. I dated one woman for a while. She was a hell of a good kisser and taught me well. I enjoyed her company (and still enjoy women's company, but now as friends only). Eventually I met some guys who went to the gay bars in Lexington and I started to go with them. I did this four to five times a week. My grades suffered. But I had a ball. Every night seemed like a fantasy.

After a couple of years in college, I became aware of just how negative people were when they referred to someone as gay. It surprised me that they would accuse a person of being so horrible without knowing anything else about them. It also angered me.

By now, I was beginning to open up about my sexuality. I worked at a "family-oriented" country restaurant, where most of my co-workers knew I was gay. No one seemed to mind. I came to believe that these country middle-class folks are not as conservative as they are made out to be.

In the early eighties, my first cousin told me she was a lesbian. I was really surprised. We have always been close—thinking of one another as two sides of the same coin.

In 1983 I left work and school and returned to Hazard. That same year I went to work for Kroger, a grocery store chain. Back in Hazard, I tried to be discreet. At work, I was careful not to let people know who or what I was. I didn't do a very good job at it; I wish I could have done better. My assistant, who knew I was gay and disapproved, eventually tried to undermine me. As time passed, my own internalized homophobia emerged. Soon, I was living life as if I had stepped back into the closet. And that was painful. It was simply too difficult—being myself and living and working in such a small town, such a small store. After six and a half years, I finally left Hazard.

I moved to Lexington, Kentucky, where I have lived since. I chose Lexington because of Darryl, whom I had met in 1987. He was a part of a group of us who went on vacation (my first ever) to Key West, Florida. It was love at first sight. We fit well together and brought out the good parts of each other. We liked many of the same things—music, bad movies, good food. He made me feel like I was the most important person in the world. Oh, there were times when he was very stubborn and childish, but none of us is perfect and I was able to accept that.

Sundays were our day to drive. He would take me places where I had never been before—old abandoned schools, small towns, old distilleries along the Kentucky river, always someplace new, just me and him driving. I miss those Sundays. I don't do them by myself.

In my relationship with Darryl, I was very happy to be a part of another person's life and I was pleased to have others know of our relationship. My parents came to know Darryl very well. We made plans to live together, and we thought we had a pretty good life. It's funny how plans often do not turn out the way we hope. In early 1989 he was diagnosed HIV-positive. We had not practiced safe sex. Somehow living in a small city made me think we were immune from the disease. We both knew people who had died of AIDS, but for some stupid reason we thought we were safe. What a joke. He didn't tell me about his diagnosis until the fall of that year, six months after he knew. I was extremely upset with him for not telling me because he could have killed me. He was afraid that I would leave him.

I was fortunate that Kroger hired me in Lexington. The people and atmosphere in my new store were completely different. And though I spent much of my time worrying about Darryl, work went well. While I didn't make a big deal out of my sexual orientation, I didn't hide it either. The people I worked with were tolerant. We got along.

In the summer of 1990, things got especially rough. My Aunt Betty had a breast removed because of cancer, my father had a major back operation, and Darryl, the first real love of my life, died from complications of AIDS.

It was Sunday morning at 6:30, a beautiful sunny day. I sat there and held his hand and he just went away. I guess part of me went away that day too, a part that has only recently begun to come back. My boss, Lisa, was there to comfort me. My friends were there, so were Darryl's; his sister and mother came. The people at work who didn't know of our relationship, but knew I had lost someone special, expressed their concern. They left me alone in my silence and didn't ask for any explanations.

Lisa's husband, Chris, is dying of cancer now. He may be gone by the time this is published. Recently, we talked. She told me she knew how I felt and what I went through. "How strange of her to say this," I thought, but I also felt like all my love and pain had been affirmed.

My mother, who now knew I was gay, told me soon after Darryl's death that if there was anything, and she emphasized anything, that I wanted to tell her or talk about, that she was there. Darryl had been to my parents home many times, and they "loved him too"—their words, not mine.

After the summer was over, I immersed myself into my schoolwork and my job. The stuff I was producing in school was good—one of my wall sculptures won a "Best of Show" award. I got a new boss and we grew to like one another. I graduated from college in December 1990, thirteen years after I had begun. It was one of the happiest days of my life. My only wish was that my grandmother, cousin Gladys who died of cancer when I was in high school, and of course Darryl had been with me.

I remember sitting by the windows of my apartment waiting for everyone to arrive before the graduation ceremony, and for some strange reason I was remembering how I felt when Darryl looked at me—I would melt.

In 1991 I met Bob. As they said in the movie, *Arthur*, "I had to go to a bowling alley to meet a man of such calibre." With him I've seen parts of the world I'd only dreamed of—New York, Paris, Rome, Venice, San Francisco—even New Jersey. He is as nutty as I am. We make each other laugh a lot. I am amazed at how his brain works—he has such big thoughts. We work hard working through the hard times. I love him very much.

After almost three years, I have finally begun to get over all the grief that I've carried with me since Darryl's death. For so long, I held it all in—all the hate, the guilt, the blame, the good and bad in our relationship—letting it fester away in a cold black room. I was head of the "Let's Keep Darryl Alive Club." And, by keeping it all in, I was killing myself. I can't believe how much I could hate someone I loved for leaving me. Little by little, I let the anger and pain out. Once I started, it got easier, and soon everything started coming out. After weeks of talking and crying and even writing a letter to him, which I dropped into the river near where he is buried, I started to feel calm. It was such a strange feeling, this calm that started to slip into my mind and soul. The sadness was replaced by peace. The last time I left the cemetery, I said goodbye to Darryl, to all our lost chances and forgotten dreams. We are both at peace now. It is a new beginning.

Randy offers a look into a life that few of us are even aware of—life in the mountains of rural Kentucky as a self-defined "holler queer." His story demonstrates that stereotypes rarely capture any one individual. For the most part, stereotypes simply limit our experience.

Randy's is also a story of love and empowerment further confronting many people's stereotypes about gay people and loving relationships. His story, like all the stories in this book, demonstrates the wonder and beauty of the diversity among us.

Note your thoughts and reactions to Randy's story.

Jillaine
Smith

Oh, you mean I'm homosexual. Of course I am, and heterosexual too. But what's that got to do with my headache?
                                          —Edna St. Vincent Millay

I am the fourth child of my parents. They grew up in the depression in upstate New York. After World War II my father, recently finished with medical school, brought his young wife and my oldest sister to California where they had three more children. They were thirty-five when they had me. Dad was in the middle of a major career change that ultimately led him to become the head of a key department at a prestigious southern California clinic.

While I grew up in an upper-class environment, my parents never really joined the establishment. I perceived them as social loners, and believe I took that role on myself, never quite fitting in to any particular clique or group. My siblings, significantly older than me, were mostly out of the house by the time I reached adolescence.

As a youngster, I don't remember learning anything about homosexuality. Later, I learned that my parents knew a couple of homosexuals, but they never mentioned or discussed them. At worst, my parents kept me from much knowledge of homosexuality. But, if that is true, then it's also true that they never instilled in me any intolerance of it. Bias does exist in my family, however. My dad is fairly conservative, with little patience for people who break the law. Sometimes he lumps certain races into stereotypical groups. But I never felt his racism was very deep. I think he's too intelligent for serious racism. There were certainly racist, sexist and, later, homophobic jokes in our household, but we (my mother and my sisters) always gave him, and then my brother, a hard time for such jokes.

I was eleven or twelve when I first met a homosexual, or at least perceived him to be at the time. He was my friend's younger brother, then six or seven. He was very effeminate and, in the end, my young perception was accurate: he is now a gay man. In high school, I learned that a male friend of my older boyfriend was gay. We socialized and he would sometimes bring a lover to parties I attended. I don't recall any judgment. Probably nothing more than curiosity.

I figured that one or two of my physical education teachers were "gay" but I didn't give it any serious thought. The first lesbian I actually knew was a girl I'd known from a church youth group. Bonnie was a year older than me and very religious. I perceived her as matronly, especially in the way she dressed. I thought she would make a good mother. Bonnie came back from her first year at a midwest college with another girl, and was quite changed. Her hair was long and down in her face and she wore baggy jeans and loose shirts. It was 1976 and she was a "hippie" and was quite "out" as a lesbian. I remember being shocked, not so much because she was a *lesbian* but at how such a strongly religious woman was able to come to terms with a sexual choice (that was how I saw it then—a choice) so contrary to her upbringing. I remember feeling worried for her. But I never knew her as a lesbian, never talked with her after that time as she went back to college and I never saw her again. I've often wondered what became of her.

In college, I met bisexual women. I even met a cross-dresser. I have no recollection of anything other than curiosity and excitement. I wondered and fantasized about sexual experiences with other women and I even flirted with the only lesbian I knew (in college), but I never perceived of myself as anything other than happily heterosexual—that is, until my mid-twenties, when I fell head over heels in love with Betty, a colleague of mine.

Betty, who resisted my affections because I was a "straight girl," identified then as bisexual with a preference for women. I introduced her to my lesbian friend and watched their fire grow and grow, ever envious, wanting that for myself. Later, I did convince Betty of my desire to pursue being lovers with her and we spent most of the next seven years of our lives together. Sometimes, I think I spent most of it trying to convince her of the desire I had for her. I learned a lot about myself during this time, about alcoholism and about codependency. I now have a lot of compassion and sadness for both of us. Since our break up three years ago, I have been with both men and women. I have even tried a threesome, seeking to meet both sides of my sexual and emotional needs.

While technically I consider myself to be bisexual, I hesitate to use that or any label. I have never felt political about my sexual orientation. I have always felt, since loving a woman for the first time, that my attraction is to *people*, particular people, not just their gender. I've heard and participated in many discussions about bisexuality—none of the typical viewpoints ring true for me. I don't believe that I'm indecisive. I don't believe I "return to men" for social privilege. If anything, I was more uncomfortable when I started seeing men again. I'm also not a bisexual activist. I don't feel any need to go to support groups or march in bisexual contingents in parades.

The only time I felt "righteous" political anger was when a gay, twelve-step conference I had attended for years curtailed its bisexual workshops, excluding bisexuals from any active role or representation. I have felt much more prejudice and lack of acceptance from gays than from heterosexuals. And I find myself appalled when I see people who fight against their own oppression then turn around and oppress another group of people. To me, that is the watermark of hypocrisy—using the very weapons of your oppressors to oppress others.

I never performed the "coming out" experience with my family. I simply became "out." I never said, "I'm lovers with Betty," but I included references to her in normal conversation, just as I would about a male lover in my life. I acted as if it was normal and ordinary to spend so much time with this woman. It became known and understood that Betty and I were lovers. Ironically, the first family member to realize the nature of my relationship with Betty was my (then) fifteen-year-old niece, who quite perceptively picked up on the emotions I harbored for this female colleague of mine. Very early in our relationship, I left out-of-town rather quickly to return to San Diego where Betty was going through a very difficult time. "That was odd," my sister commented to her teenage daughter, who replied, "Looks to me like Jillaine and Betty are much more than 'friends.'" She was right.

With my family, I initially experienced a fear of rejection. But this faded after a while, especially after the first Christmas that Betty joined the family festivities. If my family had any judgments, they kept them to themselves or to each other. I think that any concerns they might have had had more to do with the emotional dynamics of our relationship than with Betty's gender.

Most of my friends' reactions were positive. Many of my female friends' first reactions were wondering if I had ever felt "that way" towards them. Sometimes I got the impression they were disappointed in my negative answer! In one case, when a former classmate of mine, who expressed an attraction to me, learned I lived with a woman, he said, "Well, I guess I prefer hearing that than hearing you're with a man." The comment didn't sink in until much later when I realized he perceived relationships between women as not serious enough to damage his efforts at winning my attentions. In his eyes, I was still "available." Most of my straight male friends were titillated—as if my new-found orientation offered the possibility of expanded sexual experiences for *them* (threesomes). Only one female friend couldn't "deal with it." Her initial reaction was, "Oh God, my husband isn't going to like this." We fell away for several years, but today she is much more accepting and even curious. I think all of my female friends were drawn to consider their own level of attraction for other women.

On one occasion, I did make a conscious choice to stay in the closet. Early in my relationship with Betty, I met an old childhood friend for lunch. We hadn't seen each other in years, but I had always felt an intimate bond with her.

At lunch, she told me of her new found faith in a charismatic Catholic sect. Every word out of her mouth was about the importance of God and religion in her life. At the time, I was strongly biased against any organized religion, especially one that had somehow managed to convert this woman who *looked* like my old friend into someone so unrecognizable internally. I spent most of the lunch weeping, experiencing her change as a loss to me, unable to accept it as a gift in her life.

And I was unable (or unwilling) to increase the gap between us by admitting my own new found identity. I was afraid of losing even more of this old friend by having her judgment (which I was sure would be there) thrown at me. I saw her again quite recently. We spent the afternoon together. She is still quite religious, but I am less critical. However, I was still unable to tell her of my years living with and loving a woman. For some reason, I felt the need to protect those memories and feelings from someone I was sure would judge them negatively, although now I'm not so sure she would do so.

In other areas of my life, I was mostly out from the beginning and especially after we moved to San Francisco. In "the city," I met many lesbians and gays and I heard many "in the closet" and "coming out" stories. And, I heard horror stories of discrimination. I could never relate to them, as I have never perceived myself as experiencing discrimination at work or elsewhere. My girlfriend was beat up for her orientation, but I have not directly experienced discrimination or violence against myself.

In my work, I practiced what I did in the other areas of my life—I never made a big deal about my orientation. I simply incorporated my lover into my life. I "became" out. I know this is going to sound arrogant, but I believe that, at some level, I convey a self-acceptance and self-esteem, competence and intelligence to which people respond favorably. My sexual orientation is just one more aspect of me and not my entire identity.

When I feel in love with Betty, we were colleagues in an academic department at the University of California. Our co-workers watched or didn't as our relationship developed. I neither hid nor flaunted my orientation. It was simply a part of who I was.

If I came out at all, it was to myself. I never expected to fall in love with a woman—it was a big surprise to me, but I enjoyed it and revelled in it. I had momentary doubts the first time I placed my mouth between her legs, but that passed very quickly!

If there is any "message" to my story, it is that I believe that if we develop and express our strengths, we become more well-rounded, balanced human beings with healthier, happier life experiences. We are much more than our sexual orientation or sexual expression. Our sexuality is just one aspect of us—an important aspect—but not our entire identity.

Jillaine provides us with a look at the bisexual community and, at the same time, encourages us to consider if there is any value in labelling people. She would rather be thought of "as a person who has an attraction to people" rather than a particular gender. Jillaine grew up in an environment where people of varying sexual orientations were accepted, or, at least, not rejected. She does not recall having any judgments about a gay male friend of her boyfriend, just curiosity. Wouldn't it be wonderful if we approached differences with curiosity rather than judgments?

Jillaine's experience demonstrates that such judgments are learned and that we can teach differently. Jillaine also puts sexual orientation into perspective (as do other storytellers) when in her concluding statements she notes that "our sexuality is just one aspect of us—an important aspect—but not our entire identity." Our hope is that as you read these stories this point becomes crystal clear. People are people regardless of their sexual orientation, race, ethnicity, religion, national origin, physical ability, or any other categorizations we can come up with.

Note your thoughts and reactions to Jillaine's story.

Susan Gonzalez

I am not afraid of storms for I am learning how to sail my ship.
—Louisa May Alcott

I think of myself first as a deaf person, then as a lesbian. After that, I think of myself as a womin and then as a Latina. [Editor's note: Womin is an alternate spelling of woman that is used by many feminist scholars and writers. Womyn is the plural form (women).]

Deafness is usually discovered in infancy—most people are diagnosed between six and twelve months. Born in 1966 in Redwood City, California, I was five years old before I was diagnosed as deaf. I'm not sure why it took so long for my parents (and the doctors) to discover that I was deaf. Sometimes, I think it was because as an only child I learned to read lips at a very early age and I was very good at it. I don't remember a time when I couldn't lip read. And, as there is no history within my family of anyone being deaf, my parents certainly didn't expect nor were they attuned to looking out for a deaf child. Even today, no one knows why I am deaf—my middle ear is mixed up and my inner ear is missing.

My father didn't know how to deal with the fact that I was deaf. As a result, he did nothing except sit at the kitchen table and watch T.V.; Mom did everything for me. And, she did it so protectively.

At age five, she enrolled me in an Aural/Oral program. Sign language was not permitted in the program or at home. I was simply expected to speak. Over the years, I learned speech reading, phone education and a host of other techniques all designed to enable me to *pretend* that I wasn't deaf. Anyone who signed was punished (hit with a ruler; sent to the principal's office). This approach to handling deaf children was common in the sixties and seventies and wouldn't change for many years, not until the growth of the deaf movement began in the late eighties. I didn't learn how to sign until I was twenty years old.

My father was half Mexican; half caucasian. My mom is caucasian. They took care of me by feeding me, providing shelter, sending me to school, and so on. They didn't really know how to nurture me mentally and emotionally. Until I was fifteen, all I did was argue with my father. Then in 1980 we both discovered we loved the San Francisco 49ers, who were B-I-G. We spent many hours watching football together. When Reagan began his run for the presidency, Dad began to talk to me like a real person. It was the first time he spoke to me without giving me an order or demanding an apology. He died three years later at age forty-nine of an unexpected heart attack.

Throughout the years, Mom played the role of peacekeeper. It was a difficult, if not impossible role for her, as Dad demanded she side with him in the arguments we had. Later, I learned from Mom that she and Dad stayed together because I was at home and that they had planned to divorce when I left for college. Ours was not a happy household.

At school, I was enrolled in the Aural/Oral Program, a group of between twelve and twenty deaf kids. Three of us from the program went from kindergarten through high school together. We were considered "different"—we talked funny; wore things in our ears; and through the eighth grade never really mixed with hearing kids—and I felt "different." By the time I reached high school my grades were good enough to "mainstream" me out to other classes, like history and P.E. For the first time, I began to interact with other hearing kids. On a one-on-one basis, I was treated well. But in groups, I was isolated, always the outsider, never a part of the *in-group.*

In college, I became friends with Sara and started to fantasize about her. (My first fantasy had occurred when I was eight or nine. Maria and I were students together at Bidwell Elementary School. She had such long, waist-length black hair and big brown eyes. I would spend hours watching her play tether ball, all the while wishing we could be friends. Even then I thought, "Maybe I'm not like everybody else.").
But, I was at UC-Davis for the education, so I didn't act on any of my fantasies. In fact, I didn't tell her that I was a lesbian for many years. That communication was the last time I ever heard from her.

In 1989, I told Mom that I was a lesbian. She had been asking me why I was out so much. At the time, I was attending San Francisco State, working on my Masters degree. So, I said to her, "Well, I'm dating someone."

"Oh, when will I get to meet him?" she asked.

"There is no him, Mom," I said.

"What do you mean?" she said.

"I'm dating a *womin,*" I replied.

"Why? What for?" she asked, not able to figure it out.

"Because I love womyn, Mom," I added.

"Oh, that's bullshit," she stated and then added, "That's just a phase you're going through."

"No," I said, "I don't think so."

To this day, Mom thinks it's a phase I'm going through.

I met Elise in 1990 at San Francisco State. I was in the Womyn's Center looking for a self-defense class for womyn. I started to sign. She said, "Wait, I'm very slow." And I thought, "Oh, not another one." She asked me to help her with her signing and said she wanted to take me to coffee. I gave her a piece of paper with my name and phone number on it. We met weekly for signing and coffee. We started to take classes together. In October, she asked me out on a date. We went to a movie. I asked her what she would do if I made a pass at her. She looked at me. I kissed her. She kissed me back and we have been together ever since. (She still has the piece of paper with my phone number on it.)

When we first met, Elise said she was hearing. Later, she admitted that she had a hard time hearing and that she had never had a hearing test. I took her for testing. It turned out she is borderline hard of hearing. In some situations, she's hard of hearing; in others, she's fine. She currently lives in the state of Washington studying law at the University of Puget Sound.

I've always known I was a lesbian. It's just like I've always known that one day I would teach, one day I would live in San Francisco (I do both of these today). I've had very few problems coming out. People who I have come out to have either supported me or dropped me as a friend. I figured those who couldn't handle my being a lesbian had a problem, not me.

I never had a problem at work until, ironically, I started working at the California School for the Deaf (CSD). In my first year of teaching I tried to start a support group for deaf gays and lesbians (there were many deaf gays and lesbians on campus and many experienced a great deal of difficulty being both deaf and gay/lesbian). But I was just given this incredible run around by the administration. On one occasion, I set up a panel of gays and lesbians and, along with another teacher, invited them to come in and talk to the students. Both faculty members and the administration had a "shit fit" and immediately set up a "normal family panel" where a husband, wife, two kids *and their family dog* were brought in to speak/sign. This panel immediately followed the gay and lesbian panel. I was amazed to find so much homophobia in the deaf community. I expected that because of the oppression deaf people have experienced for years that they would be more accepting of others who are different. But that is simply not so and I saw much prejudice—

racism, sexism, homophobia—during my tenure at CSD. I concluded that the deaf community is so far behind in these areas because for so long they have had someone *run* things for them and, as a result, they tend to do what they were taught by their teachers, parents and others in authority. It is only recently that deaf people have come to take their power and are doing things for themselves. For many years, the deaf community has lived in denial. "If one doesn't see it, hear it, talk about it, then it doesn't exist."

I currently work in the San Francisco Unified School District at Caesar Chavez Elementary School, where I teach first and second grade. There are about twenty deaf kids in the school and six of them, all from hearing parents, in my class. There is a lot of wonderful support at the school and many other gay and lesbian teachers. The faculty is very warm and accepting. And, we have lots of interaction with the kids. I teach in American Sign Language (ASL), which is amazing considering that I couldn't even learn sign when I was the age of the kids I teach. I love it there.

My whole life is around the deaf and lesbian communities. I work to help bring these two communities closer together. I like to tell people that we are everywhere (and break the denial) and let them know that we are not dirty or vile or evil people (and counter what's so often said about us). I don't have a very big message to send to people. We are just human beings, like everybody else, and like everybody else we want to be treated with respect. It's a simple thing.

Deaf, lesbian, woman, Latina. Like many of our storytellers, Susan has multiple identities to manage. She grew up feeling different first because she was deaf then because of her other identities. Her experience differs from Jana's and Jillaine's in that she felt she was always aware of being a lesbian. As noted earlier, this simply demonstrates that there are differences in who we are *and* how we relate to our sexuality just as there are differences in how heterosexuals relate to their sexuality.

Susan shows how powerful denial can be when she says, "if one doesn't see it, hear it, talk about it, then it doesn't exist." Susan is right when she says that those who can't handle her being a lesbian have the problem, not her. Denial is the problem and Susan, through her multiple identities, has learned to move beyond that denial to a place of acceptance.

Note your thoughts and reactions to Susan's story.

Dean Moncayo

I swear to the Lord
I still can't see
Why Democracy means
Everybody but me.

—Langston Hughes

I was born and raised in Novato, a small town in the northernmost corner of Marin County, California, in May of 1963. I am the youngest of four children. My mother is a native Heilstsuk Indian from Canada; my father is Spanish-American Indian. My parents seldom discussed their heritage. I never heard them speak of being proud Native Americans. My parents were both sent to Christian, Eurocen-tric schools where they were told to "fit in" by ignoring and denying their cultural background, which is why they raised us as if we were white.

From an early age, I felt more at ease and less inhibited with boys than with girls. I also realized at some level that this made me different. My first "boyfriend" was a kid in the neighborhood named Patrick. We were in kindergarten. We sought refuge in each other's company. In spite of our somewhat limited social capacities, we developed a strong friendship—we were intensely fond of one another. On several occasions I tried to kiss Patrick or hold his hand. He always resisted and once said, "Boys don't do that." I asked him how he knew that and he said, "...I dunno." I didn't know either but I did know that somewhere along the line my feelings toward other boys intensified. Other kids began to make fun of me and I began to hide my feelings. In school I focused on solitary sports and activities that did not require contact with other boys.

In the fifth grade, a boy named Greg moved into town. I remember thinking how pretty he was. He had a very smooth body, blond hair, and blue eyes. And, he seemed very intelligent, especially for a fifth grader. Greg and I became instant best friends. We did everything together, walking to and from school, listening to music, going to the movies, concerts, and eventually, sleeping in the same bed. I remember feeling awkward because I was unable to express how I really felt for him. I didn't know how to deal with the feelings I had or how to share them with him so I never told him how much I liked him. The feelings I had for Greg felt natural but I was acutely aware that I needed to hide them.

At home, we had a sideboard that was just off the dining room. My dad had bolted the top half to the wall so that it wouldn't tip over in case of an earthquake. My mother had all these pretty porcelain plates and figurines on it, and on the bottom shelf were photographs of us children at different times in our lives. I often gazed at one photo of my brother posed at the batter's plate in a baseball game ready to swing the bat. He looked so competent. Then I'd look at the one of me in which I was standing in front of a sliding glass door looking out. My hands are raised and resting on the glass in the photo. It was taken from outside giving the illusion that I was trapped inside. I've always remembered that image of being trapped. Being trapped is how I've felt most of my life.

As the youngest kid in the family, I had to fight for attention. My two older brothers got full attention from our father. By the time I came along, my sister, who was two years older than I, had absorbed whatever energy he had left and I received little attention. I was hurt. I wanted him to teach me how to play basketball, football, or even baseball.

My mother put me in the pee-wee softball league when I was a kid. We played on Saturday mornings in the summertime and, God, was it hot. We wore helmets that were always too big for us, the kind that when I ran, it jogged around my head like those big leather socks they put on golf clubs. I was up to bat. My mother sat in the bleachers along the third base line with all the other mothers. I was nervous. I had never really practiced hitting a ball. I was standing, trying to be just like my brother in the picture, posed and smiling, and I looked at the pitcher and stared into his eyes. They were beautiful and nearly hypnotic. We nodded at each other and he smiled back. He threw the ball and it sailed perfectly over the plate...strike! He threw a second pitch.

Strike! The guys were all yelling at me, "Swing, Moncayo...swing!" My mother sat there in the bleachers smiling—wearing glasses that reminded me of Jackie O. and looking beautiful. The pitcher wound up and threw the third pitch. Mesmerized by him, I struck out. Those few moments of attraction caused me to fail, I thought.

I never did well at team sports after that. Always the last to be chosen for any team, I played more poorly than I was capable. I felt awful about myself as a result and soon hated all sports. Usually, I would do what I could to avoid playing at all by saying something like "my stomach hurts" or "I might break my glasses." The excuses were always half-baked and poorly delivered. In return, I was called a sissy and a queer.

Things got worse in junior high school. Sissy and queer became faggot and dick. Even the coaches seemed to side with the budding heterosexuals. Not only was I different because I was homosexual but I was also a person of color, a Native American Indian. I had virtually no tie to my Indian ancestry. My lack of experience with Native American culture diminished any value or sense of worth I could have received from my indigenous background. I felt very alienated and incapable of coping. I escaped to a world of drugs.

The first time I used drugs was in the sixth grade. I was paralyzed with fear at having used them and became determined not to use them again. But, by the seventh grade, I was a regular user. I liked psychedelic drugs like acid because they totally massaged my brain and masked my pain. I also used pot and alcohol even though I didn't particularly care for their effect on me. By the end of junior high school, I gave up on the psychedelics because they no longer worked their magic.

The majority of my friends in junior high and high school were female. Other than Greg, with whom I continued to have a close but nonsexual relationship, I found it almost impossible to develop casual friendships with guys. Those who hung out with me ran the risk of being labelled a faggot or a pothead and few were willing to risk such accusation. My female friends were accepting and liked me because I seemed to understand, if not what they were going through, that there was more to life than school. I never denied that I was gay. I survived by seeking an environment where I could exist without controversy.

Looking back, I see that I was in a lot of pain. I wanted to be everything that I wasn't. I was growing up feeling different than the other kids and I was growing up differently than how my parents wanted me to. I felt that no matter what I did I couldn't please them. I found some relief in expressing myself through music and art. I joined the school band where I played the trumpet (Greg played the piano masterfully). I also began to draw. I also continued to use pot and alcohol. This combination of boys, girls, music, and drugs was powerful. It was exhilarating.

My art work was well-received by both the faculty and the student body. While I was finally getting some positive attention, I noticed that my geography teacher was getting a lot of negative attention. He had a shaved head and wore aviator glasses with mirrored lenses, ruffled shirts with collars the size of South America, rings on every finger, multiple earrings, leather pants, and platform boots. He was the focus of constant ridicule and I watched in amazement as he walked across campus with his head held high. No one on the faculty ever discussed the obvious, nor did he. I recall thinking that his behavior was indicative of his own self-acceptance and pride—two concepts which I lacked.

I became more involved in the music scene. Music was my calling, my sanctuary. I believed I had the ability to create and succeed through music. I began working as a volunteer for Bill Graham Presents (BGP—one of the country's biggest concert production companies). I was fifteen and commuting to San Francisco on the weekends to work the big shows. I thrived on the experience and, eventually, became part of the BGP management team. These experiences made me even more different from my suburban peers. The small stream that had separated us became a river. I had less in common with the town in which I never really fit.

My art teacher encouraged me. She told me to stop worrying about peer approval and just, "do it, follow your heart." By eleventh grade, I stopped attending school except for my art classes. As a result, I didn't graduate. I was devastated. I pretended everything was alright but, on the inside I seethed. I responded by getting more and more into drugs.

I told my parents I was gay when I was eighteen. They said, "Well whatever, if that's so, then that's what you choose," and the subject was dropped. But, before long, they asked me not to bring my gay friends to the house (I could bring straight friends but not my gay ones). I chose to tell my parents because my older brother, who is also gay, was not out to our parents and I decided I could not live in the closet like he did. He had moved to Los Angeles, effectively limiting his contact with our family. He was in a committed relationship for eleven years (the longest of any of my brothers or sisters). My family seemed to accept his lover as a friend of the family. But nothing was ever said about their relationship. When my brother's lover died of AIDS, they acted caring and concerned, yet no mention was made about the illness. Pretense and denial ran strong in my family (at times,

I wonder whose choice makes the most sense, as he maintains a strong relationship with both of our parents while mine is more troubled).

I worked for BGP until I was twenty-three. Eventually, I lost my job because of drug use. I became a cocaine addict. Cocaine ruled my adult life just as acid had during junior high school. I began to sell bedding and art and spent most of the money I earned on drugs. My life was a shambles. My memories of these years are vague and unclear. Around the age of twenty-five, I was in a single-car accident. I fell asleep at the wheel and cracked my skull. I was in a coma for ten days. I woke up and realized I needed to makes some changes, so I did a "geographic" (a move to another place) thinking a change of locale would solve all my problems. I packed up my belongings and moved to Vancouver, British Columbia, where my mother's family lived. It was 1986. It took a while but I found a good job there. I also found a great deal of discrimination against Native Americans. In California, I might be confused as Mexican-American or some other ethnic group but in Vancouver I was clearly Indian, and Indians were an oppressed group. I stayed in Vancouver for a little over a year but throughout felt oppressed. My "geographic cure" didn't work (I still had the same old problems) and I returned to San Francisco.

This time, I was introduced to amphetamines, and that was the beginning of the end. Soon, I was homeless. For a while I stayed with friends rotating from one place to the other. Then, I lived in the garage of my friend, Darryl. Darryl was an amphetamine addict—he died in a dumpster in the arms of my boyfriend shortly after my move. My boyfriend was a heroin and speed addict—had been for over a decade. He was a toxic bomb ready to go off. My life was a mess.

The big earthquake hit in 1989 and I hit my bottom. I began a slow climb out of the mess my life was in and reached out to my family. My mother found me a room in a boarding house where I simply had to show up for two meals a day.

At the boarding house, I talked and talked and talked. One day, I called suicide prevention. I spoke for hours. The woman I spoke with suggested that I go to a twelve-step meeting. She said there was one that day and I could go and just listen. I went to my first twelve-step meeting for alcoholics. I became clean and sober. For a year, I stayed at the boarding house.

By 1991 my life had turned around. I had developed a sense of spirituality, learned a new craft, and found work in a woodworking shop. I strengthened my ties with my family—especially with my sister, who was a great support to me during this time. Currently, I am attending San Francisco State University and hope to become a furniture designer. For the first time in my life, I am happy. I finally feel that I am taking responsibility for my life.

At San Francisco State, I have begun to explore my heritage as a Native American and how it relates to my gay identity. I have found wonderful support from the chair of the Indian Studies program. I have learned that in traditional Indian culture the gay male may often be revered in a role such as a shaman or medicine man because he possesses both male and female qualities. The ability for a male to see through female sensitive eyes is a quality valued for that role. I hope to pursue a role as a gay man in an indigenous community, although at this point I have no idea what that role looks like or how it will be. For now, I am happy and proud to be a gay man *and* a Native American and know that my life is headed in a wonderful new direction.

> As a child, Dean, like Tom and many others, had an early recognition that he was different. Dean felt less inhibited with other boys and he only judged this difference as negative when the other kids began to make fun of him. In response, he began to hide his feelings. Yet, his feelings felt natural. Having what feel like natural and pleasant feelings and at the same time sensing that they need to be hidden creates a painful, often confusing dilemma for young gays and lesbians. Not surprisingly, this dilemma often leads to feeling alienated and incapable of coping. Like many young people in this situation, Dean escaped to a world of drugs. After many years, he bottomed out and began the long journey back to self-acceptance. Today, he is proud and happy to be both a gay man and a Native American. His experience illustrates both the strength of the human spirit and the need to help children express, rather than conceal, their feelings, needs, and desires.

Note your thoughts and reactions to Dean's story.

Zoe Thurau

The greatest enemy of truth is very often not the lie—deliberate, contrived and dishonest—but the myth, persistent, persuasive and unrealistic.

—John F. Kennedy

I was born and brought up in Mexico City in the 1960's. My parents are both European: my mom is English from an Irish background, my dad German. He escaped Nazi recruitment in 1939 by emigrating to England. My dad and his brother were put into English boarding schools while my grandparents were interned on the Isle of Wight, much as we interned the Japanese in California during the same time period. My dad became more English than the English, and to this day uses English expressions I've only seen used in books. My mother was the youngest of twelve children, ten of whom made it to adulthood. She was born on the day her mother's favorite son was buried. Her oldest sibling was twenty-one at the time. My grandmother died when my mother was nine, and though several of her siblings were married with kids of their own, she and the sibling closest to her in age were put in an orphanage. She felt abandoned—a feeling that has followed her throughout her life and was passed on to me. I think my mother believes she has no family. I don't feel I have one either and I'm not close to anyone in my family.

My dad, along with many ex-servicemen, graduated in Mining Engineering. The competition was fierce for the jobs in the European mines, and when my father was offered a desk job in Mexico for a couple of years, my parents jumped at the opportunity. Along with my sister who was one and a half at the time, my parents went to Mexico City in the early 1950's and stayed there for almost twenty-five years. They are conventional people, and conservative in the sense that I think they would have voted for Reagan—both times—had they been able to vote (the three of us are permanent residents and therefore cannot hold office or vote).

I was born in 1963 and grew up as a little English kid with other influences. Even now, after fifteen years in the States, I still come across words that Americans don't use that I do, I still spell neighbour with a "u," I say bath with an English "a." But I don't consider myself English, would never make England my home. I'm the only one in my family who feels this way. My initial contact with "the States" was very positive and resulted in my developing a strong affinity for the U.S. When I was six, my parents separated, and my mother came to the States to live near her sister. I lived with her for six months before we returned to Mexico City, where I spent the next four years in a French lycee (school). That six months is the most independent I've ever seen my mother. My dad, who was my childhood ally, moved away from home. As my mother was usually gone, and as my father had been my primary parent, I felt a terrible aloneness having him not be there. He also travelled a lot for his work—months on end at times. My memories of my childhood are of being alone or being with my friends and their families, but not having one myself.

At eleven, I was sent to boarding school in England, as my father believed the English system of education was the best in the world. After two unhappy years, I was transferred to another school, and after two even more unhappy years, my father gave in to my occasional pleas to come live in the States. During these four years, I lived in the country in England. My sister was at Oxford, my mother in Mexico, and my dad in New Jersey, where he had moved. That scatteredness characterizes my family: we are emotionally and physically distant from one another and generally have been. In fact, during my whole life the four of us have only lived together for four years.

In high school, I was considered smart. I graduated with advanced placement credit which entitled me to one year of college credit. I attended Smith College, my mother's college, much to the disappointment of my parents, who would have preferred I go to school in England like my sister. I had a wonderful first year and floundered through the rest of it.

As in many families, my parents never mentioned sex or talked about sexuality. I was never told about my period, "boys," contraception or drugs. I do remember homosexuality being referred to in my father telling the story of an old beau of my grandmother's whom he looked up in London on a trip. He laughed and said no wonder he had "thrown my grandmother over." "He was as queer as a three-dollar bill," he said. My mother, in a disparaging tone of voice, would refer to certain men she came across in the theater as "queer." Their actions would invariably be something she disapproved of or even despised.

Homosexuality was also invariably male, in these few examples in my family, and also in my experience in society as a whole. Women either were supposed to be non-sexual (virginal) or weren't sexual when they were supposed to be (frigid) or were sexual in ways they weren't supposed to be (whore, nympho, etc). No matter what, women's sexuality only existed in relation to men.

I started masturbating (such an odd-sounding word for such a fabulous thing) when I was twelve or so, just after I got my period. I had my first sexual experience with another person when I was twenty, and she was a she. I didn't think her being a woman was odd—I was surrounded by women. Smith was a women's college, so she was just a person to me, and a fascinating one. What to me was remarkable about my first lover was the fact that I had sex with another human being. That fact was much more important to me than her being female. The sex seemed very natural. In fact, I remember she asked me if I was sure I hadn't done this before. This was a time of discovery. As I came out, I kept being asked to define myself by both straight and gay people. "Was I gay?" "Was I a lesbian?" "Feminine?" "Androgynous?" "A dyke?" I learned "lesbian" is an invisible word. It's a reference to a poet, Sappho, who is believed to have headed a colony of women-loving women on the isle of Lesbos, in the Adriatic Sea, about five thousand years or so ago. Common knowledge, right? It took me years to become comfortable with that term. "Dyke" was much easier, once it's negative connotations were removed. I learned that gay people used the term differently from straight people—as a value neutral term rather than as a slander. "Dyke" is a word denoting strength and therefore is a transgression for women in our society. Even women who sleep exclusively with men are called dykes if they are aggressive or even if they are assertive, i.e., step out of line. So I had to decide whether or not to "step out of line"—be a lesbian and deal with the social consequences.

I came out in 1983 in Northampton, Mass., which is known as a "lesbian capital" of the northeast. I lived there after college. There were two women's bars and no men's bars, which was unique in my experience of the gay scene. It was around this time that I began to realize what being a minority meant to me. During most of my life, I'd been a minority of one, often the only English kid I knew of at the French Lycee in Mexico City or the only Spanish-speaking kid in the very white elementary school in Massachusetts (that was confusing because I looked as though I belonged being white myself). I was the only kid with an English accent in high school in New Jersey. Here I was, at twenty, already a feminist (an unpopular minority in a rich conservative school). As I explored what being a lesbian meant—reading books (not taught in schools), going to Lesbian Alliance dances on campus (terrifying: they were all so cool, wearing black from head-to-toe, making reference to things I was completely ignorant of, not very friendly)—I discovered that even within the lesbian community on campus and in town, if I chose to belong, I would be a minority within a minority group.

In the early 1980's, in some U.S. lesbian communities it was generally cool to be androgynous. To identify as femme or butch meant one was internalizing the oppression of heterosexist roles. In other words, it was very uncool. I defined myself as and was seen as a femme—a high femme. That is, further from rather than nearer to androgyny on a scale. A femme to me is a person (woman or man) who has more feminine energy than masculine—like what the Chinese call "yin." A butch is a person who has more masculine than feminine energy, or "yang." It's hard to be more precise than "energy," but I think most people instantly identify that energy emanating from those around us as butch or femme or androgynous. These definitions are *not* to be equated with the outward appearance and behavior that our society constructs for women (feminine, being a good woman) and men (masculine, being a real man). I decided to live with lesbians to try to figure all of this out. To that end, I moved into one of the co-ops on campus which was exclusively lesbian.

In Northampton, the lesbians tended, as a group, towards flannel plaid shirts, hiking boots, a disdain for make-up and an investment in conformity. I didn't identify with either the college lesbians or the town dykes (my predilection at the time for heels and skirts was frowned on by the latter). I did invest in some flannel shirts and black items for everyday wear—to cover all bases.

There was one group that was accepting of femmes, butches, androgynous and (glorious concept) those without labels. They were the S/Mers (Sado-Masochists). Their reputation scared me, and while they seemed more accepting than any other group, the dread conformity of dress and attitudes often prevailed there too (black leather jackets, jeans, short hair, styles varying for femmes and butches). I joined the S/M community to see what I thought. These groups were important to me as social organizations and places to learn about sex and sexuality.

One of the principal conflicts within the lesbian and gay community at the time was focused on S/M. Bitter disagreements centered on power and sex. The pro-S/Mers reserved the right to define what worked for them as long as it was safe, sane and consensual. The anti-S/Mers wanted the right to proscribe "acceptable behavior" and they

saw S/M behavior as unacceptable. While whips and other accou-
trements were alien to me, and their use disturbing to me in some con-
texts, I wanted the right to define myself on my terms and let others do
the same—however threatening to me. I've yet to find any other group
as educated about sexuality in general or as committed to defending
the individual's right to define her/himself as this community.

The more I participated in the dialogue, the more I became aware
of feeling like "the only one" again and how that reality had perme-
ated my life. This time, though, I was part of a group, however het-
erogeneous it felt. I gained strength from my alliances and from defin-
ing myself, rather than accepting and wholly believing others'
perceptions of me (like most twenty-year-olds). I discovered I could fit
in if I wanted to, and I often didn't want to. I came to see that being
true to myself was the most important single thing in the world to me,
underlined by the certainty my background had taught me that there is
no one else to count on but myself. I came to believe that the more I
held on to my integrity, the less others could use me against myself. I
discovered I was brave and ignorant about myself and others. For the
first time in my life, I felt a tenuous solidarity with a group. I found
out that love and sexuality are powerful and positive forces, and that I
was willing to commit myself to defending their expression.

I came out to my parents during this time. My mother surprised me
by asking me if my girlfriend at the time was my lover (never under-
estimate your mother). We had a reasonably sane conversation (over
avocado salad in a restaurant). Just before my plane was due to leave,
she voiced her fear: "But, you'll be so unhappy, so rejected.... You don't
have to be one of them; why don't you change (and buy acceptance,
gain tax-breaks, health insurance, the right to work, keeping one's
kids—tempting arguments)?" As I addressed each issue, she went on
to the next "but" and finally accepted, unhappily and resignedly, that I
had chosen my path and was not going to be deterred. I felt seen and
unseen. I felt seen by her in that she accepted my certainty (a first in
my experience with my mother), yet, unseen by her never asking, then
or since, what this was like for me, what the process had meant of my
reaching the decisions I had. But then my mother hadn't asked those
questions before I came out to her. Since my coming out she has never
referred to anything in my life other than work. I guess she fears my
home, friends, volunteering, travel and belief in a universal force
greater than myself might have a connection with my gayness or others' (she would have been right). We've spoken less and less over the
last eight years and, while I've remonstrated about this, I find it as hard
to accept her the way she is as she does me. We don't find much com-

~~mon ground to connect on anymore.~~

My father was and is a different story. He wrote me long, convoluted creeds at irregular intervals for years about the immorality of homosexuality (much to my surprise—I'd never gotten this much attention from him before). He sounded to me like a fundamentalist who was also a philosopher, rigid, but capable of imagining, of thinking. He often has used that capacity for thought to support his rigidity (I don't understand what motivates him). As the letters accrued—unanswered and, eventually, unread (I had no idea where to begin to respond, how to even define a frame of reference for communication), it occurred to me he was protesting too much. My father rarely asks what others think or why, but even for him, this outpouring was too verbose, too vitriolic. I wondered if he was repressing his own interest in homosexuality (if I can try and imagine my father as a regular person, and not just a sexless parent). I remember his saying in passing that he was "too fey" as a young man in college, so he decided to take up mechanical and mining engineering (and be a real man) rather than follow his interest in philosophy. What's sad is I know both my parents would say they love me—and would mean it, as far as it goes. There are certain things I'd always do for them, and they for me—helping one another financially or in a crisis—but they aren't the first or even the third people I'd go to when in need. We've lost one another.

Until I was twenty-eight, I lived on the margins of society economically and sexually. I moved to San Francisco sight unseen soon after college. It was west, California, far away from my parents on the east coast, by the ocean, near Mexico, gay-friendly (as much as any place is—maybe the gay-friendliest-of-the-available-options). Very importantly, it didn't snow and there was no humidity. I'm still here. I waitressed part-time for my first four years in San Francisco. My parents are under-earners (i.e., do not earn what their education and skills are worth) and so am I. My tax returns were about $500 above the poverty line during those four years. I now make $18,000 a year—about one quarter of the cost of my Ivy League education. My parents live on Social Security and the interest of $30,000 a friend left my mother. They didn't buy their first house until they were in their fifties—very unusual for their generation. My mother needed a hysterectomy and waited four years until she could qualify for Medicaid to get it. So while my dad made a middle-class income ($50,000 during the early 1980's), they lived a lower-middle-class if not working-class life economically. I'm working to break this (family) pattern. Until recently, I focused on my spirituality, sexuality and family background. Now, I am turning my attention to my work or career.

Like many others in the mid-eighties, I joined a twelve-step program for people affected by another's addiction, after identifying that my mother was a prescription drug addict and my father was a co-dependent. I am an incest survivor (not from either of them, but from a mother figure). Three years into the program, I realized that of my mother's nine siblings, half the women and all the men are alcoholics, and the rest of the women are co-dependents. Most of them are dead from their respective diseases. I gathered this information from my mother when I asked her about family diseases, so I'd know what to put on doctors' forms. She said those who died did so of heart disease, and added, as an afterthought, that some of them had been alcoholics (she thinks because she hardly ever drinks that she's not affected).

I got into therapy to deal with all this and to try and get a handle on my ineffective behavior patterns and my powerlessness over repeating them—like under-earning, for instance. Thereafter, I began to choose co-dependents rather than addicts as girlfriends and friends. In various S/M pro-sex organizations, I learned a lot about being clear with boundaries—both in bed and in life, taking responsibility, taking up space in the world and having a voice. I also learned to identify and discriminate between what I found exciting, scary, disturbing, and tried to let people be who they are, as much as possible. I brought spirituality and imagination into my bedroom. I developed a relationship with what I consider to be "god," which is now the foundation of my sanity and my life.

I owe a lot to the generations before me, especially the butch-femme lesbians and drag queens of Stonewall, who have promoted and fought for gay visibility, and made it safer for me to be out. In the restaurant business in Massachusetts and San Francisco, there were always a lot of other gay people, including, at times, my boss. Though it was (and continues to be) scary not to censure my conversations, no one in the workplace has overtly hurt me because of my being a lesbian. Actually, the only bad experience I have had coming out has been with my parents.

Two years ago I made the decision to join the mainstream more, and to focus on my work and career. I got involved with a woman who has worked in corporate America and earned a lot of money. She wore pastels and wanted to have a commitment ceremony and then have kids. I went to work for a commercial (as opposed to retail) French bank as an independent contractor (wearing my leather jacket and purple-and-midnight-blue jeans to work). It turned out that all the independent contractors at the bank were gay, as was the vice-president (the only women there in a position of power) who had hired us. I made it a point to try to connect with people at work that I wouldn't necessarily speak to because we seemed to have so little in common. Almost all the low-level workers at the bank were women, most women of color. They were almost all straight, conservative, married. Some avoided me, but this might have had as much to do with my outspokenness about life in general as it did my gayness. Who knows? Dialogue, if no agreement, ensued. I think I made them think—which is not always comfortable for either party. Now I work as a wholesale tour operator. Our clients are European and South American travel agents, and I use the three languages I speak (English, French, Spanish) every day, which was a goal of mine.

In my present job, I was the only gay person in a group of nine for most of the first year. It was a drag being the only one of something—again. Invisibility can be just as difficult as overt harassment or subtle censure. When I revealed that I was living with and sharing my bed and my life with the woman of pastel corporate fame, there was silence at first. As time went on the silences often turned into conversation. Some of the people turned the focus of these conversations on their relationships, rather than on mine. I was allowed to speak, but I wasn't acknowledged. When that happens I feel invisible, as if I'm not there, as if I don't exist. I know some people are uncomfortable and don't know what to say, some are afraid to say the wrong thing, some aren't interested, and some don't know how important it is to me to be acknowledged. After a year, another lesbian was hired as well, so my sense of being alone diminished.

I hope this book helps to alleviate the fear people have in daily, casual interactions, and helps others to be inclusive, to not leave anyone out for whatever reason. I know I, too, am afraid of differences in others, of their unfamiliarity. Although it is draining to have to speak out, I choose to do that rather than remain silenced. What I strive for is to be comfortable with myself. I know I can be opinionated. I am a visible person, which can be scary at times. I'd bet some people at work are more annoyed with me for insisting on clear, across-the-board benefits that are written down and known to all than they are with my political views or my sexuality. Speaking against silence is a hard choice to make every day, and I sometimes am silent when I hear a racist remark or hear a woman referred to as a bitch or see politicians promulgating hatred so calmly. I find some straight people at work confide in me when they don't in others, and I believe that has a lot to do with my approach to living my life. The people who have actively tried to silence me at times during my work history have been people who don't want to break their silence as workers or gays or women.

Voicing my sexuality continues to be as important to me as my being brought up in Mexico, as my English parentage, as my European and American educations. Now that I'm thirty, my focus in life is continuing to create a loving family. My partner Lisa (she of corporate, pastel fame) and I have been together since early '91 and have agreed to have a commitment ceremony (an acknowledgement and celebration of our commitment to one another). I plan to have a child within the next two years. All the attendant doubts as to when I'll ever be grown-up enough to handle love's responsibilities assail me, but in the end, my everyday life is grounded in faith, love, hope, and self-knowledge. I am blessed.

In Zoe's family, as in many Judeo-Christian cultures, discussion of women's sexuality, let alone homosexuality, was discouraged. As Zoe notes, "women are not supposed to be sexual." This created a huge challenge for a young woman looking at her sexuality. Zoe's story is one about self-definition, learning to define both her sexuality and who she is. She began by looking at the labels used to define women who love women—dyke, lesbian, gay, and so forth. Her experiences in the S/M community further developed her sense of boundaries and definition of self and she then began to define herself rather than accepting and wholly believing others' perceptions of her.

Zoe realized that being true to herself was "the most important single thing in the world to her." Zoe admits that she too is afraid of differences in others, of their unfamiliarity, but she chooses to confront those fears. Our hope is that this book will help alleviate the fears that many have about people of varying sexual orientation by helping you to become more familiar with this "difference."

Note your thoughts and reactions to Zoe's story.

Eric Bean

I'm everything you were afraid your little girl would grow up to be—and your little boy.

—Bette Midler

I'm convinced that my coming out began at the same time that I escaped from my mother's womb. Hell, had I been born in the disco era of the seventies, I would have had a microphone in my hand lip-syncing Diana Ross's "I'm Coming Out." And, had therapy been as popular in the 1950's and 1960's as it is today, I would have been used as a role model on how to raise a homosexual.

I was the youngest of four boys. Separated in age by about five years, each of us has different impressions of our parents...it's as though we each had different sets of parents. My oldest brother was the apple of my father's eye. My father was twenty-eight when he had his first son. My father was a young, vital man climbing the corporate ladder. He gave his first born all that his money could buy and a couple of things not for sale...time and attention. The next child born had severe birth defects, and lived most of his life in an institution. He died when he was thirteen and I was five. The third son came four years later, in the shadows of the firstborn child prodigy and the breech birth baby who never had a chance of a normal life. By the time I came along, neither my mother or father wanted another child (or so my father told me on a few occasions). Actually my father would boast about the moment I was conceived. He was in between a hernia operation and a business trip to Europe. And, as the story goes, the condom he was wearing while having intercourse "burst in all the wrong places." When my parents discovered that another child would soon be theirs, they began a campaign for it to be a girl. Sissy, at times; chick with dick on many a Halloween night; but never a girl was I.

In addition to my brother's death, my most vivid, though not my fondest, memory of my early childhood was of that awkward year of school...kindergarten. It was Halloweeen, and my mother dressed me up as a girl and made me go to school looking like Heidi. She did a superlative job because my teacher swore I was a girl. She said that Eric was just absent that day. Whether or not my teacher was serious or poking fun I'll never know, nor do I want to.

So, we now have the early beginnings of a real faggot. An overbearing mother who resented giving birth to yet another boy child. And an absentee father who would rather watch football than be around his sissy son. Freud would have been proud.

When I was eleven, a male relative began to sexually molest me. He was sixteen. And here's a true confession: I think I must have liked it because it happened more than once. During this period of discovering I had a penis and how to use it, my mother was becoming increasingly ill. She had been in and out of the mental wards of hospitals, had experienced electric shock therapy, threatened to leave my father every other day, and tried to commit suicide. Yet, we did not know her true diagnosis until 1970, when I was fifteen. She died of a brain aneurysm that had been impossible at that time to detect. During her illness, which lasted about three to four years, I was her care partner. A role I'll take with me to my grave.

So, given my upbringing I figure I could have become (a) a transvestite, (b) a football player, or (c) your run-of-the-mill homosexual looking for fame, fortune and romance in the big city? (Either "a" or "c" are acceptable answers.) Thus, one can sense my difficulty with the notion of "coming out." I never was "in" except for those developmental nine months and my college days. At my Protestant-affiliated university, I was what you'd call a BMOC—Big Man On Campus—and did not want to jeopardize that status. Instead of exploiting my sexual desires then, I took recreational drugs...what a pity.

Now it seemed right to unleash all of that sexual energy. Immediately upon graduation, I left Ohio and moved to New York City. My father, who had long since remarried, did not want me around. His wife wanted me to take any job and get out of their home. I did not fight it.

New York seemed the logical place for me to go. My oldest brother lived near by in New Jersey. I had close college buddies living in Brooklyn, and that's where and with whom I took my first New York residence. Imagine, I lived with three of my best friends (we're still friends even now!), all of whom were heterosexual, in a two-room apartment in Flatbush. As much as I loved these people, the environment got extremely claustrophobic. Tall, blond, and sexually inexperienced, I would escape this straight den to explore Manhattan's gay culture with my eyes (and yes, other body parts) wide open.

I lived my life like many other gay men in the late 1970's. It was a wild, exciting, and sexually permissive era for gays and straights alike.

Who would have known what danger lurked in and around us? Eventually this hedonistic lifestyle grew old. I was building a career that I was proud of. I had many serious and casual friendships. Yet I was missing that one all-important relationship. I wanted to be "married" and establish a home for me and my mate.

After a year of "shopping around" for a spouse, I quite unexpectedly met Alan. It was lust at first sight, and before I knew it, we were the couple that other couples emulated and singles envied. After careful consideration, we both knew this was the real thing, and began to establish our lives together.

Alan cooked and managed our money, and I did everything else. We established a beautiful home, knew each other's colleagues, friends and families, and never once felt ashamed, embarrassed, or dishonest. We just were. There was no need for a debutant ball. (Damn!) Granted, we lived in a very tolerant city, and gay pride was easy. We were lucky, most who knew us respected us. Our marriage was as real as the matching bands we wore on our fingers.

My father died in 1982 after a year-long battle with lung cancer. For the first six months of his illness, I travelled once a month to be with him. I rarely got to see him during the latter part of that year. I was forced to make an awful choice between spending time with my father or my spouse. My spouse was hospitalized with a blood infection and immune deficiency (AIDS, although it was called GRID at the time). I chose to be with Alan and hoped that my father would understand. I think he would have made the same choice. Anyway, he had a good care partner—his wife.

AIDS became a permanent part of our lives. Alan lost the battle after a diligent nine-year fight. He wanted desperately to live, to nurture our relationship, to show me, once again, how much he loved me. The details of his illness are much too devastating to describe. It's how and why he endured the combat that's important now.

I developed full-blown AIDS in 1992. If letting people know you're gay is difficult, try telling someone you have AIDS. Fortunately, I have a strong support network who accept me with open arms and kisses. And besides, I lived with the best role model for over a decade.

I recently learned that I have three to six months to live. That kind of news makes me question many things, including the approach I take to tell you my story—I wonder if, for the sake of what I think is humor, I am leaving out the kind of details that would move you to help kill this disease, to become more accepting, more tolerant. Have I let you know how much I loved Alan? Have I told you how my family of gay friends has rallied around me to care for me? Have I let you know how close my (straight) brother and I have become?

The truth is I simply don't have the choice to detail these avenues of my life. *All* of my energy is devoted to living. So Miss Ross, you can chirp about "coming out" all you want. I'm OUT, now, then, and forever.

Eric lived in New York City in the 1970s. On the surface, Eric's life looked like one of the many gay men written about in novels and, therefore, embodied many of the stereotypes of a gay man. However, his story and life go beyond that when he talks about being a caregiver to his father, then his lover and other friends. His is the story of a person with AIDS who chose to focus on living rather than dying. Eric wrote his story during the last month of his life.

Before he died, Eric worried that his light-hearted story telling didn't express the depth and richness of his life. While Eric came out with a Donna Summers' flair, he lived his life as a loving and caring man. Eric crossed the magic line well before his death in May, 1994, of AIDS-related complications—a few years after his lover, Alan, passed away.

Note your thoughts and reactions to Eric's story.

Michel (Mitch) Perez

To understand everything makes one tolerant.

—Madame De Stael

My mom moved with my father to the United States in 1960. She's from Rabat, Morocco; he's from Budapest, Hungary. Quelle Combo! She, the youngest of eight children, was raised in a Safardic (North African Jewish) matriarchy; he, a single child in an atheist home. When they came to the United States, they decided on Cleveland, Ohio (of all places). I was born in 1961 and a few month later my father was history. Nothing like being a single, working woman with a kid in a new world, nothing like it. Years and many tears later, I would mutter under my breath to my mother, "Welcome to the American dream, Ma." She would never hear me—I made sure never to say it loud enough for her to hear. Denial was crucial, especially when dreams and hopes were continually destroyed. We lived an endless realm of suffering and basic survival.

Mom's native tongue is Arabic, a language never passed on to me—the racism in this country made sure of that. It was not safe. I was never told directly; I didn't need to be. My mother would say, "Why?" and add, "Why teach you Arabic; you have no use for it *here*." She would marry two more times (I have a brother from her second marriage; he's three years younger than I). Mom picked some real losers as far as I'm concerned, but she sure has the survivalist work ethic down. She's a very strong and powerful woman, principled, truthful, passionate, stubborn, a fierce loving person. My respect for her is eminent and concrete. I talk about her, because to know about her is to know about me. In retrospect, she gave me the gift of courage and wisdom.

Ya know, my life was not this beauteous thing, sooo wonderful that I would sing praises and rant and rave about the parent. My life, in fact, was fatalistic, full of pain, cynicism, rage. The list goes on. I grew up working-class, moved quite a bit during my first nine years. Life with Ma and bro was marked with violence, emotional isolation, desperation. No one was listened to, no one had a voice. It was war. We had no common language of the heart. Unable to be strong together as a family, we survived alone, as strangers bonded by blood. The irony is, a pure love existed. We just didn't have the tools of expression for it. That would come later, almost two decades later.

I'm seven, seven and a half, something like that. We're living in Florida, on Miami Beach! Well, sorta. Actually, we live in this one room, roach-infested "residential motel," about a block from the boardwalk. Mom's trying to find steady work and deciding whether to settle in Miami or move on. Meanwhile, this is *total* vacation to me—no school, no supervision, just freedom. I hang with a new set of friends. There's two girls about my age. I am smitten. Impression is 99 percent of the game, so I tell them my name is Michael and I'm a child stunt actor for the movies in Hollywood, California. I say I'm visiting, taking a break. Even at age seven, I knew I was different.

One day the kids come to the door and ask for Michael. With her French accent, Mom said "there's no Michael here, only Michel (pronounced Michelle)." I came rushing out and we all ran outdoors. The kids asked me what was going on. I said Michel was French for Michael (ironically, my elementary teachers had often called me Michael; I was always correcting them). My new friends seemed to accept my explanation. I don't think they were willing to jar their reality.

I'm eight. We're in Columbus, Ohio, and the Vietnam war is in full swing. Things feel heavy. My consciousness seemed to begin around this time. It was a crisp fall day and I was with this little girl that I liked. She was the kind of girl that I thought would never like me. We went to her house and she encouraged me to get dressed in her brother's Levis' and white starched tee-shirt. We spent the afternoon dancing to the Archies' "Sugar-Sugar." We went to the park recreation center, where my mom showed up. "Where have you been?" "Who's clothes are those?" she screamed. I was humiliated. My mom's behavior told me what I did was bad. I never saw the girl again, even though we went to the same school.

It was Thanksgiving time. Then a student cared for us, as mom worked nights. It was 3:00 A.M. and we were driving to an army base to pick up her brother on the way to Thanksgiving dinner at her house. When they met, they hugged and held each other for a long time. I got the feeling that he was ready to go off to Vietnam and I had this profound sense that something very important was happening to me. I didn't have the words to describe what was happening, but I knew intuitively that the world wasn't fair; that in fact, it was a scary place; that there were nasty forces at work. And, at that moment, something changed in me. From then on things seemed different. Music meant more, as did emotions, feelings. My political consciousness was born in that VW ride to and from the base.

Through the years, Mom and I battled over my personal rights (clothes, needs, and so on). *It was war!* Eventually, I wore her down. She got tired of the bitter, drawn out fights and the endless questions.

"Why can't I dress like the rest of the guys?" I intoned.

"You're not a guy," my mom would yell back and add, "Why can't you wear dresses?"

"I hate dresses," I replied.

My big coup was purchasing a three-piece brown velvet suit from J.C. Penney. I fought for months for it. Then I wore it only once. I don't know why, but something about it reminded me of the time in Florida that Mom bought me a bikini and made me wear it just long enough to have my picture taken in it. After the photo shoot, I took it off and never wore it again.

I'm twelve and in Montreal for a cousin's bar mitzvah. It's a great summer 'cause I get to wear all his clothes. He wears a tailored grey-blue linen suit, bow tie, crisp button-down white shirt, and patent leather shoes. It's a killer! The family bought me a real dress, floor length with puffy sleeves, the color of cotton candy. It was forced drag! What injustice. I could hardly grasp the unfairness of it. I sat solemnly during the ceremony. At the party, I got drunk for the first time in my life and soon the dress turned into the linen suit and everything became okay. I had found another way, through booze, to be myself.

Things seemed to come together that summer. I saw concretely that I liked girls and realized just how alone I was. I had this little secret— I was different—and I couldn't tell anyone for fear of my well-being. Later that summer, when we returned to L.A., where I now lived, I made a pact with myself. I vowed to be myself even if that meant I'd be alone the rest of my life.

At fifteen, I got addicted to drugs—I had no social skills, no peer group. I isolated, spent the entire summer alone. After ninth grade, I stopped going to school (I lost all interest in it). No one seemed to notice. I thought it was a class thing, i.e., the authorities just didn't pay much attention to the children of single working mothers, even though I had been a top-notch student. On my own, I became an avid reader. I practically lived at the library. I lived in intense isolation. The only group I had ever belonged to decided (as a group) not to hang out with me. I was "too rough" and "too sarcastic" I learned many years later.

My addiction—to speed and alcohol—grew, and I fell into the L.A. punk scene of the late seventies. The politics of the punk scene were "fuck you." That allowed me, for the first time, to be myself among others.

At sixteen I had a boyfriend named Bill. He was great. Six-foot-two and gorgeous, Bill provided me a front, and I paraded him around for all to see. People told me I was lucky. One day he gave me a locket. I just couldn't lie to him anymore. I mustered my courage and told him I was gay. He screamed, "Me too!" We were hysterical with laughter and maintained a great friendship and our secret. Telling Bill about myself was the first time I had a friendship wonderful enough to risk telling the truth about myself.

At seventeen I was using Mom's home like a train station, coming and going. I learned a lot about power struggles and dominance around this time. At one point, I had been on speed for a week. Mom tried to talk me into going into a home. I interviewed with the staff but refused to go. Later, we got into a raging fight where she ordered me to leave. I refused, locked myself in my room, and began throwing furniture out the window. Mom called the police and I was declared an "incorrigible minor." Mom had me put in Hamburger Home, a half-way house originally established for young starlets new to the Hollywood scene. Mom said she couldn't handle me anymore. It was a very difficult act of *tough love* for her.

Being full of girls, the home became a coming out party for me. I was in heaven! I hooked up with the gay and lesbian center in L.A. and started going to groups. After awhile, I got a job with the California Employment Training Agency (CETA). Soon, I was introduced to the women's community and I started to become politicized. It was here that I met Phranc, a well-known lesbian folk-singer. She was "the most on the coast." Androgenous, cool, slick, creative, she had her identity "in tact." She had style, finesse, and she knew how to get the girls. Phranc, a wonderful singer, was my first role model.

Up until then, I had been open about being gay, but hidden about my gender issues, which produced in me much shame. I was such an oddball. Active in both the punk scene and the lesbian/feminist movement, I'd go to a lesbian/feminist group and then head off to a punk show and "slam" (a dance popular in the punk scene), like a pig. Even though I had some identity problems in these groups, I knew I found a home in queer culture and I owe much to the gay/lesbian community for their helping me to be who I am.

At twenty, I attended my first Gay Day event in San Francisco and shortly after moved to "the city." Leaving my mom was intense. It felt like a "tearing away." I just told her I was leaving for San Francisco and that I'd never speak to her again. It was cruel, but it was the only way I knew how to leave.

Within a week, I found a job, and shortly thereafter I found Scotts. Scotts was a tough bar, full of butches, leather-clad motorcycle women, and old-school dykes. I felt right at home. I learned from those women—about loyalty and ritual, about being a butch, a femme—and I felt taken care of. I lived at Scotts for several years.

This was a time of breaking free, of finding my identity, finding myself. I worked as a bike messenger, where I could get by as a guy, and hung out with other messengers. At twenty-seven, I declared I was a boy—not a man—a boy. I had no men role models, at all, ever. Men were perpetrators, abusers, so I felt like an adolescent boy. This made it difficult to feel like an adult, so from time to time, I would revert to the role of a butch woman. As I look back, I always saw myself as a boy, but because of what society said about these issues, I pushed these thoughts to the back of my consciousness; otherwise, I wouldn't have survived.

Coming to terms with these gender issues was a slow process, bringing about major depressions throughout most of my life. After each bout of depression, I felt I could "see again." For a while, I thought I was a centaur (half male, half female). I began to talk about these issues, not saying I was a transsexual, but in terms of male identity. I found others who felt the same way and made contact with transsexuals. I also learned about the coming out process transsexuals go through. I had great fear. Overwhelmed by uncertainty, I worried incessantly about losing my friends. Some depressions were worse than others. In 1992 I wanted to commit suicide. I ended up in a psych ward, having felt that I had lost everything—friends, relationships, sense of who I was, community—everything. This "bottoming out" gave me the opportunity to rebuild my life from a point of truth without the debilitating fear of uncertainty. In the hospital I said, "I am a transsexual." It was remarkable for although I had no shame in being queer—in fact, I felt power, strength, and pride in being queer—I had great shame in being a transsexual.

I began to work on accepting myself, especially my own sexism. The decade I had spent in the queer community would help me come to terms with myself; so would my therapist, who specializes in transsexuals. Once I began to accept me, without judgment and self hatred, I could begin to examine the big question, "What is it I'm looking for in life?" and begin to be myself. Only then could I let others know me. I worked hard and when I met my current partner I let her know me on our first date. I said, "Look, I'm a transsexual."

She said, "What's that?"

I said, "Think about it."

She said, "Oh, okay," and told me that while she lived as a heterosexual, she thought of herself as a bisexual without bisexual experiences. Since we don't really fit any couple labels (heterosexual, gay) we define ourselves as a queer couple. My friends, many of whom are from the recovery community (I have been drug and alcohol free for many years now) have been incredibly supportive.

In the end I concluded that I get to create myself. I can rely on "who I am inside" and match that with physicality. I am currently on male hormones and plan to have upper body surgery. I'm not decided on lower body work. Today I have male role models (adults) so I can evolve past adolescence.

Generally, I feel respected. I'm seen as male, addressed as male. People who have known me a long time take a while to adjust. Some friends still refer to me as *she*. One said, "Oh, he, she, it—what does it matter?" I said, "It matters. I'm not an it." If people don't like me or take me seriously, I don't know about it. If people are *transphobic*, [Editor's note: Transphobic refers to a fear of or a negative emotional or physical response exhibited towards transgender persons.] I say get yourself educated, learn about it. In San Francisco I have the resources I need to live my life as a man. The diversity of the city and the accepting cultures and communities make for a good life here. Ironically, in San Francisco people are so aware of transgender issues that I don't "pass" as often. I'm very lucky to live my life here.

I finally reached a point where I had to tell my mother and my brother. I recently flew to L.A. to tell them. Over the years, my mother has accepted a lot of things about me. When I told her I was gay she said, "Oh, I knew you were gay before you knew." So, I knew when I told her I was a transsexual, I would be accepted. There is a lot of love there.

I spent the first few days of my visit getting my mom used to my tattoos. On this particular trip, there seemed to be a lot of family things going on. I thought, "Maybe I should wait for a better time" and wondered if there would ever be a "better time." One day, she said my voice seemed to be lowering and asked if I was smoking too much. I took this as my opportunity to gather Eric (my brother) and Mom together and said, "I need to talk to you." I sat them both down. I could hear my pounding heart. I looked at them both and thought of the people in San Francisco that I had talked to before I left. I recalled their advice to "tell my family how I felt." I thought of Leslie Feinberg's book, *Stone Butch Blues*, in which she told the story of her coming out in the Midwest as a transsexual in the sixties and I remembered her incredible fight to live and what she said about self respect and respect for others. I said, "This is very hard for me," and added, "I'm scared." I took a deep breath and said "There is no good time for this. I'm a transsexual." They both looked at me. I told them I felt I've been male my whole life and related past incidents, like the bikini story and the many fights we had in stores over clothes. My brother looked at my mom. Mom looked at my brother. She started to cry. I explained I was in therapy, in treatment. She said aloud, "I can't control this" and began to repeat the phrase over and over again.

I loved my family and knew they loved me. I wanted to protect them, but I couldn't. I owed it to them and to me to let them know who I was. My brother became "Mr. Fixit." I said, "Eric, leave her alone; let her have her feelings." He turned to me and said, "It's okay. I love you as you are." "It's what's inside that counts," he said. We sat in silence.

I asked if they needed anything from me. Mom said, "It's like a death." I knew I couldn't begin to even imagine what a parent must feel like to learn that a child is a transsexual. Mom said she wanted to be alone. I left feeling a real sadness and I became really scared.

In the morning, Mom gave me a kiss on the cheek and said, "I'll be home." That told me it would be okay, 'cause a kiss on the cheek was a ritual between us. I felt reassured. When she returned home, nothing was said (it was as if it never happened). I wasn't going to push it. I'd done what I needed to do. I couldn't make her understand. I could only tell her.

The weekend came and my partner joined us. As the three of us were prepared to head out the door for dinner, Mom, in her great French accent, said "Alors, Madame...Monsieur...Mademoiselle...Which one is it?" She chuckled and added, "Are you ready to go?" I took it as a good sign. I had already decided that if she needed to address me as her daughter till her dying day that would be okay with me. I simply needed to tell her who I am. It was as important to me to accept her on her terms as it was for her to accept me. The day we left, the three of us (Mom, my partner, and me) sat down one more time. Mom said she was concerned about my health. I explained the differences between hormones and steroids—gave her the facts. She asked my partner how she felt about my being a transsexual. She said she was okay with it. Then, Mom asked me to keep my given name and then said, "You know Michel is French for Michael?"

"Yes, I know," I replied.

Mom looked at me and said, "My son, Michel."

I said, "Yes, your son, Michel."

Most of us know very little about the lives of transsexuals. As such, the knowledge we gain by reading even one story can be immensely valuable. While no single story represents the diversity we find among transsexuals, we learn through Mitch's story that the process of acceptance is similar to that which any person goes through regardless of what it is she or he is learning to accept.

Named Michel at birth, Mitch began to take on the persona of the opposite sex at age 7. At 8, Mitch began to cross dress. At 15, Mitch experimented with drugs and by 17 was open about being gay but hiding his gender issues. At 27, Mitch declared himself male and began in earnest a process of acceptance which also brought about periods of depression.

His decade of declaring himself queer and his time in therapy both helped him to accept himself as a transsexual. Only then could he let others know him, including his partner, his mother, and his brother. Mitch drew upon a book he had read, *Stone Butch Blues*, to tell his family. Mitch's brother was accepting from the outset, but his mother said, it's like a death. And, just as it takes time to accept death, it would take time for Mitch's mother to accept his change. And, like the other family members in this book, Mitch's mom came to accept her son.

Note your thoughts and reactions to Mitch's story.

Lynne Jassem

> ...*if you removed all of the homosexuals and homosexual influences from what is generally regarded as American culture, you would be pretty much left with Let's Make a Deal.*
>
> —Fran Lebowitz

I'm a lesbian (not a thespian, but a lesbian), which feels really weird to say. I don't know why. I guess it's what remains of my own homophobia.

I was born in Manhattan in 1946 and moved to Queens with my family when I was two. My mother was a Rockette. Later, she worked for the City of New York. My father owned a five and dime store. My parents, both born and raised in Brooklyn, were Jews, although my mom was only half Jewish. Both of my two brothers were bar-mitzvahed. I was raised to get married, which is why today I need a wife.

My growing up occurred during an age where things were shifting, when women's lib was just taking hold—the sixties. I can remember at three years old wanting to be a boy. I also constantly fantasized about women. I saw women walking down the street and I "fell in love." When I was about four or five there was this very butch woman who lived in my neighborhood—Hew Garden Hills. I wanted to grow up and be like her. It's amazing because, well, she was ugly. But she dressed like a man and I was terribly attracted to her. I used to shop these little stores on Main Street with my mother and we'd see this woman and I'd say, "Oh mother, I want to be just like her when I grow up." Terrorized, my mother would smile at me and say, "Yes, honey." But, it was like my goal.

My family was very male oriented. It was the fifties where "guys will be guys" and they got to have all this fun. Girls didn't get to do anything and I didn't like that. It was very humiliating being a female. Consequently, at age forty-six, I still associate my lesbianism with masculinity. In maleness, I see a power and a strength. I'm learning, as I get older, that there is a different kind of strength that women have that isn't as verbose, that isn't as out there.

When I was six, I spent hours on end in the basement, putting on my brother's tie and dressing up in his clothes. I played "office" or I became Gene Kelly doing his number from *Singing in the Rain*. I always wore a necktie and a little hat and I constantly spoke in my deepest voice. My mother thought I was adorable. The neighborhood kids thought I was queer. For years, they beat me up. They'd yell at me, "This isn't Halloween, you know." They didn't like it that I was dressing like a boy.

Once my father took me into the gas station. I was wearing a little baseball jacket and one of those hats with ear flaps. The guy at the garage said, "What's your name son?" and to my great delight I said, "Billy." I now have a show called "Billy" that I wrote and performed all over America, about me, about how I used to wear my brother's boy scout uniform and all that kind of stuff. It seems weird to many people because I look so feminine. It's hard for people to imagine that inside this feminine creature lurks Errol Flynn, Marlon Brando.

I was seven or eight when my mother got me into show business. This was a real problem for me as it created a kind of schizophrenic personality—I'd be performing on TV, in the Borscht Belt, and in the Catskills. Or I'd be auditioning and I'd have ringlets and banana curls, and wear short hooped skirts, crinolines—the whole bit. Since I always wanted the job, I'd be 100 percent girl. But, as soon as I got home I'd take off that whole chasarie and go outside and play with the boys. By now the kids were used to me; in fact, they'd call me Casie. I'll never forget those days of playing with the boys. They were so much fun—so very physical—and I loved the sports, playing hardball, running.

I also loved dancing, though I didn't like show business because people kept trying to make me something I wasn't. One day, my dancing teacher made me sing "In My Sweet Little Alice Blue Gown." I wanted to put a bullet through my head. I was a tough little kid, a tomboy, I thought of myself as a boy, and this song was such a soft, feminine, whimpy, sugar-sweet song. That was not who I was at all. It was very humiliating to portray that in front of the whole school. After much pleading, the teacher developed a medley for me called, "If I Was a Boy." "If I was a boy I'd leap through the air, like the great Fred Astaire, without a thought or a care." Everyone thought I was "real cute."

At eleven or twelve I developed ulcerative colitis from the pressure of show business. I was very sick. Unable to attend school, I watched television all the time, except for the frequent visits to the bathroom. Nobody knew what was really going on, so they filled me with opium and cortisone. I ended up weighing seventy pounds.

For several years, life just stopped. It came to a crashing halt. I didn't eat and I didn't get out of my pajamas. I lost track of time, I was totally incapacitated. I suffered so much physically that it affected me mentally and, by the time I was fifteen, I was put in an experimental psychiatric ward. Ironically, this is where I met my first lesbian.

I has a room at the end of the hall in Mt. Sinai Hospital. One day, I saw them bring this young woman in. In a matter of twenty minutes, she had on men's pajamas and a man's bathrobe. She had totally slicked back her hair. *She was a dyke!* I walked around saying, "She's a dyke, a dyke, a dyke, a dyke." And, I befriended her. I wasn't attracted to her because I didn't like such butch women, but I was fascinated by the fact that she was a lesbian. I didn't understand everything she told me, but it simply didn't matter. She was nineteen and lived in the West Village with her lover. She stayed home everyday and cleaned the house and cooked the meals while her lover went out to work. I couldn't figure this out as it didn't fit the butch/femme stereotype I had heard about. I told her, "I want to be a lesbian, I want to be a lesbian." "I think I am a lesbian," I'd say and then add, "But, when I get married...." And, she'd say, "Oh, then you're not a lesbian."

One day the two of us snuck out of the psychiatric ward and went up to physical therapy. My new friend closed the door behind her, looked at me and said, "Well, Lynn are you ready?" I burst into tears. "I'm only kidding," she said nervously and left me to "collect myself." Shortly after I got out of the hospital, I called her. But she was nuts. She told me all kinds of crazy stories about locking herself in closets and shaving her body. She started a relationship with this very effeminate guy. He looked like a girl and she looked like a guy. Suddenly, the whole world seemed sordid...underground...and bohemian. It just had all this mystery to it. I decided I didn't want to be a lesbian. What did being a lesbian mean anyway? I wondered. If a woman loves another woman, does that mean that I have to be a guy? A part of me thought that. So, I kinda put being a lesbian on hold and I went out with boys.

I attended college in Miami. I believed in free love or so I thought. But, the fact is, I hadn't had sex. I started to hang out with the theater group and I became more and more drawn to lesbians and began meeting lesbians who did not look like men—who looked like women and were attractive. That terrified me; I felt such incredible loneliness, shame, and confusion. I wanted to kill myself but, instead, I began to take drugs—speed and acid. I barely coped. I went out with boys again and wound up having a gay boyfriend. We were at this party—both drunk—and I said, "You know Barry, I think I'm a lesbian." and he said, "You know Lynn, I think I'm gay." We just looked at each other. The next morning he didn't want to talk about it, but he spent the next year driving around the men's gay bars, cruising people with a Groucho Marx nose and glasses on. Eventually we talked. We hung out together and protected each other from the threatening world. I started following women. There was this one woman—her name was Victoria—and she hung around all these gay men (I had begun to spend most of my time with gay men also). She had long red hair and was small and thin. I developed this crush on her. I knew where she had lunch, where she had breakfast. I knew what time she would be in the cafeteria, what time she would go to the library. I followed her around campus. I never spoke to her, I would just appear out of a doorway and stand in her path and stare at her. This went on for a couple of months. She would get this look of terror in her eyes. One day, she finally said, "Hello," and I grunted, "Huh." That's all I could do. Shortly after, I attended a party where I stepped outside for air and ended up sitting right next to her. I thought I would die of cardiac arrest. I managed to say, "Some party, huh?" and that was that. I never saw her again.

As I inched closer to graduating I concluded I was the only virgin in all of Miami and became determined to have sex. I met a woman—I thought was straight—who seemed attracted to me. I told everybody that I was going to seduce her. One day she invited me to sleep over. In preparation for my "big night," my friends plied me with pills (drugs were flowing in those days), and I went. We ended up sleeping in the same bed. (Surprise!) Sometime in the middle of the night, she said, "Oh Harry," or something like that and rolled over onto me. I took that as "an invitation" and I "went for it." After about twenty minutes, she "woke up" and said, "Oh, what's going on?" Boy, I never knew what sex was until I met this woman. She became my first lover. Her name was Adrienne.

On campus, I thought of myself as the philosopher of the college theater group, the Bishop Berkeley of Miami U. Before long, I was tap dancing. "Where did you learn that?" my friends asked in disbelief. Upon graduating, I moved to San Francisco to enter graduate school and decided to take tap lessons, but found out that I was more advanced than the instructors. So I began to teach and, once again, found myself performing, rekindling a career in the theater which lasted for many years. I started to work with a group called the Cockettes, at the Palace Theater. They were a wild, flamboyant group of drag queens who put on a midnight show to an even wilder audience. I played Bess Martyr in *The Amazing Nancy Drew*. I got to work with Mink Stole, Charles Pierce, and a host of other characters.

I pursued my masters in philosophy. It was now the seventies and we used to sit around and ponder, "Are we gay women or are we lesbians?" I didn't find the women in San Francisco very attractive. I liked feminine, very stylish women, and the look among women in San Francisco during that era was very "frontier-like." Most of the women were in flannel shirts, with combat boots. I attended this consciousness raising group in a church basement. I wore my little mini-skirt and long earrings. I remember this gorgeous woman, dressed in leather from head to toe, and I thought, "I could do leather."

Soon, Adrienne joined me in San Francisco. She had a sister who adored me, that is, until she found out that Adrienne and I were lovers. Then, she refused to talk to either of us. Adrienne's sister became engaged and the entire family flew out from Florida for the occasion. They refused to include me in any of the festivities, which infuriated Adrienne and me. We were very idealistic. "They have to respect us," we thought. One night, the family was having this big party and Adrienne and I went to "demand respect." Instead, we got abused. I was badly beaten by Adrienne's soon-to-be brother-in-law. A big football player, he was twice my size. He picked me up and held me over the balcony of a six-story building. He was going to throw me. Adrienne's mother yelled out, "Don't throw her, Jack, don't." So, instead, he kicked me down three flights of stairs and strangled me. A handful of family members pinned Adrienne down so that she couldn't help me. Her father was one of these. Only one person did anything to stop it and all he could say was, "Leave her alone; leave her alone." Jack stood up and said, "Now, I want you to get YOUR LOVER, ADRIENNE out of here." He then dragged me down the remaining three flights of stairs and grabbed my hand, forcing it backwards. I felt my hand breaking. Just then some neighbors came out and he remarked, "Oh, don't worry; just a little disruption." When we got to the front door they let Adrienne go. She came running down and Jack said to her, "Don't come near here and don't say a word or I'll break her (my) hand." We got into my car. Her father and mother came running towards the car. Adrienne rolled down the window and her father socked her in the face. I stepped on the gas and zoomed away. I was hysterical.

I had fingernail marks on my throat and body where he had scrapped me and bruises on my spine, as a result of falling down the three flights of stairs. Soon after, I went to court. The district attorney held a hearing. Jack arrived with depositions from everyone at the party saying that I had disrupted the party and attacked him. I said, "Look, I'm five feet, two inches tall and I weigh ninety-five pounds. Do you seriously think I would attack a six-foot-three football player?" I was told by my attorney that the family's attorney would make mincemeat out of me. "If you want revenge," she said, "hire a bunch of women to steal his car or picket his office," and added, "The court's simply not going to help you." I left and spent the next two years thinking anybody who wants to can beat me up.

Adrienne severed her relationship with her family after that. We were together about three years. Eventually, she left, married, and had a child.

My mother was very upset upon finding out I was a lesbian. But in time she became accepting. Somewhere after a series of lovers, I said to her, "Maybe I'll go out with men again." And, she said, "Oh, no, don't!" My father died when I was about twenty-six, before I had the courage to tell him that I was gay. But, I remember one time he said to me, "You know, these gay men come into my store all the time, and it's really a shame how people discriminate against them." I felt that was his way of saying, "I know and it's okay."

After a couple of years in San Francisco, I decided that there just wasn't enough going on to make it in the theater here and I moved back to New York. I started going to every audition imaginable. I was in heaven. Soon, I was doing everything. I wrote, I directed, I choreographed and I performed. I worked backstage on sets. I worked with companies, I worked solo, I did duets, puppet theaters, black light, fashion shows, industrials, and even movies.

And, in the midst of this, I met a woman named Diane. Diane and I were together five years. I had known her for eight years before we went out. She had a crush on me. It took a while before I fell in love with her, but eventually I did and we formed a family. Diane had a huge home in Manhattan. We had a home in the country. She decided to have a baby and I decided to be a part of it. I took Lamaze with her (I was her coach). In the delivery room, people kept coming in asking me, "Who are you?" But, I didn't care; I knew who I was. I was the first person in the world to hold the baby. I even cut his cord. I cared for him as if he were my own. But, as time passed, I learned that I wasn't "a parent's parent." I was much more like "a visiting aunt." Oh, I did love him and we were a family and, for a while, it all seemed so ideal. Towards the end of our relationship, I developed colon cancer (for the second time) and underwent surgery to remove a tumor. My hospital room was filled with friends and ex-lovers. The support was incredible. But Diane met someone else.

During the breakup I resumed drinking—something I had stopped doing two years earlier. I have a very addictive personality and have constantly wrestled with being obsessed about something—work, sex, drugs, drinking, whatever. I've been clean (no drugs) and sober (no alcohol) for over three years now.

It took the breakup to help me see that I needed to "clean up my act." It was then that I left theater and returned to San Francisco, where I now live. I've begun a new life, with a new career as a real estate agent. A part of me loves it here and another part feels like "a fish out of water," which is pretty much the way I've felt most of my life, with one exception. And that is, I accept and am comfortable that I am a lesbian. I was a thespian—that feels really weird to say.

At three years of age, Lynne fantasized about women. Lynne grew up during a time when homosexuality was considered a mental illness. Learning about homosexuality was left up to a child's own devices. Consequently, for most kids, it was a terribly confusing time. Lynne began to think in terms of butch/femme. Though she realized her same-sex attraction early on, it took Lynn time to accept herself for exactly who she is. Along the way, she toyed with drugs and alcohol, addictions that many gays and lesbians have faced. This is especially true as it is so tempting to try to hide through drugs the pain and shame they might feel as a result of their same-sex attraction and the messages they receive from our culture. Not only did Lynne end her addictive habits, she came clean about herself and accepted her sexual orientation.

Note your thoughts and reactions to Lynne's story.

Frank Y. Wong

I can't understand any discussion of gays and lesbians as if they were something immoral or unsatisfactory—they're doing just what nature wants them to do.

—Buckminster Fuller

Homosexuality is recorded in Chinese civilization and reached a peak during the Sung Dynasty (circa 1000 A.D.) Many gays during this dynasty gave Chinese civilization some of its greatest literature. For the most part, the various forms of Buddhism and Taoism do not see homosexuality as a sin. In fact, in Mahayana Buddhism, being gay is due to one's karma. Today however, most Chinese think that gays are abnormal. They generally tolerate homosexual acts so long as men "procreate" and keep their homosexuality to themselves.

My name is Frank. I am a Chinese-American, born in Vietnam (formerly South Vietnam). My parents, ethnic Chinese, were born in China. They and their parents moved to Vietnam after the Chinese Communist Government took power in the Motherland in the late 1940's.

Even for people who are familiar with Chinese cultural practices, some explanation is usually required to understand my family background. My father, the youngest of five children, came from a very wealthy family. Following Chinese tradition, my paternal grandparents arranged for my father, at age sixteen, to marry one of his first cousins, a daughter of his aunt. One is allowed to marry a first cousin as long as she or he is from the maternal aunt's side (a tradition based on no scientific evidence). The woman my father married at sixteen is not my biological mother but according to custom, I call her "Mother." Their union resulted in nine children. Like other ancient cultures (such as Indian and Arabic), Chinese culture allowed male polygamous marriages. Although this practice is no longer legal in China, it was common among my father's family and other wealthy families when he was young. Thus, when my father was about thirty years old, he met another woman roughly his age whom he married and with whom he eventually had two more sons and a daughter. I was the second son and the middle child of this subset of the family. According to the same custom, I call my biological mother "Aunt." Although my father was well versed in traditional Chinese culture, I sense that he met and "fell in love" with Aunt (my biological mother) in an almost Western way. Educated by the French, he raised us in a less than orthodox Chinese fashion.

Fortunately my two mothers got along well with each other. I attribute the harmonious relationship between them to the facts that my father maintained two households and that both my mothers are faithful Mahayana Buddhists. Mahayana Buddhists believe that Buddha is God while Hinayana Buddhism (the original belief), which I practice, honors Buddha as a mortal human being. My father was not very religious, nor were most of my extended family (aunts, uncles, cousins), which is atypical of most Chinese.

Communication in my family was very complex. At home I usually conversed with my father and "Aunt" and, sometimes, my "mother" in Cantonese. With my paternal grandfather, my father's brothers, and other extended family members I spoke Chiu-Chownese. "Aunt" had to learn to speak Chiu-Chownese when she married my father. My father and I also, occasionally, spoke in Mandarin and French. I attended a multilingual, Catholic school in Vietnam and classes were taught in Vietnamese, Mandarin, and French.

Growing up in my family was not easy. Because of our lineage and social status in South Vietnamese society (we were a prominent business family), I realized, even as a young child, that we were somewhat different from others. Lineage and customs are so important in Chinese families that a different name is given to designate similar kinships (e.g., cousin from the mother's side versus cousin from the father's side). My father's first name indicates his position within a span of twelve generations in the extended family.

Looking back, I suspect that my parents were often torn between the demands imposed by Chinese tradition and their Westernized experiences. My father gave some of us Christian first names and Chinese middle names. It was also complicated by the visibility my father experienced as a highly successful businessman. He was repeatedly asked by the president of South Vietnam to become a naturalized citizen. He compromised by changing his Chinese name to a Vietnamese sounding name while remaining a legal alien. We, his children, were Vietnamese citizens. Like my father, I have often felt torn between the push and pull of differing expectations.

In Chinese families, emotion is seldom expressed or talked about. Yet, my father openly showed affection for "Aunt," though not for "Mother." He also showed affection for his daughters and his youngest sons, including me. Yet my three older brothers, expected to adhere to strict roles, were shown no affection whatsoever.

I spent summers with my "mother" and the rest of the year with "Aunt." When I was about five years of age, I had my first sexual experience with one of my half brothers. He was a year older than me. I recall it as an enjoyable and pleasant experience and one to which I attributed little thought or significance. I think my parents were aware of the incident—they probably thought it was just child's play—although they chose to say nothing about it. My brother and I continued to "play" for about two months until I returned to my "Aunt's" house.

Upon my return from the summer of my first sexual experience, I had several encounters with one of my father's gardeners. He was seventeen, a pleasant, well-built fellow, who initiated these encounters (by today's standards, he might be accused of sexually abusing me). Like many Chinese, the gardener found a girlfriend once our encounters ended. I recall these experiences as enjoyable, pleasant.

About this time, my parents decided to move our immediate family to Hong Kong. They had lost all confidence in the South Vietnamese government and selected Hong Kong because our extended family already had businesses there. Although a British crown colony, Hong Kong was predominantly a Chinese society with few political overtones (or at least, that was the case in the early sixties). So, in 1965, at the age of six, I went to Hong Kong. Eventually, my father's side of our extended family joined us. The family's business headquarters were relocated there as well.

The move was exciting—Hong Kong was a very modern society—and it was difficult. While I spoke Mandarin, French, and Vietnamese, I did not speak English, which was the official language of Hong Kong (it is now bilingual). I also found it difficult to live in an apartment, after being raised in the large open spaces of South Vietnam. And I missed my friends and the relatives who stayed behind. To overcome my anxieties, I channeled all my energy into school.

I attended a private bilingual school. I was a straight-A student, yet bored by the curriculum that emphasized rote memorization. To fill my time, I read incessantly. When I was thirteen and fed up with traditional schooling, I pleaded with my parents to let me transfer to a more innovative international school. After much persuasion and many antics on my part, they agreed. In my new school, I learned how to think as an individual. It was a rich experience—a classic case of "East meets West"—and I grew as a result of wrestling with such conflicts. I also began to play competitive badminton, I took up swimming and I began to travel the world, which my parents generously supported.

I loved my newfound independence. I maintained a straight-A record, but unlike most Chinese teenagers, I did things just to annoy my parents. I was becoming quite Westernized, and my parents became increasingly worried about my behavior. At a loss as to how to deal with me, they decided to send me to live with my older sister and two brothers, who now resided in Canada. They hoped that my older siblings would know how to deal with me. I welcomed the opportunity and left for Toronto in 1975 at the age of sixteen (I later learned that my parents were also preparing me for the future, as they thought that eventually Hong Kong would return to China, as it will in 1997).

In Toronto, I attended a private, Catholic high school. My parents hoped that upon graduation I would attend the University of Toronto, one of Canada's most prestigious universities. My father and "Aunt" also wanted me to major in business or "something useful"—meaning financially profitable. "Mother," however, simply wanted me to be happy in whatever I did and hoped that I would be spiritual.

I opted for the University of Guelph, a medium-sized university fifty-five miles west of Toronto, where my parent now lived. The distance enabled me to live apart from my folks, who by now thought of me as "unusual." "He's not your typical Chinese," they would say.

Once on my own, I developed a thirst to learn more about Chinese civilization. I became vice-president of the Chinese Student Association and was active in many campus activities, including varsity badminton. I majored in philosophy, which disappointed my father and "Aunt."

I began to seriously date a Chinese girl whom I had met during my last year in high school. My parents seemed pleased. While we liked each other a great deal, our relationship ended when she moved to Vancouver. I still had not come to terms with my being gay.

When I was a senior in college, my father developed lung cancer. He was a very stubborn man and refused many major forms of treatment. He remained ill while I finished college and got my first job, as a mental health counselor in Rochester, New York. He died on November 16, 1982.

I went to Hong Kong for the funeral. His death brought about many squabbles in our extended family, especially in regards to the family business. According to Chinese tradition, the last male in the patriarchal family becomes head of the extended family and controls the family businesses. Thus, one of my uncles took over, creating a family uproar that would rival any seen on the T.V. programs *Dynasty* or *Dallas*. As a result, our family name was constantly in the media. And there was litigation, which took nine years to resolve. As faithful Mahayana Buddhists, "Mother" and "Aunt" did not intervene in these squabbles, and in the end my immediate family lost almost everything—money and lineage. My three older brothers, who had seen it as their duty to protect and maintain the family name, felt great shame. My greedy uncle disgraced six generations of the family name.

Like "Mother" and "Aunt," I stayed out of the squabbles—a stand not very popular among some of my siblings. Yet, I was determined to maintain some sense of myself, not wanting these squabbles to draw me back into the family whirlpool. Nevertheless, I became quite depressed about my father's death. He and I had a lot of unfinished personal business and I wish that I had been able to tell him who I really was, despite how difficult that would have been given our cultural heritage.

Following my father's death, I met several individuals who significantly affected my life. I found myself attracted to an older man. I was taken by his blond hair and blue eyes and flattered that he was taken by me. For the first time in my life, I fell in love, and we began what turned out to be a very short-lived relationship. There were troubling signs from the very beginning. Claiming to be an heir to the Upjohn Pharmaceutical Company fortunes, he was constantly broke and, like a fool, I constantly gave him whatever money he needed. I soon discovered that he was lying about a number of things, including an affair he was having with someone else. That was all I could handle and I ended the relationship, which cost me so, both emotionally and financially.

I was hurt and lonely. Shortly afterwards, I met a Hungarian-American woman. She was six years my senior. I also met a man who was ten years older than I. I dated both of them simultaneously and told each of them about the other. Neither seemed to mind. They turned out to be my best friends, accepting me completely—the good and the bad parts—and treating me like an individual. They keenly understood how conflicted I was by the demands imposed by Eastern and Western cultures. Their advice to me was always "to be myself."

Because of these two dear friends, I realized that I needed to work on some of my personal issues. I started seeing a therapist. Therapy helped me to come to terms with many of these conflicts and address the relevant issues surrounding my homosexuality and my family.

Given what I learned about homosexuality and Chinese civilization, I concluded that most of my family would allow me to quietly do my gay thing as long as I married and had children, but my experiences and therapy taught me to be true to myself. I simply wasn't prepared to lead a double life. I tried to communicate some of my feelings to my immediate family, but most of them preferred not to know. As a result, my relationship with my family has been strained. There were two exceptions, however. My two youngest sisters understood completely and, to this day, have been very supportive of me. Despite this strain posed by my family, I felt rejuvenated by my therapy and plotted a new course for my life.

I went to graduate school at Texas A&M University, where I attained a Ph.D. in Social Psychology. Both the majority of my fellow graduate students and faculty were supportive of my being openly gay. Following university, I joined the staff of Hofstra University, in Long Island, New York, where I currently live as an openly gay man.

I have lived in the United States for twelve years now. My relationships with my family are slowing improving. While most of them still prefer not to hear about my being gay, and I respect that, if the subject comes up I do not budge. I am being myself today.

In addition to dealing with my homosexuality, as a Chinese man I have also had to deal with racism. At times, it seems that being Chinese has often been more difficult than being gay. I have had little problem with being an openly gay psychologist and in other work settings. More difficult, perhaps, is having to deal with others who assume that simply because I am gay or because I am Chinese, I know everything there is to know about being gay or Chinese. I don't. But I do know that being gay is a part of the whole of me, an important part. I would like to think that being gay is just another adventure in life...

Frank's story demonstrates the role that culture can play in dealing with issues of sexual orientation. His efforts to integrate eastern and western cultures show the conflicts that those from different backgrounds often experience. Add to these differences how each culture treats homosexuality and you can see the challenges that gay, lesbian, and bisexual people often face.

Although born thousands of miles from the United States and raised in three different countries, Frank went through a process to accept himself as a gay man that is similar to that of all of our storytellers regardless of their national origin.

Note your thoughts and reactions to Frank's story.

4

Deepening Knowledge
Stories from the Workplace and Stories of Spiritual and Religious Development

You've looked at sexual orientation in the home, among friends, and in the community. Now that you have a sense of the diversity of this community, let's deepen your knowledge by zeroing in on two other important areas: work and spirituality.

In this chapter you'll identify the impact sexual orientation and the closet have on workplace productivity and learn how five individuals—two straight men, one heterosexual woman, one gay man, and one lesbian—have come out at work. Later in this chapter you will deepen your knowledge of religion and spirituality with regards to sexual orientation. You have already read Rabbi David Horowitz's story and, in reading his and most of the other stories, you probably noticed an emphasis on the spiritual aspect of the lives of our storytellers. Coming out and coming to acceptance are spiritual processes. In this section you will read about the son of a southern preacher, an African American Methodist minister, a gay Mormon, and a born-again fundamentalist Christian.

STORIES FROM THE WORKPLACE

In chapter two, we said that most families have adopted a U.S. Military-like policy of DON'T ASK, DON'T TELL when it comes to sexual orientation. We also said that such a policy destroys intimacy in the family as it forces people to run away, hide out, or be someone different than who they truly are.

Most businesses, like families, also operate in a DON'T ASK, DON'T TELL environment. Not only do businesses face similar losses (in intimate relationships, effectiveness, productivity, and so forth), they also face huge financial losses, because a policy of DON'T ASK, DON'T TELL has a tremendous and negative impact on performance and the bottom line.

Performance and the Bottom Line

In our earlier book, *A Manager's Guide to Sexual Orientation in the Workplace*, we demonstrate that when people lack knowledge, as they do in a DON'T ASK, DON'T TELL work environment, workplace performance deteriorates. In fact, a lack of knowledge is one of the primary causes of performance problems in organizations. In the manager's guide, we point out that even when people do possess knowledge they often lack the skills to translate their knowledge into effective action. Emblazened with the fear of saying or doing the wrong thing, which generally stifles action, most people at work do nothing. As a result, important issues are not addressed, productivity deteriorates, and more and more of the twenty-five million gay, lesbian, and bisexual customers in the U.S. are speaking out. They are also organizing to invest their $500 billion in purchasing power *only* in companies that acknowledge their existence and aggressively support their equal (not special) rights as human beings. Companies, from APPLE to Xerox, are taking notice and addressing these issues.

The Link Between Sexual Orientation and Performance

A high-level manager recently asked, "Does sexual orientation impact performance?" That's a good question and, surprisingly, the answer is, "Absolutely!" When managers send signals or messages that it is not okay to be gay in the workplace (and they do), they negatively impact performance. Some managers send blatant signals such as statements like, "Who do you people think you are talking about your sexual orientation in public?" or "We don't want any of *them* in here." More often, the messages are subtle, such as "Gays and lesbians are okay so long as they don't talk about it." Whether blatant or subtle, the messages are the same to sexual minorities—you can't be yourself here and, when people are made to feel unwelcome, their performance is negatively impacted. If heterosexual employees were made to feel that their sexual orientation were not okay, their performance would suffer also.

When these messages or signals are sent, many employees feel forced to hide their sexual identity. This (hiding) takes a tremendous amount of psychological and physical energy. These employees divert their energies to protect themselves by covering up facts, keeping low profiles, lying, changing pronouns, and so forth. Anyone who has ever hid a significant part of their life can understand the energy hiding takes—the boss who is hiding a recent diagnosis of cancer, an employee who is hiding that her son is dying of AIDS, two employees who are hiding their intimate relationship, or a co-worker who is hiding an addiction or a family illness.

While most people recognize that hiding wastes energy, they often continue (both knowingly and unknowingly) to send signals and messages that encourage people to hide.

Whenever a manager or co-worker tells a homophobic, racist, or sexist joke, the message is being sent that it is not okay to be yourself. Every time we exclude sexual minorities, we reinforce the message that sexual minorities are not welcome. Often this is done inadvertently—for example, in a training class where all role plays contain references only to opposite sex couples, or in invitations to office parties in which husbands and wives are encouraged to attend but no attempt is made to include same-sex partners. Although seemingly subtle, these acts reinforce the message that one needs to hide simply to survive.

When people feel excluded, as sexual minorities often do, they are much less inclined to devote energy toward making the organization successful. Ask yourself how likely you would be to go out of your way to help an organization that tells you there is something wrong with who you are, that says you're not welcome. The answer is, "Not very likely."

If you are heterosexual and have any doubts about the effort it takes to hide, try this simple experiment for a day or even during a fifteen minute coffee break. Go the entire time without making a single reference to your spouse, children, family, significant other, or any other statement that would give even a hint of your heterosexuality. In trying to hide your sexual orientation, you will experience the difficulty that sexual minorities face. It becomes almost impossible to answer even the most simple questions like, "What did you do over the weekend?" "What are you planning to do tonight?" "Do you have a family?" Most people cannot go two minutes without revealing their sexual orientation. Those who resort to hiding who they are, end up feeling dishonest, powerless, and often disgusted with themselves, traits not especially conducive to improving workplace performance.

Another response people have to being made invisible is to "act out" or "act up," rather than hide. Forcing people to be invisible has led disabled people to wheel in protest down America's main streets, AIDS activists to shout down Presidents, women to break through the doors of the U.S. Senate, people of every color to march arm-in-arm through towns and villages around the world, from Selma, Alabama, to Johannesburg, South Africa and, it has led gays, lesbians, and other sexual minorities to stand up and shout out, "We're here! We're queer! Get used to it!" Not only can you get used to it, you can also come to enjoy and find value in embracing this diverse group of co-workers, employees, bosses, and customers.

In the following stories you'll discover how productive work relationships can be destroyed when these issues are ignored, witness the impact the closet has on gay and heterosexual workers alike, and recognize the unfairness that occurs when people are not treated as equals. You'll also read the stories of heterosexual managers who recognize the importance of these issues and take action to deal with them in a way that supports, rather than undermines, top-notch performance.

In this section you'll read the stories of a gay man (Joe Wilcox), a lesbian (Lisa Busjahn), and three heterosexuals (Constance Holmes, Danny Langdon, and Dale Barr) that focus specifically on work.

Joe Wilcox

This above all to thine own self be true.

—William Shakespeare

The first gay-related memory I can think of was the feeling of warmth and strength I got when my father taught me how to tie my shoes by kneeling behind me and reaching around me to tie the laces. While I didn't have a knowledge of sexual feelings at the time, I did notice that his touch was different from that of my mother.

I was raised in a large Catholic home in suburban, New Jersey with four brothers and two sisters. While I can't say that my childhood was idyllic, I considered it relatively normal as compared with other kids. I recall that my parents weren't demonstrative in their expression of emotions, and throughout my childhood I tried to be perfect in order to garner their affection and approval. This perfectionism showed up in my schoolwork, in the work I did around the house, and even in the way I related to my brothers, sisters, and friends. Being polite and well mannered was always extremely important to me. To this day, these manners can be seen in my work life and relationships.

As I grew older, and reached the age of twelve or thirteen, when many boys started becoming interested in girls, I began to worry much of the time about my ambivalent feelings toward girls. While I always enjoyed being around girls, there were no new feelings inside me that compelled me to want to write notes to girls or carry their books. I began to do those things anyway in order to be like my peers and attributed my disinterest to the thought that I must be very late in maturing and that those feelings would come when I matured.

I had been minimally exposed to homosexuality through stereotypes on television and the comments of my friends. When I began to mature, I was disturbed to notice that my fantasies generally did not include girls, but centered on men or other boys in my life. I looked up the word faggot in the dictionary—a bundle of sticks used to start fires. Not much help. Later, I learned that those bundles were used to burn witches, heretics, and homosexuals. I read in another book that many adolescents go through a phase in which they have homosexual feelings. Greatly relieved, I looked forward to passing through and beyond this unpleasant phase of my life.

In the interim, I had two minor affairs with boys toward the end of my high school days. I tried to put this "phase" behind me. In anticipation of becoming a healthy heterosexual, I began to look at women and comment on their physical attributes to some of my friends. I collected the requisite pinups of the time—Linda Ronstadt and Loni Anderson—despite the fact that I still couldn't understand the attraction. I decided that by doing the things my straight friends did I would become more like them and hopefully hide my secret at the same time.

It became more and more difficult to deny the fact that I was gay. But because of my religious beliefs, I continued to suppress my feelings toward other men, and I propagated the lie that I was a heterosexual. I tried even harder to attain a "normal" life by starting a relationship with a female friend of mine. It didn't take long till we were seeing each other seriously, and the prospect of sex became imminent. I found myself in situations in which I'm certain other men would have known what to do and the situations would have resulted in sex. With me, however, they never advanced beyond necking sessions. Thankfully, after a year of dating, she broke off the relationship to begin seeing a mutual friend. I acted upset, although inside I was relieved that the pressure was off, and I would only have to talk about women and not feel impelled to perform.

When my father died while I was still in high school, I actually felt somewhat relieved that I wouldn't have to tell him about my being homosexual. In fact, I was so afraid of the prospect that my family would disapprove that I moved out of the house and decided never to tell them about myself.

In my junior year of college, I was assigned a roommate in the dorm and found myself attracted to him. I began to unravel the lie I had perpetuated of being straight and started to admit to myself that maybe these feelings weren't a phase after all. Coincidentally, I also started to wonder if my roommate might be gay. I listened to some of his phone conversations and watched for any hints in his behavior that would tell me about his sexual orientation. Finally, I read a card from a man I had believed to be his lover. The card confirmed to me that he was gay, and I confronted him with the knowledge. Ironically, it was this discussion that began my coming out process, wherein I admitted to myself and to my roommate that I was gay. Though we never did have a physical relationship, we often went out together and met many other gay men who went to our college. I will always be grateful to him for introducing me to gay life.

I did a lot of carousing during my last two years of college. I was very conservative in choosing partners, however, and I was determined to find a long-term partner, whereas many of the men I met were only interested in short-term or no-term relationships.

I stayed very secretive about being gay and told no one except other gays. The only exception to this was when I told a woman whom I had recently met at college. She told three of the friends I had established in prior years. "I just don't want to hear about it," one of them said and all three began to distance themselves from me.

My first job after school was as an insurance and patient billing coordinator in a large doctor's clinic. The atmosphere was very open, and I knew many of the people I worked with from outside organizations. I told many of my co-workers that I was gay. They seemed to accept it well. In retrospect, the environment in that office allowed me to be myself and without the constant worry of being discovered, I was able to give most of my energy to my job.

While everyone I worked with knew I was gay, I was still unable to come out to my family. I was simply too afraid. There was an often-told story in my family about one of my brothers who used to go out with his high school friends to pick up gays at a local cruising spot and then beat them up. This story was always good for a laugh. They laughed especially hard at the notion of harming an "unsuspecting, nellie faggot." I would pretend to enjoy the story, but my insides hurt each time I heard them speak. I learned that cruising in public places was dangerous with people the likes of my brothers.

At the age of twenty-two, I began a relationship that I call my first real love. Keeping the relationship secret from my family became increasingly stressful. Then, too, I had difficulty reconciling my sexuality with the rules of the Catholic church. I began consulting and confessing with a priest on a weekly basis to try to come up with some way that I could continue to practice Catholicism and still maintain my relationship. The pressure was intense. The lack of integrity I had with my family, the idea that I might have to leave the church, which had been a source of great comfort to me in the past, and the day-to-day stresses of maintaining a relationship were too much for me. I was overwhelmed with conflict and shame. Shortly thereafter, each of these pressures were resolved.

First, I was involved in a car accident which required me to live with my family for a short period of time. During that time, my mother read one of my personal journals which described in detail my relationship with my lover. She wasn't happy, nor did she confront me directly. However, my sister did, and I ended up coming out to her. Before long, I was out to my entire family.

Then, after two years of being together, my lover left me. It was extremely upsetting, yet it propelled me to develop a network of friends who were able to help me get through a difficult time. I took the break up as an opportunity to make some other big changes in my life.

I did some very deep soul searching where I seriously considered joining the priesthood. I realized that I could never maintain a vow of celibacy. By now, I had developed a very close relationship with God and had a very clear experience of who God was in my life, which was different from what was being taught by the Catholic church. Soon, I chose to leave the Catholic church.

During this time, I changed jobs and went to work within the corporate offices of Manufacturer's Hanover Trust, a very conservative New York City bank. I threw myself back into the closet, where I suppressed my enthusiasm, creativity, and energy. I commuted to work by train from New Jersey to Manhattan every day and developed a small group of commuter friends, especially two men and two women. One of the men, Donald, lived near me and we would walk from the station to our neighborhood. Soon, I began to wonder if he might be gay. I dropped a few "hints" and found out my suspicions were accurate. Donald and I became very friendly after that. He sometimes became the topic of discussion with the other commuters. One of the women told me that the others thought that "Donald was a faggot," but she didn't believe it because he had a beard and moustache. This bit of information panicked me and I made sure that I never gave any of them any indication that I too might be a faggot.

Working in New York was exciting (my father had commuted to New York as an executive, and I had always aspired to do the same), but my job wasn't. In an effort to hide my home life, I acted very serious and businesslike. As a result, my employers saw me as dull and lifeless. They treated me as though I weren't able to pick things up quickly, though in fact I learned quickly and was bored by most of what I did. Their assessments of me in performance reviews were always adequate or good, but in their eyes I never excelled. This was an enormous change from the way I was perceived at the doctor's clinic, and it was a difficult one for me to accept, as I felt devalued.

During my first year working in New York I went out a lot. I missed living with someone and I was very lonesome. I wanted to share my life. I had a very good friend with similar aspirations, and together we cruised the only known social outlet for gays—the bars—looking for mates. In 1985, I met Thaddeus. We began to see each other seriously and soon fell in love. After three months we decided to live together.

Even though I still seldom discussed my lifestyle with my family, I wanted them to know Thaddeus and to know that I thought of him as my life partner. Finally, something happened that brought me fully out of the closet with my family. Thaddeus and I were preparing to celebrate our second Christmas together. My mother decided that she wanted all of her children, sons-in-laws, daughters-in-laws, and grandchildren to come home for Christmas. For the event, she scheduled a well-known photographer to take a family portrait. Since I had made it clear that Thaddeus was my spouse, he was invited with all the other in-laws. It was Christmas Eve day and our house was extremely chaotic. Eighteen of us—my mother, seven children, four in-laws, and six grandchildren—all were crammed into my mother's house for the holiday photo session.

When the photographer arrived, she busied herself with the equipment as my mother gathered all of her brood into the living room for the photo shoot. The photographer then began to arrange people. She put my two oldest brothers with their wives and children and then she pointed to me and asked, "Are you married?" For the very first time that day, my entire family fell silent. Not even a peep was heard from the babies. I mumbled an affirmative grunt, and she asked, "Where is your lovely wife?" I thought my entire family would die. I pointed to Thaddeus and she looked behind him and asked again where she was. This time, through my embarrassment, I distinctly pointed him out. She looked at us both and put us into position. She then went to my next brother and asked, "Are you married?" When he said, "Yes," she added, "To what?" At that, everyone broke into hysterical laughter. Regaining her composure, the photographer began shooting away.

This incident gave my family what they needed to make my homosexuality okay with them. It also made possible subsequent discussions that since have made it comfortable for me to be gay with my family. And, in some way, it educated the photographer to think twice before automatically assuming everyone is a heterosexual.

By now, I was out everywhere but work. After two years at the bank, I changed jobs and joined Atlantic Mutual, a mid-size insurance company based on Wall Street, working in the human resources department. The company had been established for one hundred and fifty years and was considered one of the more conservative companies in the industry. At first, I opted to keep secret about being gay for fear of losing my job. While I was certain that my bosses wouldn't have fired me solely for being gay, they might have felt it was "poor judgment" to come out and used that as the reason for losing trust in me.

I excelled quickly at my new job as an analyst and began to establish myself as a hard working and energetic employee. I was quick to take on additional responsibilities and was viewed favorably by most of the people with whom I worked. Soon I was promoted to supervisor and then to manager.

By the time I had been with the company for five years, I had slowly picked out people with whom I worked that I felt I could trust, and I told them the "secret" of my sexuality. Then something happened that made me realize that my secret was not quite as hidden as I had thought. Following a day of heavy snow, my supervisor informed me that she had tried to call me to let me know that the office would be closed. When the operator couldn't find my name listed with directory assistance, my supervisor said that she tried to remember my roommate's name. I was shocked that she knew I had a roommate. As casually as I could, I asked how she knew my roommate's name. She told me that she had seen it on my life insurance beneficiary information.

I used that opportunity to begin talking more freely about Thaddeus. I spoke of vacations we had taken, mentioned our checkbook in conversations, and told about our sharing a car. I even brought Thaddeus to the annual holiday party. I made it apparent to everyone that Thaddeus was more than just a roommate.

About this time, I became more socially and politically aware. I read everything I could about gay and lesbian issues. Soon, I realized that by being open at work I could help represent gays and lesbians as being visible and equal (and sometimes superior) contributors to the work force, which led me to an important decision. I would discuss being gay as if I were straight. For example, if someone asked me about my personal life, I would feel free to tell them about my relationship with Thaddeus, if that was pertinent.

The first few times I said the word gay in public, I could feel my ears turn red and the room get warmer as I waited for a reaction, positive or negative. Sometimes the words rang very hollow in my head as I confronted the awkward situations these conversations seemed to create. But mostly, I felt freedom and that outweighed the slight embarrassment I sometimes felt.

I had one setback in my newfound policy of honesty. I was invited to dinner by the president of my company with nine other employees in recognition of our participation in a company sponsored health program. During dinner, the president's wife asked me if I was married. I told her I wasn't legally married. She nodded her understanding and went on to tell me how, despite her husband's protests, her son had lived with a woman for a period of time, but it was alright now because they had married. She then asked my girlfriend's name. I got very embarrassed and tried to change the subject. She persisted and asked why I wouldn't tell her the name of my girlfriend. By now, we had attracted the attention of the other dinner guests. I was mortified and asked her to stop asking. She ended the conversation by winking and saying that she understood. I have no idea if she really understood. I do know that I felt angry and ashamed that I didn't have the courage to talk about Thaddeus as the other employees at that dinner spoke of their spouses. While I excused myself by acknowledging that I simply didn't feel safe sharing about my life with the company's first lady, I resolved that I would never suppress myself in a similar situation.

In the years that have followed, I have been proud of the many times that I have told the truth despite my discomfort and my fear of possible financial loss. During these times, I have not received one negative comment or reaction to my coming out directly at work. My bosses have all been very supportive of me. In fact, I sense that they have a renewed respect for me and the integrity with which I am living my life. I know I do.

I can't say that I was very thrilled when I first realized I was gay. I can't say that coming out to friends, family, and co-workers has been enjoyable or painless. I also can't say that my life has been easy. But, I can say that I wouldn't change one thing about my life today or my history, since my history is what made me who I am.

I have become a respected colleague in the field of human resource systems, both within and outside of my company, and I expect my career success to continue. Over the years, Thaddeus and I have grown both personally and as a couple, and we have a loving and empowering relationship today. We are approaching our tenth anniversary. Most importantly, I have learned that maintaining my integrity about who I am is the most important thing in my life.

Finally, I have learned that coming out, for me, is a continuous process, and I am now out to most everyone in my life. I intend to continue this process to be who I am, and to make the fact of my sexual orientation a matter of public knowledge, free for the asking. I hope that this will enable people to see how very much alike we human beings are, and that we (gays and lesbians) are not to be feared. I hope too that telling my story will help others find the courage to become more accepting human beings.

Joe's story shows how making assumptions (as both the president's wife and photographer did) can, inadvertently, create great stress and discomfort for everyone. Had either used the tools contained within this book (in line with the DO ASK aspect of this book), they would have avoided creating such situations. Joe's story also illustrates how gay employees often take such negative experiences and use them to develop positive future actions (the DO TELL aspect).

Joe's story also highlights the fear many sexual minorities face and that causes some to remain closeted throughout their corporate life. This fear was in evidence in the authors' stories and is one that almost every sexual minority faces at some point. The skills and tools that you will develop by reading this book will help you create an environment in which sexual minorities can devote less effort to hiding and more to productivity.

Note your thoughts and reactions to Joe's story.

Constance Holmes

...accept one another then, for the glory of God, as Christ has accepted you.

—Romans 15:7

There are only seven or eight all-black cities in the United States. Mound Bayou, Mississippi, a rural community of twenty thousand located in the Delta, where everybody is black—doctors, policemen, teachers, and politicians—is one of them.

I was born in Mound Bayou in 1958, the youngest of eight children.

My father, who had a seventh-grade education, was sixty-one years old when I was born. My mother, who also ended her schooling in the seventh grade, was half his age. We were a farming family, and like many black families, very religious.

My father raised soybeans, cotton, and corn. The entire family worked on the farm. Most of my siblings were much older than I, and given my father's age, he and I generally "supervised" the work the other family members did. We would ride around the farm in my father's pick-up truck. Every once in a while I smile and think that was my preparation for supervising people in my work today.

I idolized my father. He was a well-respected man and very loving. More than anything, he believed that education was the one way for us to make it in the world. I remember him saying to me, "Girl, get your lesson." Because of his beliefs, I and all seven of my brothers and sisters are college educated, a remarkable achievement given the most he probably ever made was $10,000 in any given year.

He didn't consider himself poor though, in part because he owned his own land, and partly because in Mississippi in the 1950's one didn't need much money to survive. I'm not sure how he did it, though, as all of his children attended private Catholic school. This was unusual, not simply because of the cost, but because we were devout Baptists. I remember studying catechism from Monday through Friday and singing hymns and participating in church activities during the weekend. I liked church, though I really didn't "get out the Bible" until I was an adult. My favorite activity was participating in the "speeches," which the kids gave at church. I think that was my preparation for my first career as a radio announcer.

Growing up, I spent most of my time with my father or alone. I seldom played; I was the "mature" kid, the one that would help the younger children get started playing and then leave. I liked being around older people, which is true even today. When I wasn't with my father, I read. I seldom watched television. On Sundays, in addition to attending church, I visited my cousins.

The towns adjoining Mound Bayou were racially mixed. My father would take me there twice a year to shop for clothing, the one thing we couldn't buy in Mound Bayou. That is where I first ran into whites and Chinese. The Chinese owned the grocery store and the whites owned the clothing store. I don't recall anything remarkable about seeing different races. In fact, it seemed quite natural.

Ironically, my first taste of discrimination occurred in Mound Bayou. I was in kindergarten. Even though we were all black, I remember thinking Mrs. Springer liked the lighter skinned students better, even though I was a better student. It wasn't that I felt singled out; I didn't. But I did feel that I wasn't getting the opportunity to shine because I was darker skinned.

During most of my growing up, I didn't experience much discrimination and never on a daily basis. I knew that it happened to others, but because our town was all black and because I so seldom watched television, the extent of prejudice in America was unknown to me. For example, I was about ten when Martin Luther King was killed, but I felt very distant from the events because of the peaceful life I was living.

I knew little about homosexuality. It was seldom talked about within the black community. While there were some homosexuals in the community—many worked as nurses in the hospital—I didn't know any of them personally. Nor did I believe that there was anything particularly wrong with homosexuality. I simply didn't think in those terms (right or wrong); that is, until a very religious friend pointed out a reference in the Bible and told me that homosexuality was not acceptable. I was left feeling confused. My confusion was compounded by the fact that there were gay musicians in most of the black churches, yet many black preachers spoke of the evils of homosexuality. I didn't understand how either the homosexual or the preacher reconciled these conflicting positions. How a preacher could have someone in his church who was gay and, at the same time, talk about it as a problem, or how homosexuals could subject themselves to such preachings and still go to church simply didn't make sense to me.

I met my first gay person when I was in college. I worked in the hospital with a guy whom I thought was gay. It was just an impression, but I believe now it was accurate. He never said he was gay; in fact, he often talked about having a girlfriend. I never saw him with any girls nor did I really believe that he had a girlfriend.

At Jackson State, a mostly black college in Mississippi, I majored in Radio and Television Communications. When I graduated, I got my first job in radio. My boss saw my talent more than the color of my skin. This was also true in my second job, where my boss used to call me his "black pearl." I did not find this offensive, and when he decided to leave, he offered me a job.

The first time I experienced blatant racism was when I was working on an internship program. My roommate was a white woman. The person next door used to play her radio very loudly. My roommate would usually go next door and ask her to turn it down. One day, however, she asked me to do it. So, I knocked on door of the apartment. I could hear the woman approaching when I heard a man's voice say, "I betcha that's the police." The woman looked at me through the peephole and I heard her say, "Oh no, that's just the nigger next door." She opened the door and I told her what I wanted. She was polite, but I was hurt and somewhat concerned about my safety. I wondered if this is how all whites really felt.

In 1980, I entered graduate school, where I majored in Instructional Design. I was the only African American in the program. In 1982, I began to work as an intern at Arthur Andersen in St. Charles, Illinois.

St. Charles, like the graduate school I attended, is almost entirely white. For the first couple of years I felt as if I was giving up my life for my career. I hardly had any black friends and there certainly were no black men to date. So, I threw myself into my career. After about three years, I decided to move closer to Chicago, where I would meet more blacks.

My work as an intern lead to full-time employment with Arthur Andersen, and in January, 1983, I was made a training evaluation specialist. During the next several years, I went through a series of promotions. In 1991, I was made a director and now supervise about forty-five people.

Arthur Andersen has about twenty-five to thirty directors in St. Charles. I am the only black and one of five women directors. The people within Arthur Andersen have been very supportive of me, and my career has progressed nicely. I certainly don't experience any blatant discrimination. At times, I theorize that clients don't take to me as well as they might to a white male. My work has gotten more difficult as I move up in the organization. The difficulty has less to do with my work talents than with my ability to socialize, to network. I think that if I were a white male it would be easier.

In 1992, I had my first real association with an openly gay man. He was a person on my staff. I didn't know him well, but when I heard he told his work group that he was gay, I decided to talk to him. I told him that I thought he was a brave man and I wanted him to know that I would be there to support him if he needed me. I knew it would be difficult for him. I guess because I felt different from most of the people around me, I could understand what he might be going through. I wanted him to know that he mattered to me and I wanted him to know that I would support him if anyone tried to discriminate against him. There seems to be little, if any, negative consequences. It just hasn't been an issue.

In 1990, I chaired the diversity committee of the National Society for Performance and Instruction (NSPI), my professional organization, and then served as a member of that committee. When we began that work, I thought of diversity in terms of race or culture. As time passed and I learned more about others, I expanded my thinking and now realize that diversity is far broader, including gays and lesbians, and people with other differences. I have been around a number of gays and lesbians in NSPI and can honestly say I am comfortable around all of them.

I think gays and lesbians have a tough life because they can't be themselves without being concerned for their own well-being. Even though they have some limited legal protections, gays and lesbians are not totally accepted. They can't walk down the street holding hands with the people they love and feel safe. I know they can't talk about their spouses, their lovers, and be accepted and not have to worry about it. I think if there were an opportunity for straights to walk in a gay person's shoes, the world would be more tolerant of differences. Everyday, I think about my color. I imagine homosexuals think every-day about being a homosexual.

Last night I went to buy some gasoline. There was an Asian man at the station who spoke very broken English. The attendant asked him for his license number. The Asian wrote it down and handed it to him. When he left, the attendant said to me, "They have no business here in the United States. If they can't speak English, they don't belong here." I turned to him and said, "You know, we have to be more tolerant of people." I was very pleased with myself for not colluding with his prejudice. It really didn't matter whether he was Asian, black, gay, or whatever.

Recently, I spoke to a group of high school students in Anchorage, Alaska. One of them asked something like, "Do you ever wish you were different?" I told them I don't question who I am (I am an African American woman). I said I would probably have a different life if I were of another color, but I've had a wonderful life and every year gets better. I have a mission in life—to make sure other blacks make it. I don't quibble that I'm getting older either, or that I'm changing, or that I am getting gray hair. These experiences have all made me a stronger person. They have made me who I am today.

I learned about work from my father, but I learned about acceptance from my mother, a giving, kind woman. That's part of how I grew up. I have nothing to lose by accepting people as they are. They don't hurt me in any way. They don't take anything away from me. Being accept-ing makes life easier.

Constance Holmes tells how her own experiences of prejudice have helped her become a champion of an all-inclusive workplace. Like Dale Barr (who's story follows), she became supportive as a result of interacting with a gay man at work and then, like Vince, integrated her experiences of prejudice with those of her gay co-worker. As a result, she began to understand how it is important to support *all* workers. She experienced further insight and growth through her work as the chair of NSPI's Diversity Committee. By her active involvement, she realized that diversity was not just about race or culture but about inclusion of all people who are different including sexual minorities. Her experience demonstrates that working to create an all-inclusive workforce provides opportunities and experiences that will increase one's confidence and competence.

Note your thoughts and reactions to Dale's story.

Danny Langdon

No democracy can long survive which does not accept as fundamental to its existence the recognition of the rights of minorities.

—Franklin D. Roosevelt

It always seemed to me that the town I grew up in made it virtually impossible to learn to be prejudiced. Twin Falls, Idaho, was a community of sixteen thousand hard working, independent farming people (almost entirely white). It was a safe place to walk around, to be a little bit mischievous, and a "happy days" kind of place for a teenager. There was one black man, who ran his own shoe shine business, and I spent hours hanging around listening to his stories over and over again. There was a Jewish shoe merchant who gave me fatherly advice and allowed me to x-ray my feet any time I wanted to on the store X-ray machine. There were a few Mexican farm laborers who lived on my side of the town. It was not until very late in life that I got even an inkling that any of these ethnic differences might have mattered to some people. I learned from my mother that each person was a person.

I was born on November 16, 1938. My father died of a heart attack when I was seven years old, so I cannot speak to any influence that he might have had on my development. My only recollection of his death is of a little boy (me) asking why everyone was crying. My mother, however, is another story. She was, and is, a model of the way I would hope every person should be—tolerant, understanding, firm about what is and is not right, compassionate, just, a good listener, a reinforcer, and many other superlatives. She organized and ran her own scrap iron business for forty years, was Mother of the Year in our state and runner-up in the nation, and was far ahead of any liberalized male or female who ever wrote a book or marched in a march. She raised eight children, saw five of us through college, and has grieved the loss of two children. I learned a great deal from this woman, especially about caring.

I used to watch her in her business dealings with others. I distinctly remember a person who tried to pull the wool over her eyes, only to find that such behavior was far from satisfactory and a quick admonishment set the record straight. I also saw her give more than an extra allowance of time and money to those who were in need—bums, as they were called in that day and age. She had a set of hospital beds that she gave away, likewise food and clothing. How could a child learn prejudice around such a person, around such a community? In reading Ashley Montagu's book, *Touching: The Human Significance of the Skin*, I noted his observation that those who have been tenderly held and loved in their youth are the best adjusted in later life. I was tenderly held and loved by my mother. Given the people around me, I am not surprised I turned out to be an accepting human being.

I was twenty-three when I first saw the ugly face of prejudice. The year was 1961, and I came face to face with an event that tore at the reality of what I thought the world to be. Certainly I knew of the civil rights movement—T.V. had come to my hometown. Also, I was in college and colleges typically were at the forefront of what was going on (e.g., civil rights, the Vietnam escalation). But, I had not felt this or other prejudices directly in my soul.

I was in graduate school in Missouri. My graduate advisor and six of us made a trip to Kansas City to attend a meeting of educators. Along the way, we stopped at a small cafe and sat joking, prepared to place our order for lunch. Stoney-faced, the waitress informed one of my colleagues (a black man) that she could not wait on him, that he would have to leave the establishment. Without having to say as much as a single word, the six of us rose as one and left to eat elsewhere. I was shaken by an attitude of intolerance such as I had never seen, and I was puzzled by what could ever have brought that person to treat another in such a way. It was only the breakthrough of this and subsequent encounters that have led me to realize that prejudice, on the part of anyone, is a learned behavior. I also concluded that anything that is learned can be unlearned—although with much greater difficulty. I have subsequently seen people learn to be prejudiced and others learn how not to be prejudiced.

I came to experience and cherish my friendships with gays and lesbians rather late in life. I can't really recall knowing a gay person when I was a kid. I vaguely remember others talking and joking about "queers" or "homos," as they were called in those days—but never, never myself (my mother would have been too disappointed in me, and I respected her judgment). In retrospect, there were high school friends that I might have surmised were gay, but I remember in the mid-1950s nobody, and I mean nobody, ever said they were gay. I was in my early twenties when I first saw what I believed was a gay person. There were some guys walking down the street and I said to someone else, "I bet they are homosexuals." It was a simplistic, silly statement that by itself proved how little I knew or had experienced when it came to gays.

In 1962, I joined the Peace Corps. I spent two years in Ethiopia, on the horn of Africa. I recall thinking that a couple of the volunteers were probably gay. I don't know exactly why I had this thought; after all, I had never even interacted with either of these people. One was an art teacher and I thought his gestures were effeminate. Later, when we became good friends, I found out I was wrong; he was straight. I also found out that another Peace Corps volunteer, who I took for an "ordinary Joe," was an "extraordinary Joe" (gay). It just showed me that one can never tell and one should not be so hasty to judge—as if judging itself were that significant. Better to accept than to judge.

I met my first wife in the Peace Corps. We were married in a leper colony in Ethiopia. We were together for twenty-seven years and raised two daughters, Lisa and Kimberly. After some struggles we divorced. On December 29, 1991, I married Kathleen, a woman I had known professionally for many years. We were brought together by chance and are very, very happy. It is a marriage with complete communication in all possible ways.

After the Peace Corps, I entered the "real world" and briefly spent a year teaching chemistry in a public school. In 1967, I entered the corporate world and spent the next fifteen years in various training and education jobs in Palo Alto, California, Philadelphia, Boise, Idaho, and Torrance, California. It was during this time period that I began to encounter gays on a personal level. The first of these, interestingly enough, is one of the editors of this book, Bob Powers. When Bob became active in the professional society that the two of us share it was, by his own acknowledgment, clear that Bob was gay. He was the first person who let it be known to me that he was gay. In retrospect, it both confused and impressed me. I was confused because it was one thing to know that gays existed, but quite another for someone to confront you with the fact that he was comfortable with being gay and was also proud to have the courage to talk about it. It made me think, why shouldn't he be proud? It's not like a gay person can do something, or should do something, about it!

In Bob's case, he's funny, easy to talk to, competent in his professional work, and he has become a friend of mine. His personal attributes, and his friendship, have made it easier for me to accept him and other people who are gay. That's the way they come to me—as people who are gay; the same way "straight" people come to me—as people who are heterosexual! Little did I know how important that acceptance would come to be. The lessons learned in this experience would prove quite valuable in later years.

It had never occurred to me that my own daughter Kimberly might be gay. After all, she dated boys throughout high school. She was shy and quiet. On one cold day in December, 1989, I received a phone call from a boy Kimberly was dating. I knew he was very attached to our daughter and she had broken up with him.

He was angry for being jilted and in his anger he said, "Do you know that your daughter is gay?" I was stunned.

"No, I didn't know," I thought, but I didn't say it. Instead I said, "If she is gay, it's none of your business," and hung up.

My mind raced. "Why would this person be saying this?" I wondered. "Is it possibly true? If so, what do I say? How do I react?" I told my wife, who was disbelieving. We talked and concluded that, if it were true, she was still our daughter and it would be okay. After all, we loved her and knew enough to know that homosexuality was not something one chooses. To us, irrational, bigoted people believe this is a question of choice. When it happens (becomes revealed) to one of your own and you know that son or daughter for who and what he or she is, you know it is not a question of choice. Even if it were, it would not make any difference anywhow. We decided to approach Kimberly and tell her what had happened. Kimberly denied that she was gay, but her denial seemed to lack conviction. She was nervous and defensive. We assured her that if it were true, it was okay with us. "We'll still love you," we said. We concluded that it was true—our daughter was a lesbian. My wife asked me if I believed Kimberly would change. I said no. A week later we talked to Kimberly again. We told her we loved her and that it wouldn't make any difference to us if she were a lesbian. As hard as it was for her to say, she told us it was true, she was a lesbian. We were both supportive. It was relatively easy—she's a wonderful person and a very nice person, to boot. "It's okay," I thought and I knew I really believed it, and I do to this day.

Our supportive stance seemed to surprise her. She must have been very frightened. As it turned out, our other daughter already knew. Interestingly enough, her boyfriend called Kim's place of business and, in his rage, told Kim's co-workers and many of her friends—but no one believed him. Our entire family has continued to be supportive.

When Kim told us that she had a lover, we invited Kim to bring her to our home. Kim was a little nervous, but for some reason, it seemed very natural to me. That was four years ago. Today, Paulie is like another member of our family. She spends Christmas with us. With the exception of Paulie's sister, her family doesn't know about Paulie's sexual orientation nor of the love she shares with our daughter. Paulie is a very nice person, and I'm happy my daughter has found someone she deeply cares about to share her life.

I find it perplexing that among all the disenfranchised peoples, gays and lesbians are the hardest for most of us to reconcile. At times, I wonder why and conclude that it's because homosexuality confronts our own human possibility. In other words, it could just have easily been me who turned out to be gay. I don't know why this scares some, but it does.

Most people still believe that homosexuals have a choice! Somehow, sometime, I learned that such a view was ridiculous, and certainly what I learned has been reinforced in the past few years. As with any kind of prejudice, the one perpetuating (and I use that word deliberately) the prejudice has simply lost sight of the fact that above all else, whatever the diversity, we are all human beings. No matter what craziness our parents, friends, colleagues, communities, or societies have imposed on us, the person we are judging to be so "different," so "offensive," is just like you and me, another human being. We all started out in the same nakedness and will all end up in the same dust. Homosexuals, I know, were born the way they were born, and that's the reason they are what they are. It has nothing to do with "prefer-ence." It's a basic orientation. We have to accept that fact. The lesson to be drawn from this is really quite clear. Be it one of your own or a total stranger, as humans we should be in the business of accepting and, yes, rejecting others based on what kind of person they are and not for things they have no choice over.

When I came to realize that I had a gay daughter, I was faced with whether or not to tell others that my daughter is a lesbian. In many ways, this is akin to the closet that gays and lesbians live in before they come out. Over the years, I have told some people, including some members of my family and some professional colleagues. Who I tell depends simply upon the person. I have concluded that if it's natural to be gay, then it's natural to have a gay daughter. And I do have a gay daughter, a lesbian who is the same person I remember for over twenty wonderful years as my child. I accept her every bit as much now as before. We are very close. I have an excellent relationship with both my daughters, as does my wife, Kathleen. Kimberly and I talk every other week and I love her—this first-rate individual, this tolerant, car-ing, talented, sweet, delightful, can't-help-but-like-her, lesbian daugh-ter of mine.

Danny grew up having learned from his mother that each person was a person and should be treated as such. During the mid-1950s when Danny grew up nobody ever said they were gay. Years later, he was active in a professional organization in which one of his colleagues spoke out about his homosexuality. That disclosure caused Danny to think about the subject in a way that he'd not done so before and led him to accept his gay colleague just as he did his heterosexual colleagues. Little did he know how important that acceptance would be later when his daughter came out to him as a lesbian.

Like many people, Danny had little to no real knowledge of what it was like to be gay. His real education began when his colleague spoke about his homosexuality. That prepared Danny to handle his daughter's coming out with some intelligence, care and little drama. His acceptance has made it possible for him and his daughter to develop a rich and deep relationship.

Note your thoughts and reactions to Danny's story.

Lisa Busjahn

I want, by understanding myself, to understand others. I want to be all that I am capable of becoming.... This all sounds strenuous and serious. But now that I have wrestled with it, it's no longer so. I feel happy—deep down. All is well.

—Katherine Mansfield

I grew up on a Wisconsin dairy farm during the fifties and sixties. Everyone helped with the farm work—my mother, sister, and I. We worked hard. My parents got up at four o'clock in the morning to milk. Our life revolved around considerations and events such as the size of the milking herd and how early the milk truck was expected to arrive.

When I was old enough to walk, I began following my father to the barn after breakfast. I remember trying to match the wide strides of his shadow on the sand. Sometimes when the morning dampness left the sand moist and bright, I lingered behind to leap and run among his shallow boot tracks. This was a game I loved. I played until the sun dried the sand, or the daily movement of machinery and trucks erased his steps. Then I'd catch up with him. He was huge and could do any-thing—carry bulging feed sacks above his head, pull calves, lift me into the dark holes and shelves of his tool shed to search for greasy tools. Anything! On the farm my father was God.

During most of my childhood my playground was our farm and the farms of my friends. Until I was five, my days, or as many of them as escaped my mother's protective vigilance, were my own. There were feathers to collect, milk weed parachutes to chase and a dog or two to follow. Sometimes when my mother became too absorbed in hanging laundry or weeding our garden to keep track of me, I ran the long way down through the bushes and tall grasses to the muddy creek—lured by its dark fascinations: crayfish, snakes, turtles, and sluggish trout. When I turned six, I went to work with my father on a regular basis. Afternoon milking began around 4:00 P.M. In late afternoon, a barn becomes heavy with settled aromas—the mowed-grass smell of green hay; must of wide, old, towering beams; the particular smell of corn and oats, a fragrance that almost flies, as if each oat and each kernel were separate and free in the air.

My father worked most of his life. When he was thirteen, he went to work on a farm not too far from his father's land, and had to quit high school. He spent most of the Depression working on road crews, sleeping in gravel trucks and living off of beans and cookies. His motto was, "You don't work; you don't eat." As a teenager, I dragged, moped, and complained about doing my chores, but I always had food to eat. As a result, I grew up believing in the justice of a healthy person pitching in when work must be done and feeling the love, discipline, and clarity that comes with being part of a family that works to feed itself. I also grew up knowing my father was racist and anti-Jewish. I was exposed to his tirades on many occasions.

We lived within five miles of where my mother was born, twenty from where my father grew up. They each were raised in protected, Protestant farm communities. My mother wanted to educate her children and keep up with the times; she was determined to tell me the whole truth about sex, but it was not an easy topic for her. Growing up on a dairy farm meant that I witnessed animals breeding, although I didn't understand how that related to humans any more than my friends in town did. I asked my mother many questions about how babies are made. Today we joke about how whenever I asked about babies, she would reply that I had good questions, and that someday we would go to the library to get answers together. Of course, we never went.

When my sister went to college, she left behind her treasure trove of books. I loved reading and worked my way through her childhood acquisitions and into the more adult books she brought back from school. When I was thirteen, I began to read *Giovanni's Room* by James Baldwin, a book about a homosexual. Because my mother wanted me to learn and bought me books for my birthday and Christmas, it didn't occur to me that I wouldn't be able to discuss something presented in print with her. In the evenings, we took walks and I talked about everything I read, saw, and heard. My mom patiently listened and seldom made a judgmental remark. One day I mentioned *Giovanni's Room*. It was as if I had dropped a bomb. She completely cut off any discussion and told me I couldn't read the book. I put it back and only read a bit of it now and then, tiring of it quickly. Probably because it was about men.

I had experienced crushes on girls prior to this time, but it was not until my twelfth or thirteenth birthday that I began thinking seriously about what it meant. I had my first crush when I was in third grade. I was very fond of the girl who sat behind me and began what would be my lifelong pursuit of smart women. Julie was a minor love, however. Although she was the brightest in the class, her penmanship was too perfect and her interest in following the rules too compulsive to anchor my heart.

I did not fall deeply in love until the fourth grade when I met and courted Debby—by singing "K-K-K-Katey" daily to her when she returned to the school grounds from lunch. Debby was to hold my heart for the next two years and would not have a true rival in terms of depth of feeling until I reached high school. These were the experiences, passions, and mild concerns I took with me into high school, but when I turned twelve, I was confronted by a more important set of questions.

As I mentioned, my family was Protestant. It was not only mother's desire to be open to new ideas and people, but my Sunday school lessons that let me know my father's racist, anti-Jewish diatribes were wrong. Although I have since converted to Judaism, my *introduction* to ethics began with my mother's attention and love during long walks and many trips to Sunday school. For this reason, it was very hard for me to face up to the fact that I did not want to be confirmed as a Christian.

I had learned—about the same time as my peers—the word "hypocrisy," which, of course, made me smarter than my parents and neighbors, as well as miserable. This self-perceived wisdom caused me to wish often that I could believe in what I had labeled a "Santa Claus God." Oh to be naive, I would think wistfully. As wise as I thought I was, I did somehow have enough awareness of others to know that if I said half of what was on my mind, it would cause a storm in our kitchen.

I went through the four years of preparation to be confirmed as a Christian, hoping that I would stumble into belief, or that I would find the words to explain my way out of making a commitment to false belief. I just did not believe in the trinity. I came to the conclusion that I could not be confirmed because I didn't believe in Jesus as Messiah, which was frightening because I would let my parents down, and worse, I would have to tell them about it!

I casually mentioned that I didn't believe in Christ. At that, my father came up with a new motto: "As long as you've got your feet under my table, you'll believe what I believe!" His fist slammed the table. He was a man of few gestures and little emotion, so he had my attention. I was confirmed and learned that there is nothing worse than betraying one's own beliefs. I was miserable because I didn't believe what my family, relatives, and friends believed. I was also ashamed because I didn't have the courage to say so.

I continued to read books about religion and philosophy, both fiction and nonfiction. I read most thoroughly the existentialists, transcendentalists, Buddhists, and Jews. I seemed to be drawn to Jewish thought, ethics, and action, and especially the focus of what is good and evil as framed by the Holocaust and the writing of Elie Wiesel. In the fiction of Malamud and Potok, I felt the issues of choice that were raised by the existentialists were answered in a moral context.

I didn't completely understand what that context was, however, and as I entered my sophomore and junior years in college, I became more aware of myself as a woman oppressed by male religion. I recall considering taking a course in Judaism and shuddering. What could I be thinking? I had just shed Christianity; why would I get near an older, more traditional, and undoubtedly—I thought then—more sexist religion? It would be over fifteen years before I would study the religion and its history and make my conversion.

When I left home to go to college, I lived the first year with my sister in Madison, Wisconsin. The University of Wisconsin-Madison (UW-M) was not my first choice of schools—it seemed too big and overwhelming to me, but my kidneys had failed my senior year in high school, so I had to be near UW-Hospitals for close follow-up after having a kidney transplant.

My father had wanted to donate one of his kidneys to me, and my mother, although terrified of losing him—her first husband had died when my sister, Arden, was just four—agreed that he should go ahead. I begged them not to let him give me the kidney, but he insisted he wanted to. My father loved me very much and at age sixty, I think he wanted to accomplish something truly heroic, truly meaningful to him and his family. Because of his fear of medicine and dying, it was indeed a heroic desire. There was a problem during the pre-surgery preparation, and he couldn't give me his kidney. I was very relieved. I feared I would feel guilty about not being able to be who they wanted me to be, or, worse, that I would fail myself again and act like someone I thought they could accept. In fact, the night before my father and I were to go into surgery, he asked me to go down a dark hospital hall with him to pray—a prayer he had learned through an organization he used to justify his racism and anti-Semitism. I went with him because he was about to risk his life; I hated myself, yet there seemed to be no way out.

This all happened during the year that I told Arden about my sexual orientation. She was the first person I came out to. Before talking to her, I thought about all the events of my adolescent years. I also thought about how she and my parents might say that I wasn't worthy of having received the gift of life through a kidney transplant— which I had received from a woman who had been killed in an auto accident shortly after the attempt with my father failed. I was scared that Arden would be disappointed and disgusted because my feelings for women were so against the rules, and my sister worked so hard to follow rules. It was horrible to imagine my family might not think my life worth saving because I am a lesbian—I remembered my mother telling me to put *Giovanni's Room* back on the shelf.

Arden had been very supportive and loving when I was sick and she took my news well on a personal level, but warned me not to tell my mother, and also said that she thought that lesbians shouldn't have children. Having children had never entered my mind, but I thought lesbians could probably raise children as well as anyone, and that maybe my sister was not as accepting as she stated.

When I told my mother I love women, she seemed stunned. We argued and spent the next seven years raising and burying the issue at dinners, in hospitals, during walks, and in the car. Finally after all those years of living with each other in disagreement and yet as family members, we came to realize my sexuality mattered less than either of us had imagined. We were still a family.

I outed myself at work and that too seemed natural. I was a psychiatric aide on the graveyard shift. Often there were only two of us—an aide and a registered nurse—and we handled thirty patients. We had the only locked ward in town and frequently admitted violent males who were in some state of building toward an angry eruption. This meant that one really had to trust the other staff person on the floor to keep a cool head.

The kind of stress these situations created was accompanied by boredom—most nights nothing happened. When I spent eight hours essentially doing nothing with another person I knew I might need to depend on in difficult situations, becoming personal and honest was no tough trick. The staff became very close. I was on the night shift permanently.

I chose to come out to a new-grad registered nurse. Carol seemed pretty sharp. While I had never heard her espouse the old Freudian line that homosexuality was a sickness, I was still a little nervous about coming out because of the horror stories I had heard from other lesbians about coming out to a friend or coworkers who proceeded to panic, assuming that they were about to be raped. I was also conscious of an underlying belief by men contained in the book, *Women, and Madness* that most of our attitudes and actions are crazy and dangerous. Coming out on a psych ward had its own "thrill" albeit a thrill that was short lived. In fact, it soon became boring coming out to each successive night nurse.

My experiences in coming out at work were positive until I met Mary, who was my supervisor. I had moved to Champaign, Illinois where I began work as an editor with a sports and fitness publishing company. Mary was in the process of becoming a fundamentalist Christian. Yet, she seemed openly interested in knowing lesbian women, and even courted me and other lesbians as friends. However, the more she became enmeshed in her new religion, the more intolerant she became. Mary was soon spouting her notions about homosexuality as a sin. She also began to make anti-Jewish comments.

Mary regularly spoke about her beliefs that Jews are stingy, pushy, and not "above board." I felt defensive and very uncomfortable. Although I had not yet converted to Judaism, I was in a process of reading and studying that would compel me to make that choice. Her remarks were hateful and stupid, yet, because I recognized she was ignorant, I thought the best way of dealing with the situation was to quietly and gently guide her to learn more about these issues and let go of her prejudices.

One day she appeared in my office red-faced, literally spitting anti-Jewish statements. Mary had just had a major difference of opinion with one of her authors who was Jewish. I asked her to leave my office. Later, she tried to laugh it off and begin a friendly dialogue with me by saying, "I didn't mean that. I was just joking." We had it out. I felt good about standing up for my beliefs.

A few years later, I worked in a company that created continuing education materials for pharmacists. A gay man I knew talked to the bosses about having AIDS. The bosses told him that they had no problem with it. However, they knew I was taking immuno-suppressants because of my kidney transplant so they wanted to talk to me. They asked if I would be worried about working with someone who had AIDS. I said I had no hesitations about working with a co-worker with AIDS and explained that as a lesbian, I had started writing about AIDS in community newsletters in the early 1980's. At this, I detected a shift in their attitudes, but I wrote it off as just my imagination. "After all, how could they feel okay about a gay man with AIDS and not a lesbian woman?" I thought. The meeting was abruptly ended. The bosses rushed out the door to get a cup of coffee, which seemed odd, considering there was a fairly nice coffee set-up in the office.

Soon, I was hounded by my immediate supervisor. Ron ripped apart everything I wrote, claiming this fact was misrepresented, that sentence was awkward, this comma was misplaced. He'd harangue in this way for two to three hours each morning. In the afternoon I would implement his changes. The next morning he would browbeat me again, contradicting much of what he'd told me the day before.

My desk was in a cubicle next to his office, and when we were finished discussing the material, he would go into his office and open and slam his desk drawers, expressing considerable anger. I had no intentions of quitting my job, so I took his abuse.

Soon, I learned from another gay man in the company that my co-worker with AIDS had, in fact, not come out. During his talk with the bosses, he had said that he had foolishly experimented with drugs when he was a young kid, inferring that his was not a gay-related infection. A gay co-worker (who was also not out) said that the president told him, "Lisa won't be here much longer because her personal life and politics interfere with her work."

Eventually, I was summoned into the president's office. He asked, "How do you like working here?" "Fine, I like it fine," I responded. He sighed and looked at his desk top. Eventually he said, "Things just aren't working out." Again, he sighed and we waited. Finally, he said, "I don't think you'll be working here any more." I asked if he was saying I was fired. He said, "I guess you could say that."

I was outraged and went to the city with a discrimination complaint against the firm. To my disbelief, it was denied. Even though the president of the company admitted to the investigator that he had said what my gay co-worker was willing to testify to, he claimed he hadn't meant it and, besides, that was not why I was fired. He said I was fired for incompetence.

I asked the investigator to explain how the company that had a satisfactory freelance relationship with me six months prior to hiring me to work full-time and had published two sets of materials I had finished for them, would suddenly have so many problems with me immediately after finding out about my sexual orientation. The investigator said in a meeting she had with me—with a city attorney present—that I could make an appeal to the full human rights board.

I decided to take the case to the board because I knew I had suffered discrimination. Furthermore, the city had found discrimination existed in recent cases of two male homosexuals. Even though no case had been found for a lesbian, I was encouraged by their success. However, shortly after I lost my job, my mother called to say my father was dying of lymphoma. The months of listening to my supervisor yell and badger and slam drawers had taken a toll on me and with the fears I had about the process my family was about to go through, I decided not to go through with the appeal.

I write about these two stories together—the anti-Jewish and anti-lesbian experiences—because, to some extent, I think I played a role in the first situation that was similar to the roles my two closeted coworkers played in the second. At the publishing company, there was a Jewish publication director who was above both me and my boss, and although I tried to distance myself from my immediate supervisor and squelched the "little" humiliations she tried to perpetrate against Sarah, I didn't speak about my feelings about what she said. I didn't tell anyone who could have changed the situation about the bigotry. I hated discrimination of any kind, yet it was not until Mary became so hateful and it was impossible to ignore her venom, that I was able to speak out clearly.

A similar dynamic occurred between the closeted men and me at my next job. They didn't have to come out to express outrage, yet they didn't speak out clearly to the perpetrators of discrimination about their anger and disgust. I believe that until we all begin to look at each other—Jews, homosexuals, people of color, women, people with disabilities—as human beings, precious for ourselves, we will be threatened by the brutal hatred of ignorant people. Now, when I am in situations where people are speaking hatefully or without kindness or insight about a group or a person, I remember the quotation attributed to Reverend Martin Niemoller and try to respond in a way that makes a difference:

> First they came for the Jews and I did not speak out...because I was not a Jew. Then they came for the Communists...and I did not speak out because I was not a Communist. Then they came for the trade unionists...and I did not speak out because I was not a trade unionist. Then they came for me...and there was no one to speak out for me.

In her story, Lisa tells of being fired as a result of revealing her sexual orientation—something she did in support of another employee. Her story illustrates how the reaction to her revelation adversely affected her, her supervisor, and her co-workers. Her story demonstrates the abundant energy it takes for sexual minorities who do come out under adverse conditions to protect themselves and to be treated fairly. Her story tells readers why so many in the sexual minority community choose to use their considerable energy and effort to hide rather than to come out.

Note your thoughts and reactions to Lisa's story.

Dale Barr

The only thing I want to know is whether the person is kind or unkind.

—Butterfly McQueen

I am a white, middle-aged, conservative-midwestern, Catholic heterosexual male. I have four children ages thirteen to twenty-three and am married to my second wife—a woman whom I had known in college and whom I convinced to return to the United States from England to marry me in 1990.

I was brought up in an environment that dictated a very strict code of behavior, as well as preached about the "evil" differences between my environment and the rest of the world. I was born on the day the Roman Catholic Church celebrates the feast day of Saint Blaise. Saint Blaise, the bishop of Nicea, saved a small child choking on a fish bone, and the Roman Catholic Church deemed this to be a miracle and canonized Blaise. Subsequently, every February third the Catholic church blesses the throats of their congregations. This little "miraculous" story gives insight to my childhood value system as my childhood revolved around the beliefs and customs of the Catholic church. My mother is a devout Irish Catholic, my English/Irish father is a convert to the Catholic church from the Methodist church. Like many other converts, he is more fanatical about following church precepts than those who are born into the church.

My home was in a low- to middle-income neighborhood in Omaha, Nebraska. My childhood values were strongly influenced by midwestern ethics and priorities. Omaha is a town that is divided by race and money. South Omaha is a melting pot of people who are descendants of many European countries. The people is South Omaha work at the packing houses and cattle feed lots. East Omaha is the warehouse district and railroad yards. North Omaha is where the African American population lives. West Omaha is where the white-collar affluent people live.

As in most good non-contraceptive Catholic families, my parents had several children. I was the first of seven. As the oldest I was given the grown-up responsibilities of babysitting, burning the trash (a high risk job) and punishing my little brothers and sisters if they got out of line. Assuming adult responsibilities at an early age hastened my adult psychological development.

The first time I realized that I was affected by differences and prejudice was when my parents decided to move from our comfortable, safe northeast Omaha neighborhood to West Omaha. I was upset! Why were we moving and why did I have to leave my friends, baseball team, school, and church. I asked what was going on and my parents said we were moving because "colored" people were coming into our neighborhood. They said there was going to be a crime wave, property values would drop, the houses would be run down, and our Catholic parish would lose its status as one of the more prominent parishes in Omaha. "Colored people caused these things to happen," was my parents' testimonial.

I wanted to believe them, but I hadn't seen any colored people in the neighborhood. If they were there why didn't I notice any run down houses? Why weren't my friends moving? Did I trust my parents' judgment? Did I hold the values they thrust upon me as the oldest child and was the sacrifice of losing my friends justifiable?

Torn by such questions, I confronted my parents. Their rationale seemed weak and I began to question the truth of what my parents and the church had led me to believe. I consciously began to wonder:

Do Jewish people hoard money? Do Protestants swim naked at the YMCA? Are men who dance on TV or in the theater queer? Can priests make mistakes? Was questioning authority wrong? Are women inferior? Is sex bad? I'm sure between the ages of ten and thirteen I was a trial for my parents, although I was never disrespectful.

I continued to be the "man" of the house. For years my father was in insurance sales. He left on Monday mornings and returned on Friday nights. Disciplining my brothers and sisters was my job, delegated to me by my mother. As a result, my siblings and I are somewhat distant since, after all, I was the wicked witch of their childhood.

When we moved to West Omaha, there were no stores, schools, or churches. My parents couldn't enroll me in a Catholic school, so I was bused forty-five minutes into an Omaha public school which convinced me that some of my parents' truths were false. I had always been told that Catholic schools were the best. But the public school I went to was terrific. There were art classes, shop classes, and girls with colorful dresses and nylons. There were no dull uniforms and white bobbysocks on the female student body. There were Jews, blacks, Protestants, rich and poor at the same public school. The teachers were personable, fair, and challenging. I made honors at the public junior high and one of my teachers suggested that I move on to a college preparatory high school to further my education.

I decided to take the admittance test to a Catholic Jesuit college preparatory high school. I asked my Dad for the ten dollars to take the test. I thought he'd love the thought of me going back to a Catholic school. He floored me when he said he had paid taxes all his life for public education and that I should stay in a public school. Determined to go to the Catholic high school, I paid my own test fees and tuition.

During my high school years, my relationship with my parents became distant. I loved my mom and dad but we were never close and we never shared any of the intimate details of our lives. Paying my own way through these years further pushed me into adulthood at an earlier age than most of my peers. I chose my own values and developed my own opinions. I rebelled. I became an activist against the Vietnam War. I marched in civil rights demonstrations and for ten years I supported women's and gay causes by donating money to various activist groups, although I invested little time, commitment, or heart to those causes. In the late 1970's I met two people who so touched my heart that I began to seriously look at my commitment to these two communities—women and gays. I realized that ten years of sending money wasn't enough.

I had taken a two-year work assignment on the east coast. I thought of it as the "country boy heads to the big city." In New York, I met a woman who was to be one of my colleagues. I was blindsided by her candor, her ability to confront sexism, and the professional way she conducted business. I had all of the stereotypical notions of women in the work place. But here was a woman who knew who she was, acted like it, and made sure no one discriminated against her. This single experience of working with this woman and three of her female peers prompted me to become a more active "feminist." On my return from the east coast I helped form a women's support group within my corporation. This organization, twelve years later, is still functioning and is as strong as ever.

I also developed a friendship with a gay man named Mike. Our relationship took nurturing and time. Over the years, he fed me small bits of information about the gay community which I consumed and digested until my uninformed fears of the gay community diminished. At the outset of our friendship I knew that I was out of my ordinary "comfort zone." At first I couldn't put my finger on it. Mike openly shared his feelings and spoke with gratitude about our budding friendship. He told me of his own ups and downs with a sincerity and warmth that I had not experienced with my "buds" in Omaha (I know that my friends are genuine but they have difficulty showing it through expressions of love and commitment to one another). As time passed so did my discomfort.

Mike knew himself, knew what he wanted, and knew what he wouldn't tolerate (much like the woman mentioned above). Mike could hug people. I was never allowed to hug or show affection. These were traits that I admired and aspired to. We worked together for several years. I was unaware of Mike's sexual orientation during the first year. It didn't matter because I was simply trying to develop a friendship with someone I liked and admired.

During the second year of working together I found out that Mike was gay. He did not profess to me he was gay. He simply invited me for dinner to his home where he and his partner lived. I knew that I had truly accepted gays as human beings. Mike and his lover were not freaks. The only difference between us that I could identify was our sexual orientation. I recognized Mike's deep feelings for his partner and was distressed as I thought of the intolerance they face in our culture. Mike and I have now been friends for over fifteen years and our relationship has grown to where I now consider him as one of my brothers. I am proud of our relationship and I can comfortably and openly speak about his sexual orientation.

These experiences have given me a strong desire to get to know about the lives of all the people that I work with, not just what group they belong to or where they came from. I can now see how the experiences of my youth and early adult years have been provocative and insightful for me. I appreciate and understand the difficulties women, gays, people of color, and people with disabilities have in moving public opinion. I understand and realize the fear and shortsightedness of uninformed people regarding people who "seem" different. I recall the years when I was developing my values, when I was questioning everything, and the subsequent changes I went through. That searching and development was of great value for it helped me construct an understanding of who I am, what feelings I possess, the amount of fact I base my opinions on, and the degree of fear I feel in an uninformed situation. And, it has helped me to become a healthier and more accepting human being.

I will always value my friendships with Mike and others and, as a result, I have "upped" my commitment to these causes. While I still contribute money, I also have increased my personal involvement in ending discrimination. For nearly ten years, I have worked for US West Communications in Omaha. In conjunction with my job, I have been a director on the company's diversity council. I strongly advocated giving company support group status to an internal support group for homosexuals called Eagle. This was an extremely controversial issue at US West. However, after much upper management soul searching, the company officially supported Eagle. While my role in accomplishing this was minor compared to the hard work of many Eagle members, I do believe that it took a few of us straights talking and writing letters to the right people to help move along the process of endorsement. I continue to be a strong supporter of Eagle. I am a straight man who believes in diversity and equality and who opposes discrimination of any kind. I hope I can help others become tolerant, accepting of individuals like Mike who have so touched my heart.

Dale's story shows how conservative, midwestern values can be translated to champion an all-inclusive workforce that includes sexual minorities. In his story, you see how two gay and lesbian co-workers (and Dale's openness to developing his relationships with them) provided him with new insights and valued friendships. Dale provides readers with an example of someone who took concrete action to support gay and lesbian employees at a major telecommunications company. Like Vince Patton, his support grew from his friendships and acquaintance with gay people.

Note your thoughts and reactions to Dale's story.

STORIES OF SPIRITUAL AND RELIGIOUS DEVELOPMENT

The bible says, "you shall not lie with a man as with a woman." In the same breath, it also says, "nor shall you wear gold, pearls or costly array [jewelry], nor mix fabrics, braid hair or die without leaving children."

By these interpretations, there probably isn't a person alive today who shouldn't be condemned to some eternal hell for breaking these "laws of God." Most people can't trust what they read in yesterday's newspaper. Yet many people believe they can trust something written (and constantly re-interpreted) by *humans* over two thousand years ago. Biblical interpretations and theology change. Roughly 150 years ago in the United States, some Christian organizations taught that whites were superior to blacks and that slavery was ordained by God. Clergy arguing this position claimed the authority of the Bible. Today, these organizations, obviously, do not support slavery. Did the Bible change? No, simply their *interpretation* of the Bible.

If we truly follow the Bible we note that God did not send Jesus into the world to judge (or condemn). The few Bible verses that are used to condemn homosexuals *have been* distorted, mistranslated, or deliberately misinterpreted. More importantly, there are hundreds of statements promoting acceptance, and none that promote judgment.

As you read through the previous stories, you have probably noted that religion and spirituality played an important role in the life experiences of many of our storytellers. In the following stories, you will see how religious intolerance and lack of acceptance created tremendous conflict and pain. You'll also see how some religious leaders have come to accept lesbian, gay, bisexual, and transgender people, and how their acceptance positively impacts on our fellow and sister human beings.

Despite the hatred of some outspoken religious people, we believe that most people are not so intolerant. We also believe that most people simply do not know what to do in this area so they remain quiet—leaving the rhetoric to religious extremists. We believe that some extremists hold onto their views in part because it is profitable, and, in part, because they are filled with fear and lacking in knowledge.

We think people's hearts will be opened by reading about the love, compassion, courage, and spirituality of others (like them and unlike them). While all of our storytellers draw us together, the following speak specifically of the impact that religion and spirituality have had on their lives. These stories move all of us closer to "the magic line" of acceptance and the experience of love, joy, and peace.

Frederick "Rico" Hewitt-Cruz

You gain strength, courage and confidence by every experience in which you really stop to look fear in the face. You are able to say to yourself, "I lived through this horror. I can take the next thing that comes along." ...You must do the thing you think you cannot do.

—Anna Eleanor Roosevelt

I was born in Belize (formerly British Honduras), where I spent the first five years of my life. My family moved to the deep South, where I grew up in Oakman, Alabama, a small town about forty miles from Birmingham. I do not know what precipitated our move to Alabama, nor did anyone ever discuss why we moved. Our life in Belize was never mentioned. I know there is more to this story than I have been told.

My father worked in the coal mines, which in that area of the country was considered a very good job. Several of my uncles also worked in the mines. I remember my father as a fairly innocuous man. Occasionally, he would tell me that I was a "good boy" when I did well in school, but generally he said little. He had problems with drinking and he was abusive to my mother though he never physically harmed me. My mother was a very strong woman, whose job was to take care of the family.

As a child, I was always well dressed and was clean and neat. I was known as the "pretty boy." I had long hair, smooth chocolate skin and extra long eyelashes. I looked and acted like a girl. In elementary school, there was a traditional boys' beauty contest in which the boys dressed up as girls. I always won the competition. Soon, I became known as the town sissy. I was called "Miss Freddy." For many years I did not understand what it meant to be a "sissy" or a "fag." I had several sexual experiences with boys who were a few years older than I (they were twelve or thirteen), and I simply thought that I was playing "mommy and daddy" with the other boys.

I did well in school. In fact, studies came easily, almost naturally. There were only a few black students at my school, and it was considered unusual for a black student to do well. Eventually, I was put in a gifted class in which I was the only black child.

When I was twelve, my parents divorced. My father's drinking had become too much for my mother to handle. He had stopped working and became abusive and violent towards her. I recall waking in the middle of one night to shouting voices, dishes breaking and glasses smashing. My sister and I ran to our mother's room and climbed into her bed. The next morning we awoke to see the house torn apart. And, there was blood. My mother was silent. My father was injured from stab wounds to his hand and arm. I asked Mother if she was okay and she said, "I'm okay my children; now, get ready for school." Nothing else was said.

Within less than two years my mother remarried. My new stepfather, who had been a truck driver, became a minister in the Church of Christ. He often told me that I acted like a girl. He was much more confrontational and more of an authority figure than my father. I was very afraid of him. My mother seemed to become a weaker person in his presence, and this dismayed me. I developed a great deal of resentment towards my stepfather.

At school, I was increasingly ostracized and left out of social activities. The teachers however seemed to like me, probably because I was such a good student. My stepfather often told me that I must continue to do well in school because I was a minority, but his constant ridicule about how I "acted like a girl" caused me such anxiety that my performance in school began to deteriorate.

Things only got worse when I hit puberty. I started to wear makeup foundation to cover acne scars that I developed. This only made me look more like a girl. When I was fourteen, my stepfather confronted me about my sexuality. He said, "Freddy, I don't know why you won't talk to me and tell me what your problem is, but if you don't, *I'll* tell you what your problem is." My heart began to beat fast and tears rolled down my face. My stepfather got my mother and the three of us talked for hours. I told them that for a very long time I had been sexually attracted to boys. I explained that I had tried to change. I even masturbated to pornography of women in hopes of making myself straight. I had prayed to God to help me, but nothing happened. My parents were very attentive. They listened with great care. After I finished talking, my stepfather said, "I knew that all along, son." We finally reached an agreement that I would go see a counselor, which I did. That didn't work. I tried going to church more, dedicating "my life to God." "God will fix me; He will change me," I thought. That didn't work. Thinking I wasn't trying hard enough, I read my bible *more*. I prayed *more*. Nothing happened. I stopped wearing make-up. I cut my long, beautiful hair. I started to wear loose clothes. I actually *acted* like a boy. Nothing changed. I was still attracted to boys.

I began to have "slips," whereby I would have sex with a boy and then repent. I resumed putting on make-up, lightly at first, then with a more heavy hand. Losing any hope of becoming straight, I was soon back to my old ways, which angered my parents. They began to verbally attack me, especially my mother. "You like them boys sticking their things up you," she said with a mean spirit. These attacks would be followed by weeks of silence.

Eventually, I gave up entirely. I was tired! I tried everything I knew to change. "Maybe God wants me to be just like I am," I said to myself. So, I went about living my life as a gay man, despite the abuse. And there was much of it, and not all of it from my family. Several of the older kids and adults began to sexually abuse me. An older girl toyed with me sexually. The father of a friend of mine began to call me a sissy, and then proceeded to coerce me into performing fellatio for him. He said I was so pretty that I should be a girl, then he would turn around and tell me that if I were a girl, I wouldn't be as pretty. This activity went on for some time. All the while, he presented himself to the community as a straight married man. People began to abuse my sister, asking her questions about me. Soon, she developed migraines.

I felt as if I had put a stigma on my entire family. So, I tried God and church once again. I prayed again and again. I repented again and again. And, I was "saved" again and again. I had up to three and four ministers standing over me praying that my soul would not be damned to Hell. *Nothing!*

I was known all over town and within a fifteen mile radius as that "black faggot" in Oakman. I couldn't walk down the street without being called queer; nor move through the school hallways without being pointed at or whispered about. The pressure of being called the town queer made my life very difficult. I started dating a girl in a desperate attempt to change that perception, but it didn't work.

During my junior year, I met a "pretty white boy." He was essentially a white version of me. We became friends, and for almost a year we had a strong and intimate sexual relationship. However, the town began to talk about us and no one liked that a black sissy was with a white guy. Soon, my friend began to hate me because of the talk around town and shortly thereafter our friendship ended. I was deeply saddened. People continued to call me a fag. In an attempt to inoculate myself from the pain, I would respond with, "Yeah, I'm the best one I know."

Thanks to my academic performance, I was the first recipient of a scholarship given to a black student by my school. I was very proud, but two days before graduation the principal called me into his office and told me that I would not be able to walk across the stage at graduation to accept the scholarship. He said that there had been several threats made on my life. Because graduation was to be held outside, he thought it would be better for me not to participate, for fear that something might happen. I still received the scholarship but I was crushed by the experience.

Around the same time, another devastating experience occurred. Since my stepfather's entry into the ministry, I stayed active in his church. I sang regularly with the choir and often sang solos in church and at weddings and other social events. One Sunday, my father invited a guest minister to preach to the congregation. He began to speak of the "abomination of homosexuality." The congregation seemed very still. I could hear my heart beat. Suddenly, he called my name and asked me to come forward. I was told to stand in front of the entire congregation. I was dressed flamboyantly. I looked up and saw my mother and stepfather sitting quietly, their faces expressionless. I knew the names of every person in that church and, in front of these silent people, I listened to this visiting minister attack me. He told me that my homosexuality was the work of the devil and that I would burn in hell if I did not change my ways. He shouted, "Repent and beg forgiveness." In my terror and shame, I begged repentance, I begged forgiveness, and I promised to alter my ways. In a way, I was grateful, for I believed every word spoken that day, including the promise that I would be cured. After the service, not one person said a word, although I sensed that many people felt sorry for me. I went home. My parents were sitting in the living room. As I entered the house, they just looked at me, remaining absolutely silent. I was in great pain. It hurt that they offered no comfort after such an enormous public humiliation. I swore I would never again stand in front of a congregation, and I quit singing.

I decided to go to Pennsylvania to see my biological father, who was ill. He had only seen me once for a brief period since he had left six years earlier. When he became aware that I was gay, he shunned me. Feeling abandoned, I joined the Navy in order to escape my family and the pain associated with Alabama and, then, Pennsylvania.

For some reason, I thought that the Navy would make me straight. In the beginning of my Navy career, I was not sexually active. I simply focused on being a good sailor. Several individuals made passes at me, but I ignored them. I had joined the Navy with the hope of becoming straight. I was in boot camp in Great Lakes, Illinois, where our every move was monitored. I was terrified of doing anything anyway. During the second month of boot camp a guy came up to me and told me he knew a place were we could go. My loneliness for another gay man bested my fear, and we met. Afterwards, I cried the entire night because the illusion that the Navy would make me straight had been shattered.

The company commander at Great Lakes liked me and called me in to say that he was sending me to corpsmen school in San Diego, where I would enjoy work in the medical division of the Navy. When I arrived in San Diego I noticed that my class was full of effeminate men and "sissies." I then realized that, in the Navy, being a corpsman meant you were likely to be gay. My company commander must have suspected me.

My hair was short but I still looked liked a girl. But no one teased me and I established some friendships with other corpsmen who were obviously gay. After a few weeks in training, a lieutenant commander called me into her office and told me that she really liked me but noticed that I appeared to be somewhat effeminate. She said that it did not bother her but that it might bother others so she suggested that I be careful. She was rumored to be a lesbian and it was clear that she did like me, so I started working on being more butch.

While stationed in San Diego, I had met a civilian who worked for the Navy and was a friend of a friend. She was Puerto Rican and I thought she was incredibly beautiful. She was thirty-six years old but looked twenty-one, which was my age. She had been recently divorced from a marriage of fourteen years. She also had a female lover. By now, I had become sexually active with other men. Neither of our sexual lives were an issue for the other. The fact that we both had a homosexual orientation just added to the growing friendship that we developed. In 1988, we decided to marry. In some respects, it was a marriage of convenience. She received a dependent card (her lover was in the military), and I received slightly higher pay for being married. But we had not married solely for the benefits. We cared for each other and had an incredibly good time together.

This was a very positive time of my life. My "wife" helped me to see life differently. We never did have sex, but we had a tremendous friendship. She had two brothers who were gay, and her family was very accepting about that. And they really liked me. It felt good to belong to a family that accepted me for who I was.

My family reacted somewhat differently. My sister was bothered by the fact that I had married a "white" woman. My parents simply wanted to know when they could meet her. They were probably pleased that I married. I don't know.

In October 1989, I moved to Texas to attend lab school and my wife moved to Virginia Beach with her lover. As I often spoke of my wife, I was perceived as straight but very open-minded, since I would go out dancing at gay clubs. At about this time, Perry Watkins came out after sixteen years in the service. He was discharged but then reinstated because it was shown that no one had asked him if he was gay when he joined. This was a heartening piece of news for me and other gays in the service, and I felt safer, though not safe enough to come out, as I knew this issue wasn't "put to bed." So I stayed in the military closet. Fortunately, I still had my marriage to protect me. While Miriam and I are still legally married, we have had little contact since San Diego.

After attending lab school in Texas, I returned to San Diego and was called to serve in Desert Storm. I was in Saudi Arabia from August 1990 to March 1991 and worked in a medical unit about twenty-five miles from the front. At one point, we had something of a cultural exchange with servicemen from Britain who joined our unit. It soon became clear that one of the British guys was gay and he was ostracized. Space was tight and one had to give up on any thoughts of sex while in this situation. It was a long seven months.

Shortly after Desert Storm ended, I decided to fly home to see my parents. I was ill-prepared for the surprise that awaited me. I flew into Birmingham and then we drove the forty-five minutes to Oakman. As we approached Oakman, hundreds of people lined the main road holding signs and American flags. I couldn't imagine what they were doing. Then, I realized that they were waving to me and were shouting, "Welcome home." I was confused. I wondered how this town that had so abused and ostracized me could now be honoring me.

We drove on to the town square where there were even more people. The mayor and members of the city council were there, as was a local representative of the National Guard who presented me with an American flag. The mayor announced that the town was having a dinner in my honor at a "restored southern" town just outside Oakman. The town was a commercial venture something like "Dollywood." The event was something like a local fair, with carnival booths, rides and games, as well as crafts and women in aprons and bonnets cooking hominy in large pots. On the stage, the mayor introduced me as an alumni of the local high school (the one at which I was not allowed to attend the graduation ceremony—no mention was made of that). I was asked to say a few words. I said I was glad to be back and thanked them for the support they had given me and others through their cards and letters. Then I added, "We, the American people, have shown the participants of Desert Storm that we know how to come together despite race, despite color, and despite our other differences. And I hope things will continue that way now that Desert Storm is over." For a moment, there was an awkward silence, then applause. The children of the town followed me by singing a number of patriotic songs. My mother said that she and my stepfather were very proud of me.

Following the songs, I mingled among the crowd. It had been four years since I left Oakman. I knew most of the people at the event and many acknowledged me personally. Some avoided me. I acted like a politician, diplomatically shaking hands and paying particular attention to the children. I was amused by the children and how they would respond when I asked if that sign was for me. With big smiles, they would say, "Yes." I felt like a celebrity. I also felt a strange mix of pride and resentment. I knew that behind all the pretense much hatred and prejudice remained.

After the "event," my mother told me that the church had initiated the plan to honor me. During Desert Storm, I banked all my earnings and sent some of it to some of the people back home. I sent a few checks to my grandmother, a woman on our street, and some others who I sensed might be in need. I did not intend for these actions to be public knowledge. My mother told me that on one Sunday during Desert Storm, a woman to whom I had sent fifty dollars got up and spoke about me. She said that here I was at war yet I didn't act like I was the one in need of support. She said that the money came at a critical moment for her. She also recounted how I had been the choir director, had sung in the church and done a number of other things and that I had probably been hurt in the church as well. After she spoke, my grandmother stood up and said, "And he sent me a check for one hundred dollars." As my mother told me this, I felt like crying as this woman was the first person to acknowledge my hurt and I appreciated her acknowledgement.

After my four years were up, I left the Navy in October of 1991 and entered the workforce as a health care professional. Today, I work as a lab technician at a major health center and plan to continue my studies toward becoming a physician. I still live with pain. I probably always will. But, I don't regret the past, for I know that it has led me to where I am today. I freely acknowledge that my inner desire is to be with another man, and I don't think it has anything to do with my hypothalamus or any other thalamus. The reason why I am gay doesn't matter. God knows why I am gay and that's all that matters. My folks have made great progress accepting me just as I am. My mother recently said to me, "All I know is that I carried you for nine months and gave birth to you. God made you and God don't make mistakes!"

After many years of hard work, I finally stood up in front of the entire congregation of my church and said, "I am a proud, twenty-six-year-old African American gay man."

Rico's story is one of great pain, much of it triggered by narrow religious teachings and because he was ostracized and taunted by his school mates and shamed by his religious leaders. Rico escaped to the military and tried desperately to be "straight." As many others have done he decided to marry—which in certain ways made his life easier.

In an ironic turn, Rico returned to his hometown as a hero for his work in Desert Storm. That visit began to heal his pain and helped Rico move closer to the magic line of self-acceptance. Like many, his road was slow and marked by great confusion and pain. Rico's story clearly demonstrates why we need to educate our youth about issues of sexual orientation. No family or friend would willingly put a child through the kind of experience Rico went through. Imagine how different things would have been for this young man had he been taught that God loves all people—gay and straight alike. Rico's determination to be himself is a testament to his courage—courage that is vastly greater than that shown by many of our religious leaders who fail to lead in this area.

Note your thoughts and reactions to Rico's story.

Reverend Cecil Williams

The beginning of love is to let those we love be perfectly themselves, and not to twist them to fit our own image. Otherwise we love only the reflection of ourselves we find in them.

—Thomas Merton

I've been around gays all my life. "Sissies," we used to call them in San Angelo, Texas, where I was born in 1929. I don't recall the word "sissy" as a derogatory term, but I was pretty clear I didn't want to be one.

I was the fifth of six children and the most mischievous of the kids. People paid attention to me. I don't know if that's because I was the most talkative or the most vulnerable. In the 1930s and '40s in Texas the minister was the spokesperson for the community, and the church was the place to be. We were United Methodists; we cried out "amen" and clapped during services. At any rate, I was named "Rev" by my mother (she wanted a minister in the family) when I was just a kid and the name stuck, like molasses.

My mother was a strong woman. She took care of our home and our family. And she worked alongside the town's only African American doctor as a nurses' aide. She was a member of the "Eastern Stars," a group of African American women, many of whom trained as nurses, aides. My father worked as a janitor until the outbreak of World War II, at which time he began work as a cook in various restaurants. He was a great storyteller, as well as a big "ham." We played a lot. I'll never forget him putting on one of mother's dresses and a pair of her shoes, prancing around the house and entertaining us for hours. We laughed a lot in our home.

As was typical in many black families, my mother's parents also lived with us. Papa Jack, my grandfather, was half Mexican and half black. He actually helped found the city of San Angelo and was well-respected, even by many whites. And did he ever take advantage of that respect! There were many times when bill collectors would come by and Papa Jack would say, "You'll git your money when we have some," and then chase them off our property. Everyone would laugh and these usually gruff white men would say, "Okay, Papa Jack." Like many of us in the black community, my grandfather used humor and anger to survive.

My grandmother was Native American. She was a quiet and still woman who often sat silently for hours, but her presence was always felt. Whenever she had had enough of Papa Jack's storytelling she would tell him to shut up. My grandmother sang often. She sang to survive.

Laughter and song somehow liberated us from oppression. In San Angelo, Texas, we were often abused and misused because of the color of our skin. I grew up with signs. I vividly remember my mother pointing to the sign over the water fountain at J.C. Penney and telling me, "Never drink out of that fountain. That's for whites only." She showed me which bathrooms I could use, and when there was only one I knew that it was for whites only. I knew too that we were prohibited from trying on clothes in the white stores, except in storage rooms or in the back of the store.

One day, my mother took me with her to the white grocery store. We stood in line at the checkout stand. As each white person approached, my mother would step aside and let them pass in front of us. No one ever said thank you or excuse me. When there were no whites in line, the surly grocer checked us out. As we were leaving the store, a police officer stopped us and said, "We've been watchin' you, and you ain't goin' to git away with stealing nothin'." Immediately a crowd gathered and began to taunt us. They insisted that my mother empty her grocery bags. As she did, the officer checked each item of food against the receipt, hoping that he would catch us stealing. It was a humiliating experience.

Yet, when we returned home and told our family what happened, we acted out the entire experience as if it were a play. The police officer and members of the crowd became the cast and we acted out these parts, embellishing each of these characters. "There was this ole bag of bones, with a nose three foot long and clearly out of joint," my mother said referring to one of the crowd. We laughed ourselves silly. This is how we coped, how we survived.

These events made me realize that we were different. But our differences and the abuse we suffered bound us into a close and loving community, where we honored and supported one another. For example, my older sister had a child out of wedlock. No one in our immediate or extended family judged her; we supported her, just like we supported the many homosexuals in our community.

The first homosexual I really got to know was Tommy Brooks. I was eight or nine. Tommy was a musician and when he sat down to play the piano we just stood back in awe. People would say admiringly, "Oh, that's Tommy Brooks." Music was so important to our community and Tommy taught us how to harmonize—how to *really* sing—and he cared about us. He was well-known and well-liked. He was just one of the many creative people we knew to be homosexual. And the interesting thing is that Tommy was *never* put down.

When I was about twelve or thirteen, I began to take piano lessons. I wanted to play like Tommy. After only three months, my piano teacher told me I was very talented. That thrilled me, as music played such a big part in the black community. I had visions of being a great pianist. These visions were shattered when my friend Chucky told me that I was going to be gay if I continued to play the piano. So, I quit. I honestly believed that the piano would make me a sissy. After all, Tommy was gay and my friend Kenneth became a sissy when he started playing the piano, I thought. I can kick myself for being so silly, for stopping. It's sad; I could have been good.

As a teenager, I recall sitting around with friends talking about sex and girlfriends. One of the guys there was gay. We knew it was harder for him than the rest of us, being black *and* gay. I knew what being black was like. So, I knew being black *and* being gay had to be harder. There were other gays at school. We laughed about them but it wasn't the threatening kind of laughter that one would associate with prejudice; it had more to do with acknowledging being different than anything else. I also had a couple of gay cousins. We didn't reject them. They were, after all, a part of the family. So, I grew up generally comfortable, even playful, around gay people.

One of my junior high school teachers was gay and he used to kid me. One time, he put his hand on my leg in front of a group of people and said jokingly, "Cecil, you've got the prettiest legs." I looked at him and said gruffly, "Take your hands off me." It wasn't frightening. In fact, we all laughed—times were simpler then.

When I got to college there was this fellow named Fennel who was clearly gay. He and I both lived on the first floor of the men's dormitory. One night, he came home beaten and bloodied by some white people and said, "I want it to be known that it is because I'm black that they beat me," but we knew that it was because he was black *and* gay and maybe just because he was gay. Fennell was deeply hurt. That's when I realized how much hatred there was against homosexuals. I will never forget Fennell's hurt. He never left the campus grounds after that incident.

Following college, I attended graduate school at Southern Methodist University (SMU). I was one of the first five African Americans to attend Perkins School of Theology at SMU. Everyone knew there were gays at Perkins, although it was kept very quiet. Soon after my arrival, a new friend came up to me and kissed me on the forehead. He said, "Ah Cecil, you are soooo handsome." It made me a bit uncomfortable and I told him so. But, soon we got to laughing about it. There were others. Some told me they loved me. I would usually say something like, "I'm sorry, I don't feel that way." But it was okay. I knew what it was like to be attracted sexually. Like most kids, I had been trying to prove I was a man since I was in junior high—chasing after the prettiest girls and having them chase after me. I get angry when heterosexuals say that homosexuals only think about sex. That's all that most young people think about, regardless of their sexuality.

After SMU, I took a number of jobs, failing miserably to start a church in Hobbs, New Mexico, succeeding somewhat as a chaplain and teacher at my old alma mater, Sam Houston. While I had met many gay men over the years, I knew few lesbians until I entered the University of California in Berkeley, where I did further study. After Berkeley I returned to the Southwest, but within a few years I was back in the Bay Area and became very involved with lesbians and gays.

I was appointed minister of Glide Memorial Methodist Church by my bishop. Located in a seedy, rundown section of San Francisco called "The Tenderloin," Glide was a dying church. My Bishop gave me a "free pulpit," and I set out to make one change after another. From the outset, I have guided Glide to be a church of acceptance. And over the years, Glide has accepted the forgotten as well as the famous. Everyone from hippies (Jerry Rubin), to revolutionaries (Huey Newton, Angela Davis), to celebrities (Oprah Winfrey, Bill Cosby, Maya Angelou), to world leaders (Bill Clinton, Nelson Mandela) have passed through our portals. Today Glide is one of the fastest growing Methodist churches in the nation (eight hundred new members last year alone). It is also the most diverse church in America, probably the world—almost a quarter of the congregation is composed of people of color and a third is gay and lesbian.

From the moment I set foot in Glide, I attempted to connect to all of the diverse people within the community. The four of us on staff began to bridge the religious community with the gay and lesbian community. In 1965, we began our outreach to gay and lesbian street kids. We then began a program called Citizen's Alert, where we monitored violence against gays and lesbians. In 1968, I performed the first gay union (commitment ceremony), which was a story picked up by the

Associated Press and which nearly started a religious riot, as it raised the ire of religious leaders everywhere. I worked with a number of early gay liberation groups, including the Daughters of Bilitis, and many leaders of the gay and lesbian movements like Harvey Milk, Sally Gearhart and others. For thirty years, I have been committed to developing a sense of community, including not just gays and lesbians, but people of every orientation, every color, every creed, every socio-economic group, every everything.

Yet I am shocked. Most black churches are full of gays, yet the church is more officious than any other organization in the African American community. They send out the message, "Don't come out." So members of the black community begin to feel uncomfortable when people "come out." It is a mistake. People must not be made to be ashamed of being themselves. At Glide, I don't care who you are. At Glide you are accepted!

When I was young and my hormones acted up, I thought it was my male duty to try and get every girl I could. My wife Jan has taught me just how inappropriate some of my "male behavior" has been. I have learned a great deal from her, as well as others, which has freed me from a kind of slavery that most men get caught up in. I know that most heterosexual males have an irrational fear that every gay man is going to "come on to them" the first chance they get. Now, I know this simply isn't true and I also know that if it does happen, heterosexuals are capable of learning, just as women have done, to say no!

Although Cecil grew up with an easy acceptance of gays, he knew enough about the bias against homosexuals to quit piano lessons because someone might think he was "queer." How many of us have stopped doing things we love because of our fear of what others would think of us?

Cecil was around gay people most of his life. As a result, he never seemed uncomfortable around them. This seems to validate many people's experience of getting to know people who are different from them. As they become more knowledgeable, more intimate, they experience less discomfort. Today, Cecil is minister of one of the fastest growing churches in the United States. Even though he is heterosexual, not a week goes by that he doesn't speak out about the rights of gay people. His actions are a model for others in the religious community.

Alan Ellis

Freedom is when bondage is understood.

—J. Krishnamurti

I was born in the shadows of the Wasatch range of the Rocky Mountains at Latter-Day Saint Hospital in Salt Lake City, Utah. The date was November 23, 1957.

I have often thought that being born in Utah in 1957 was like being born in 1937—socially and culturally—anywhere else in the United States. I was raised a Mormon. My family's history in the church dates back to the 1850's, and both my father's and mother's grandfathers were polygamists and each had two wives. My father was an accountant and did well in his work. In the latter years of his career, he started a number of small businesses with his younger brother. I felt that his work and desire to provide for our family were more important to him than the church, although he was always active in the ward (the local congregation). My mother's commitment to the church was never in question and she raised us to be equally committed as Mormons. For the first twenty-five years of my life, she was successful—my world view was entirely filtered through a Mormon lens.

My memory of the assassination of John F. Kennedy illustrates the extent to which the church dominated my early existence. I was told that the president was shot one day before my sixth birthday. I was aware of only one president—the one who headed three million Mormons. Imagine my surprise, four months later when the president of the church spoke at our April conference. I assumed he had been resurrected, further evidence of the veracity of the Mormon church.

At the age of twelve, I began to hear the words "faggot," "homo," and "queer." Initially, I had little idea what they meant but it was clear they were meant to be cruel. I began to wonder if these words had something to do with me.

About this same time, I recall having sexual fantasies that included other boys. Perhaps, in response to these fantasies, I developed a number of strange fears and beliefs. One of these had to do with my body. I was fourteen and my family had flown to Washington, D.C., to visit relatives. It was August: hazy, hot, and humid. My uncle and aunt invited all of us to go to the community pool. I was tall and thin. For some reason, I concluded that my bony hips were too large for a male body and I panicked, thinking they would reveal I was queer. I refused to go swimming.

When we returned home, I walked a little over a mile in pouring rain to a public telephone booth and called a psychiatrist. I pleaded for help. I tried to strike a bargain in which he would help me find girls attractive and I would pay him back when I was old enough to get a job. He seemed a bit surprised by my request and suggested that I contact the county mental health services where I would not have to worry about payment. I did. For several months, I rode my bike ten miles each way and paid two dollars per visit to see a psychologist, who eventually suggested that I was too young to know what my lifelong sexual desires would be and that I shouldn't worry so much about it.

During this time, I heard only veiled reference to homosexuality by the leaders of the church. However, there was much said about the evils of masturbation and, like a good Mormon, I religiously attempted to avoid this "sordid" activity. It was during this period that my mother, after twenty-nine years of marriage, divorced my father. As far back as I can recall, I knew my mother slept downstairs while my father slept upstairs. As they so seldom displayed any tenderness or emotion, the divorce didn't seem to change much—they simply slept in different houses now.

At the age of nineteen, I went on a two-year mission to spread the Mormon teachings to Buenos Aires, Argentina. The experience of living in another country helped me see that there were many ways to live and, at some level, I acknowledged that most, if not all, were equally "correct" ways to conduct one's life. Nevertheless, I remained convinced that the Mormon church was the true church and I hoped that serving a mission would convince God that I was committed enough to be granted my long-sought-after goal to be attracted to women.

Upon my return to the States, I began classes at Brigham Young University. Like my father, I majored in accounting, and I did well. I taught Spanish at the language training center where missionaries were trained and I was the executive secretary to the bishop of my congregation. All of my sexual energy was sublimated into my work, which I loved, especially teaching and counseling missionaries. My involvement in the church was extensive and, in a sense, I was on the "fast-track" within the Mormon hierarchy.

During this period, however, I spent innumerable late nights walking around Provo, Utah, pondering and lamenting my sexual attraction to men. I developed strong feelings toward a number of my male college friends and some of the missionaries I was teaching, but I did not act on them.

I "fell in love" with one of my roommates, an attractive and fully alive man, who had cystic fibrosis. Because of his condition, he needed someone to pound on his chest once or twice a day to clear his lungs. I enjoyed being able to help him in this way and this "acceptable" physical contact increased my attachment to him. We shared a small dorm room with beds that were within reach of each other. The sexual energy between us was strong, but we never openly discussed it. There were occasions, in the wee hours of the morning, when he would encourage me to pet his genitals. I recall shaking in my bed as I attempted to avoid giving in to the temptation while deeply longing to have this contact with him. On occasion, the longing won out. He acted as if he were in a dream state, saying his girlfriend's name (we all had "girlfriends" at the time) as I petted him. On the days following this activity, I felt unbelievable guilt. And, although my roommate attempted to talk me out of it, I went to confess to the bishop, who in no uncertain terms told me that this behavior must never happen again. He placed me on probation (a form of punishment in the church) and arranged for me to see a psychologist employed by the church.

The psychologist believed that homosexuality was a choice that could be cured, and he set out to change me. His method was strange. We took walks during which he encouraged me to look at women and imagine what they were thinking. He believed that homosexuality was simply an inability to understand women. Since I had little sexual contact with either men or women, he considered me an easy prospect for cure. I told him about a dream in which I was physically, though not sexually, intimate with a woman. He took that as sufficient evidence that I had changed and declared me "cured." I was very hopeful that his diagnosis was correct, but the "cure" was fleeting and I soon began to long for my former roommate. I wept as I thought of him and fantasized that we could disappear together to a place where neither my family nor friends would be hurt by our relationship.

In December of 1981, I completed my degree in accounting and left Utah to work as an internal auditor for a company in Minneapolis. On my way, I spent the night in Cheyenne, Wyoming. I went to a bookstore where I noticed that there was a section for pornography. I was shocked to see that some of the magazines had men on the covers. My heart began to pound. Although I was twenty-four, I had no idea that such magazines existed. Despite my embarrassment, I bought two. They had a strong impact on me, because their existence meant that there must be many other men just like me. While I was pleased to recognize that, I simply couldn't imagine what it would be like to live as a gay man. I destroyed the magazines within hours of purchasing them. Again, I prayed that I would awake to find myself sexually attracted to women.

My work involved constant travel across the United States and Latin America. I spent many nights in Holiday Inns wondering what to do about my sexual identity. I seldom thought about my work as an auditor, at which I was quite successful. I had yet to violate any of the significant standards of the church. I didn't even drink caffeinated soda.

At the end of one year, I quit my job. My managers believed that I quit because I had not been challenged by the work. That thought never even entered my mind. I left because I was simply too absorbed by the conflict between my sexual identity and my religious beliefs to focus on my work as an internal auditor. At the time, I knew of no one to whom I could turn for help either within the company or in the Minneapolis community.

I returned to school in January of 1983 and went on to receive a second bachelor's degree in psychology from the University of Utah. For the most part, I could not think of anything better to do. I took a course in social psychology that led me to question the teachings of the Mormon church. The structure of my belief system began to crumble and so did the major stumbling blocks to dealing with my sexuality.

Even so, I had not rid myself of society's homophobic messages which I had deeply internalized. In a final desperate act, I borrowed money from my father to engage in a form of therapy that promised a cure. At this time, no one in my family had a clue that I might be gay. My father, who would normally want to know the exact purpose for loaning money, understood by the way that I asked for it that I couldn't tell him anything except that it was very important to me. I felt that out of his love for me he gave me the money with no questions asked. What I pursued was called aversion therapy—a nice term for shock treatment. During these sessions, the therapist attached electrodes to my arm and a plethysmograph to my penis. Then, he showed me videos involving sex between two men. Whenever I responded physically to the videos, I would be shocked.

Several months after the therapy ended, I met a woman in one of my psychology classes, and we began to date. I was twenty-five and a virgin. We had sex and I took this as a sign that the therapy had been successful. My relief was short-lived however, and to my dismay, I found myself even more attracted to some of the men I saw the following day. I continued to date and have sex with this woman for two months but it quickly became apparent to both of us that something was wrong. I concluded that I could not successfully explore my sexuality in Salt Lake City.

I went to the library to look at a number of Sunday papers from various cities to check the want ads. As I thumbed through the Seattle paper I came across an article that featured gay Seattle and included a reference to Affirmation, a gay Mormon group. Two days later, I moved to Seattle with four hundred dollars and a carload of belongings. I was so filled with fear that I waited six weeks before contacting the Mormon group. With great difficulty, I met with the contact person. Even though I knew he was gay (and he obviously knew I was), I couldn't, after so many years of fighting it, bring myself to say the words, "I am gay."

Shortly after I arrived, I got a job as an assistant supervisor for billing in the printing department at the University of Washington. The supervisor seemed to like me and I trusted her; even so, I kept quiet about my sexual orientation.

I participated in my first Gay Pride day that summer. I was thrilled to be among so many other gays and lesbians, whose presence was still a marvel to me. Following the parade, I went to a movie with the contact person of the Mormon group. To my horror, my supervisor sat in the row in front of us. I panicked. I was sure that my male friend's "obvious" gayness would give me away, and my supervisor would know I was a homosexual. I wasn't ready for that so I pretended not to see her. Soon I heard her mention to her friend that someone she knew (me) seemed to be avoiding her. I felt like a fool and clumsily said hello. I was evasive in introducing my friend and I mumbled and stuttered through the conversation. The movie was a blur. I dreaded going into work the next day. To my great relief, my supervisor sensed that I was having difficulty and took me out for a lunch that included a strong drink. I had only recently started drinking and it had quite an effect. She said that my being gay was not an issue for her, that it was fine. I was thankful and relieved and I was struck by the thought that my first experience at coming out to a heterosexual was traumatic primarily because of my own fears.

In August, I moved to Champaign, Illinois, to begin graduate work in psychology at the University of Illinois. I stopped in Salt Lake City to visit my family. Although I had not intended to tell any of them about my sexual orientation, I surprised myself by telling my sister. I knew that my sister and her boyfriend socialized with a gay couple; still, it was very difficult to tell her. She was very supportive. She said she was also surprised. I had succeeded rather well at "acting straight."

When I arrived in Champaign, I reentered the closet that I had so tentatively left in Seattle. I feared I would fail in the program if my sexual orientation were known. There were no graduate students or faculty visibly "out" in the department, so there was no way to assess how anyone might react to my sexual orientation. I felt weak and cowardly. My first semester was marked by academic success but my discomfort over hiding my sexuality grew. I had a hard time trying to integrate who I was as a person with my role as a graduate student.

I decided to come out to another student who I thought might also be gay. I hemmed and hawed, trying to tell him. He finally asked if I was gay and if I thought he was. I said "yes," and he turned out to be very supportive even though he was straight. We subsequently talked at length about my sexual identity. Whenever I would wonder why I was gay, he would respond matter of factly, "Well, who better than you?" He helped me survive that first semester.

During the second semester, I joined a gay and lesbian support group at a local church, even though I had begun to think of myself as an agnostic. The support group offered an environment in which I felt safe to discuss my fears and, as a result, I was able to come out to several of my fellow students that semester.

Even though I continued to worry about how people would react, I stepped further out of the closet. I became involved with the university's gay and lesbian organization, which was holding demonstrations to have sexual orientation added to the nondiscrimination clause. The chancellor appointed a task force on sexual orientation which I was asked to join. My name was in the student newspaper on several occasions because of my participation. The first time that happened I stayed home out of fear of the reaction that might occur. That evening I called several of my friends to find out how people had reacted and found out there was little reaction and what there was had been supportive.

During this time, I had distanced myself considerably from everyone in my family with the exception of my sister. I could not envision ever telling the rest of my family, especially my parents. It seemed ironic and saddened me that thirty thousand students knew I was gay, but my family didn't. I became determined to tell them. I tried to reassure myself by concluding that their reaction would not greatly alter my daily existence—they could either disown me or get to know me better. Finally, I mustered my courage and when I flew home over spring break, I told them I was gay. My father seemed resigned and somewhat accepting. He said that he had always heard that one in ten were homosexuals and that there was little they could do about it. I was surprised that he knew that much. He went on to say that he had five children (inferring that there was a reasonable probability that one would be gay) but that he hadn't really thought about it.

My mother's response was quite different. In a tone that sounded somewhat like an accusation, she asked, "But you don't live that way do you?" I pretended that I didn't know what she meant by the question and let it go. It had been extremely difficult for me to tell her so I simply left, satisfied that I had told her. I knew it would take time for her to process it, as it would take time for me to share more about my life with her.

I continued to serve on the Chancellor's Task Force. My dissertation chairperson asked why I was involved. I told him that it was a good opportunity to use some of my statistical skills and that it was personally important to me since I was gay. He told me that he objected to homosexuality, but said that my sexual orientation would have nothing to do with our professional relationship. Many of my friends suggested that I change dissertation chairs, but I knew that he had written a recent glowing letter of recommendation for a gay student who was going to graduate school. He provided me with a research assistantship from his grant's travel funds that greatly facilitated completion of my dissertation. The Task Force was successful in getting the chancellor to sign an executive order adding sexual orientation to the university's nondiscrimination clause. The order had little legal power but it was an important symbolic victory.

I was now completely out (or so I thought) and was about to complete my Ph.D. I had enjoyed graduate school and was ready to enter the job market. I listed my participation on the Chancellor's Task Force on my curriculum vitae and was advised by my dissertation chair that I should remove it. He suggested that, in a tough job market, the inclusion of the Task Force might reduce or eliminate my chances for a good job. I removed the reference, succumbing once again to well-meaning advice and throwing myself back into the closet.

I was invited to join the faculty at the University of Kentucky (UK) in Lexington. UK is only five hours by car from Champaign. I was involved in a relatively new relationship at the time and the short distance was one of the factors that influenced my decision to accept the position. The psychology department at UK was well-respected and I found the department matched my temperament. I also found a larger gay and lesbian community than in Champaign, even though the community in Lexington was much more underground. Several of my fellow graduate students suggested that I avoid living in Kentucky because of the many fundamentalists in the state. But the move felt right at the time, so I began a career as a college professor in August, 1988.

Because there was no reference to my sexual preference, I had to come out all over again. I began by telling some of my colleagues and asked them to feel free to tell others, especially if someone asked. Despite this permission, many guarded the information even when asked directly by others. It was clear to me that they too had been influenced by society's homophobia and found it difficult to come out for me. To facilitate my coming out, I joined the Association of Gay and Lesbian Psychologists and listed it on my curriculum vitae. In addition, I began to do research on gay and lesbian issues. My colleagues and graduate students were supportive. Although I never came out directly in the classroom, I often spoke of gay and lesbian concerns when we discussed such issues as discrimination and prejudice in the courses that I taught.

I felt somewhat protected by the American Psychological Association's strong support for diversity. Even so, I experienced the effects of homophobia when a lesbian faculty member and I indicated interest in teaching a course on gay and lesbian issues. The Director of Women's Studies implied that if we were to teach such a course we would be unlikely to be granted tenure.

By now, my sexuality was fairly well integrated into my personal and professional life. With the exception of my sister, my relationship with my family centered on ignoring what I had told them several years earlier. Admittedly, much of this was a result of my not disclosing much about my personal life when I visited. However, it was clear that it remained an uncomfortable topic for most of my family. The few times my mother and I did discuss it we tended to do so in a very academic and intellectual way. My mother read books on the subject, but they generally were limited to those focusing on how to "cure" homosexuality. She sent me piles of brochures and such from Homosexuals Anonymous and Exodus International, so-called religious organizations that claim to have cured homosexuals. I simply threw them in the garbage.

Last year I felt it was time to more fully discuss my sexual orientation with my family, with my mother in particular. I told her that my sexual orientation is not simply some intellectual decision that I have made but that it is who I am. I also let her know that I have been in a number of relationships with other men and that my sexual identity is a part of both my personal and professional identity. Not only am I gay, but I write and do research on gay and lesbian issues, much of which is published in national and international journals. She seemed accepting but then surprised me with the news that she had written a brochure that theorized why I was gay. She had self-published the brochure and had made it available to Homosexuals Anonymous because she believed it offered support for a cure.

While I wish my mother would accept me for who I am, including my gay identity, I realize that on the issue of my sexuality we may never agree. My mother remains very active in the Mormon Church—she recently completed a mission for the church in England. She just celebrated her seventy-second birthday and it is doubtful that she will ever substantially change her opinions on homosexuality. I do feel that she respects me for my accomplishments and that she loves me. For that, I am grateful. I do regret, that despite her intentions, her writing is hurtful to me and to other gays and lesbians.

My relationship with my father has grown closer over the past few years as I have shared more about my life with him. The same is also the case with my brothers and my sister and even with my mother. I know that my being more secure about who I am and being more honest and open with them has helped all of us to not only discuss this topic more openly but other sensitive issues that we might have attempted to avoid in the past. The improved communication—even when we disagree—is helping us deepen our connection to each other.

As I look back on my thirtysomething years, I no longer wonder what the impact of being gay on my life has been. It has influenced how I accept and express who I am and the sensitivities that I have toward others and their experiences. The connections that I feel to others who are oppressed is a direct result of my sexual orientation. At seventeen, I remember staring at a dark and overcast sky and begging God to change my attraction to men. Today, I am grateful for what being gay has given me.

Alan's story describes the path many gays and lesbians take to find acceptance. The teachings of the Mormon Church clearly taught him that homosexuality was evil. Like others reacting to society's rejection, Alan tried to change. He even tried "shock" therapy in a futile final attempt to become straight.
Through a religious support group (Affirmation), Alan began

his journey to acceptance. He eventually came out to his family and publicly. He now teaches and writes about sexual orientation—a resounding final step to acceptance. His story depicts the long, sometimes difficult, road that many gays and lesbians face when they come from religious families that not only do not accept homosexuality but strongly believe that it is wrong.

Note your thoughts and reactions to Alan's story.

Luann Conaty

We ought not to insist on everyone following in our footsteps, nor to take upon ourselves to give instructions in spirituality when, perhaps, we do not even know what it is.

—Teresa of Avila

Nothing in my life prepared me for the day when I came face to face with the reality that my oldest son is gay. The subject was taboo. Let me start by giving you some idea how my attitudes were formed.

I was raised in Oklahoma, the only child of an only child. There were many only children born during the days following the Great Depression. There was nothing particularly unusual about my childhood until my father lost his job when I was six. He was unable to find work which would sustain our small family, so he went to Texas, where he could earn enough to support himself and pay the storage on our furniture. My mother and I stayed in Oklahoma. We moved in with his parents, where we lived for two years. I felt no deprivation whatever. I was the adored only grandchild of the county sheriff. He and my grandmother lived in a tiny town, where I was a rather large duck in a small puddle.

Mother, on the other hand, found this period of her life almost unbearable. She had no money of her own. The only negative impact this period had on me is that I have a near obsession with financial security. Mother has told me how difficult it was for her to ask for money for even the most personal items. My grandparents loved her as if she were their own, so I'm sure they saw to it that we both had whatever we needed. Nevertheless, Mother felt embarrassed every time she asked for anything. In this day of women's equality (more or less), I find it curious that she did not get a job herself—or at the very least, negotiate an allowance of some sort. She says the thought of going to work never entered her head. Perhaps she was unwilling to consider that she might be there long enough to get a job.

We were reunited as a family after the beginning of World War II when my father was hired at the Federal Reformatory in El Reno, Oklahoma. But the man who moved with us to El Reno was a very different person from the one who had gone to Texas. He had gone through a profound experience—he had given his life to Jesus Christ.

While that was an extraordinarily positive experience for him, it was not so for mother and me. He was consumed with studying the Bible and with sharing his newfound faith—whether the hearer was interested or not. He was absolutely convinced that what he believed about the Bible was the *truth*, and there was no discussion about the matter. For the record, fathers in the 1940's were pretty much of a similar turn of mind. "I am Father, therefore I am right," was the prevailing attitude.

El Reno was in the heart of the Bible Belt. Nothing was planned for Sunday morning or Wednesday evening by any civic group or school. Those times were reserved for Church.

People who knew my father during this period described him as generous, caring, and a good friend and neighbor—he even coached a Little League baseball team one year, for the little boy who lived next door whose father was away in the service. Yet even in El Reno, Billy Wilder was something of a curiosity. It didn't take long before people knew better than to let the conversation get around to the Bible. Billy just didn't know when to quit.

Given the environment of both my home and my hometown, I intellectually accepted the Christian teachings; emotionally, I kept them at arm's length. I didn't want to be like my father.

As an only child, I spent a great deal of my time with adults. The family across the street were about the age of my grandparents. I enjoyed their company, and spent many evenings playing cards with them. They often invited me to attend out of town basketball games with them. One of their sons, Leo, lived in Oklahoma City, and we would frequently stop at his apartment before games. Leo visited his parents frequently, as well. He was usually accompanied by a roommate, who changed from time to time, but every roommate he had was slender and small, and most worked as hairdressers.

When we visited Leo, it never occurred to me to wonder about the fact that there were two men living there and only one double bed. I was so naive I believed people only had sex for procreation, and I thought intercourse was something rather unpleasant one did in order to have a baby. It's hard to believe that a high school student could be so uninformed, but I was not all that unusual in the early 1950's.

As I reflect on those years, it occurs to me that one of the men for whom I worked as a secretary was probably a homosexual, too. No doubt, there were others who crossed my path, but as I was not looking for them, I never saw them.

I graduated from high school and entered Tulsa University on a scholarship. There I met Jane Blackford, the most winsome Christian it has ever been my pleasure to meet—loving, caring, gentle, and warm. She was never pushy or didactic; she simply talked about Jesus intimately and easily. She gave me a very different Christian role model, and I eagerly accepted Christ as my Savior and became involved in Christian groups on campus.

During this period I also met Tex Black. He was a veteran going to Tulsa University on the GI Bill. He was several years older than I, and very good looking. I fell head over heels in love. I had been very careful to date only Christian young men, for I did not want any conflict about religion in my life. Tex was not a Christian, but he went along with the program and that convinced me that he was absolutely sincere, and he was—until we married. We were still picking the rice out of our hair, figuratively speaking, when he announced, "You can forget about that church stuff now. I've got you."

I was devastated. What could I do? I did not believe in divorce; besides, I loved him. How could I have gotten myself into this mess? I believed what I wanted to believe, and now I would have to pay the price. I decided that unless Tex became a Christian, I would never have any children. I could not bear the thought of raising my children in a divided home. I was not playing games here; I was absolutely resolved to this course of action. So I went to church by myself every Sunday; I sang in the choir; and I prayed.

Two years later, Tex graduated from Tulsa University and was baptized. I was ecstatic. Within three months, I was also pregnant.

Andy was born in June of 1956, Kevin came along in August of 1959, and Linda in May of 1962. Two adorable redheaded, brown-eyed boys and a beautiful little blue-eyed blonde completed our "All American Family," as Tex called it.

However, things weren't going too well in our young married lives. Tex struggled in his career. By the time Linda was born, he had worked for six companies, and we had lived in nine houses. Eventually, I had to look at the possibility that my husband might be responsible for this erratic employment pattern. As a loving and faithful wife, I kept blaming other people for this sequence of events. Finally, he changed industries. That did not help. In 1969, when Linda was seven years old, he started his own business. I went to work in the company to help out.

My father died suddenly in 1967, at the age of sixty. While I had resisted his Bible instruction during my adolescence, as an adult, I relied on him for answers to my spiritual questions. It must have been rather obvious that my relationship with God was somewhat second-hand, because eventually a friend pointed out to me after my father's death that "God doesn't have any grandchildren." I took this comment to heart. I underwent a significant spiritual awakening and I became involved in several Bible studies.

I enjoyed being a full-time wife and mother, and I did not want to work. As soon as we could reasonably afford to hire someone to take my place in Tex's business, I went back home to care for my children. With no day care facilities in 1969, one summer of juggling children and a job was all I could endure.

When Andy was fourteen, I heard through the grapevine that he had told a friend that he thought he was gay. I was absolutely unwilling to accept even the remotest possibility it might be true. I did ask my pastor to talk to Andy. Dr. Pruett agreed, but what he told Andy was, "If you're gay, you'll just have to learn to live with it." I was outraged.

Andy went to high school, became involved with Young Life, Youth for Christ, and Campus Crusade for Christ. His friends were as wholesome and wonderful a group of kids as you can possibly imagine. They studied the Bible together and prayed for each other. I was convinced that any talk of homosexuality was gone for good.

By 1977, the financial pressures and our inability to communicate about things that mattered finally took their toll on our marriage. Tex and I were divorced. I moved into a three-bedroom apartment. In 1978, Andy graduated from Indiana University and came to live with me, and we finally had the conversation that we needed to have—about his sexual orientation.

Our memories of this conversation are so different that it is difficult to believe we could be talking about the same situation. I know that witnesses to an incident recount different details, but the only thing

Andy and I agree on is that the word "homosexual" was finally spoken between us. And, that didn't mean I accepted it.

You see, I was firmly into denial. I sent Andy to a psychiatrist, convinced that he could be "cured." What I did not know was that the doctor told Andy he "might" be able to help him if Andy were prepared to do the hardest work of his life. Andy's reaction, I found out later, was to say, "I've been doing the hardest work of my life for nine years, accepting myself as I am. Thanks, but no thanks."

Andy let me continue in my dream world; he didn't know what else to do with me. He moved to San Francisco, and I continued, in spite of San Francisco's reputation as a "gay mecca" to believe that he was "cured." I even told him that his moving to San Francisco for him was like a drunk taking a job as a bartender.

Anita Bryant was in all the newspapers; the issue of homosexuality was on everyone's lips. I would have been in the front row, cheering her on, except for the thought that it was just barely possible she might be talking about my son.

Two years later, after Frank Conaty and I were married, my daughter Linda and I visited Andy for a week, and my fragile sense of well being was shattered into a million pieces. All Andy's friends were couples, men obviously living together, or at least "involved." I could not pretend any more that Andy was going to get married to a woman and live happily ever after.

That is when my hard work began.

Stage One: I wrote to Andy often. I quoted scripture. I condemned.

Stage Two: I stopped condemning. I started listening. I cried a lot.

Stage Three: I moved to New Hampshire. No one knows my son; maybe now I can begin to talk about him. I made those first tentative efforts to speak the words "My son is gay" and I was astonished at the results. It was as if God handpicked every person I opened up to. In every instance, the response was, I have a gay brother or uncle, sister or some other relative. It was incredible. It was as if every person in the world must be related to someone gay.

Stage Four: I met Andy's friends. I found out they were likeable people. Some were outrageous. Some were shy. Some were talented. I was surprised that I genuinely liked them.

This was a long, slow, painful process. There were fits and starts along the way. I listened to a gay Christian talk about his life and heard him debate a member of the Moral Majority. That was a shock. I listened to a scientist make a case for nature, not nurture, as the cause of homosexuality. I began to put away my overwhelming guilt.

The AIDS crisis began. I was terrified that my son would die. His friends began to get sick. They began to die. When the first one was dying, his mother visited him and had to deal with the overwhelming truths that her son was dying and that he was gay. I suffered for her. I tried to imagine what I would do if Andy contracted AIDS. Realistically, I couldn't expect to go to California and stay for an extended period of time. It did not seem like a good option for Andy to come to where I lived, leaving all that would be familiar, including his friends behind. It seemed to me that the next best thing I could do would be to take care of some other mother's son who needed me. So I began to look for an AIDS agency with which to become involved.

I was still living in New Hampshire, and the epidemic was in its infancy. Support systems were barely beginning. So it was not until I moved to central Massachusetts that I found a place where I could be of use. Early in 1987 I volunteered with AIDS Project-Worcester (APW). I answered phones, surveyed funeral homes, staffed the Information Line and tried to make myself useful. But I wanted to be involved with the patients. Eventually APW started training buddies. I was in the first group. It was a wonderful experience. We were a very eclectic group. Gay men, straight men, lesbians, straight women, mothers, fathers, people with no children, ranging in age from late twenties to early sixties. We met twice a month for mutual support. We helped each other when our clients became difficult, when they lost their jobs, when they had to apply for Social Security or welfare, when they fought off opportunistic infections—and when they died. Even though that original group has drifted off in many directions, we developed such a strong bond that I still feel very close to each one of those people.

Ultimately, I dived back into the Scripture and studied the passages which dealt with homosexuality in the original Greek and Hebrew. Andy and I even co-authored a book about our experiences. I had to confront the Scripture before I could satisfactorily complete our book. I still believe that the Bible is the Word of God. I still believe that Jesus Christ is God the Son, the second person of the Trinity. I still believe that the only way to become a child of God is through the death and resurrection of Jesus Christ.

However, I now believe that God is grieved when Christians deny His grace to any human being. My Bible says, "Whosoever will may come." It does not say, "unless they're gay." My Bible says, "Come unto me, all ye who labor and are heavy laden, and I will give you rest." It does not say, "except the homosexuals." I believe that God's grace is sufficient for everyone who ever lived. I have no right, nor does anyone else, to tell someone they are too evil for God's grace. That is not what my Bible teaches me.

Today I am the Buddy Coordinator at AIDS Project-Worcester. I am working with my third AIDS client—a wonderful woman who is an inspiration to all who know her. It grieves her that she is treated differently from other AIDS patients. She is viewed as an "innocent victim" because she was infected when a medical technician stuck her in the hand with a needle that had just been used to draw blood from an AIDS patient. She says it shouldn't matter how a person becomes infected. It should only matter that he or she is sick.

In June of 1992 I was sworn in on Governor Weld's Commission on Gay and Lesbian Youth in the Commonwealth of Massachusetts. It is the first of its kind in the nation. It has been a real privilege to work with the twenty-six other people on this commission. We hope that what we are doing will pave the way for understanding and compassion toward gay and lesbian young people all over the nation. Governor Weld was moved to create this commission by a federal report which showed that over 30 percent of teen age suicides are related to gay issues. If we use the generally accepted figure that 10 percent of the population is gay, that means gay young people are killing themselves three times as often as straight young people. If we use the religious right's figure that 1 to 2 percent of the population is gay, those statistics are even more alarming.

I am convinced that one of the most important factors leading to the low self-image and to the problems that lead to suicide among this population is the attitude of a great many Christians in this country. Our gay children are told they are evil, depraved, unacceptable, disgraceful, morally degenerate, and twisted.

It is all very well to talk about loving the sinner and hating the sin, but to gays and lesbians everywhere, those words are hollow. They feel hated. And if the people who are homophobic and anti-gay would be honest with themselves, they would acknowledge that they do hate gays and lesbians.

I believe education is the answer. People like me must come forward and say, "I have a gay son. He's a fine man. I love him very much." The most valuable contribution I can make in the battle for understanding is my own vulnerability. I am not afraid or ashamed any more. I do not care what other people think. I am secure in the love of God for me and for my son. I had every homophobic hang-up you can possibly imagine, and it took a lot of work and a long time for me to get to where I am today. If I can do it, anyone can.

Luann's story reveals how even those with strongly held negative positions on homosexuality can come to a place of acceptance and support. And, like Art Moreno's story, Luann's shows how much energy and effort go into coming out as a parent of a gay person. She spent most of her life as a fundamentalist, judging and condemning. But, her desire to know her son caused her to listen and to communicate, which eventually led her to a place of acceptance and an active role in support of gay rights as a member of the Governor of Massachusetts's Task Force on Gay and Lesbian Youth. It also brought her and her son together. Luann's progression through the various stages of acceptance provides an important example of just how far one can move.

Note your thoughts and reactions to Luann's story.

5

Taking Action
101 Steps on the Road
to Acceptance

We honestly believe that most people are not blatantly homophobic. We think that most people simply don't recognize the extent of the impact sexual orientation has on families, friendship, work, and spiritual life. Even when the extent of this impact is known, many people simply don't know *what* to do when having to face this issue.

In real life, when do you tell a child that their favorite uncle is gay? What do you say when you first meet the lover, date, spouse, boyfriend, girlfriend, significant other, same-sex partner of your work colleague? How do you respond when your church leader says, "AIDS is God's punishment for homosexuals?" How do you extend your sympathy to a colleague whose long term partner has just died of AIDS? How do you acknowledge the heterosexual who stood up to his commanding officer and said, "'Don't Ask, Don't Tell' doesn't work!"?

In this section we have identified 101 steps you can take to create a "Do Ask, Do Tell" family and bring the acceptance you have come to know in this book to fruition, not just at home, but among friends, at work, and in your church. At the end of the book, you will find sets of resources (family, community, business, and religious and spiritual organizations) that can help you along your path of acceptance. We hope you will make good use of both the 101 Steps on the Road to Acceptance and the listing of resources. They will aid you in creating intimacy within your family and among your friends.

101 STEPS ON THE ROAD TO ACCEPTANCE

At Home, With Friends

1) Draw from the stories in this book to teach family members, friends, work colleagues, and members of your church about sexual orientation.

2) Tell your kids about homosexuality when they are young—before they have learned about hate. Remember, you're not teaching about sex, you're teaching about people loving another person of the same sex. (see Bob and Courtney Powers' stories.)

3) March in a gay pride parade—experience it yourself.

4) When your kids reach adolescence tell them that regardless of their sexual orientation you will love and support them.

5) Give copies of this book to other family members, colleagues, and any one else you think may benefit from it.

6) Bring your family together and talk about issues related to sexual orientation.

7) If you have a gay or bisexual family member, ask her/him about her/his life. Ask what it is like to be gay or bisexual. Let them know that you love and support them and ask what you can do to demonstrate that.

8) Write your congresspersons and other political leaders indicating your support of gay and bisexual people.

9) Adopt a DO ASK, DO TELL family policy—wear a "DO ASK, DO TELL" button.

10) Speak of your gay relative(s) to others as if their sexuality were the most *normal* thing in the world (it is!)

11) Invite your relative's partner, friends, close guests to family events, just as you would with a heterosexual relative, and welcome them!

12) When confronted, take the stance that you believe in a loving inclusive family, and it doesn't matter what a person's sexual orientation is.

13) Don't waste your energies arguing with the extremists. Instead use your energies to speak out to other loving people who need information and help.

14) Give family members (and others) books about sexual orientation and display them on book shelves for all to see.

15) Volunteer to work on a teen suicide, teen runaway or PFLAG helpline.

16) Use the resources in this book (this chapter) to further educate yourself.

17) Come out over and over again as a heterosexual with a gay child/friend/family member. Talk about how you came to acceptance and express your gratitude.

18) Stand up to homophobic jokes, comments by saying, "I know many loving gay people and I'm offended by homophobic remarks." Smile and suggest a new subject.

19) When meeting a gay couple, say, "I'm happy to meet you," and introduce them to others as appropriate.

20) Don't out others but notice signs (rainbow flag, etc.) that give permission to ask questions and *ask*!

21) If you're not sure about someone's sexual orientation, ask a question that gives them an opportunity to talk about it, if they choose. For example, ask if they saw the wonderful Gay Pride march last week (see section on "Getting Familiar with the Lesbian, Gay and Bisexual Community" in chapter 1).

22) Take a stand politically—attend school board and other meetings where these issues are addressed and speak out (see Art Moreno's story).

23) Attend gay themed movies, plays and other events.

24) Rent movies that appear in gay and lesbian film festivals. (They often are excellent but don't make it to the "big screen.")

25) Keep an open mind. Value the diversity you're learning about rather than judging it.

26) Support gay-owned businesses.

27) Write letters to the editor of your local newspaper in support of this issue.

28) Speak out at PTA/School Board meetings. Encourage others to do the same.

29) Mix your dinner parties with gay and straight people.

30) Attend PFLAG meetings.

31) Talk about AIDS and other health-related issues with your family and friends.

In Your Community

32) Volunteer at local lesbian and gay community center or an AIDS organization (see list of organization in this chapter).

33) Make use of your local gay and lesbian community center.

34) Ask your libraries to stock lesbian, gay, and bisexual-related books.

35) Ask political representatives what they plan to do to create a harmonious city, state, country that is inclusive of *all* people, including those of differing sexual orientations, and then ask what evi-

dence they can give to make you believe their statement.

36) Gather together a group of friends and family members and sew a panel for the Names Quilt to honor someone you've cared about who has died of AIDS.

37) Speak out for all loving relationships including same-sex marriages.

38) Wear a "Straight but Not Narrow," a "DO ASK, DO TELL," or other supportive button.

39) Read bisexual and gay magazines and newspapers to stay abreast of news of the gay and bisexual community.

40) Talk about the heterosexual closet. Tell *your* story of coming to acceptance.

41) Tell someone that your child, parent, friend is gay or bisexual. Tell someone else. Practice makes perfect.

42) Join forces with other groups who have experienced discrimination. Learn about and support one another vigorously as if your life depended upon it. It does.

43) Fight, with all your might, anti-gay political campaigns like Amendment 2 in Colorado or the "No Special Rights" (translation—no rights) hate campaigns in other states.

44) Smile when you say the words gay, lesbian, or bisexual.

45) Read *A Manager's Guide to Sexual Orientation in the Workplace* (Powers and Ellis, Routledge, 1995) and other books and articles related to this issue.

In the Workplace

46) Champion an all-inclusive organization.

47) Adopt a company-wide non-discrimination policy that specifically includes sexual orientation.

48) Let the message ring loud and clear that you will not tolerate even subtle forms of discrimination.

49) Attend/support attendance of others at professional conferences that deal with sexual orientation and workplace issues, like the "Out and Equal Conference," sponsored by NGLTF, or company conferences like AT&T's annual League Conference.

50) Post a Safe Place magnet or "Do Ask! Do Tell!" sticker in a visible spot in your office to denote that this is a place where one can freely talk about these issues. (A Safe Place magnet depicts a pink triangle in a green circle and can be purchased by contacting AT&T's League. See their information under "Business Organizations" at the end of the book.)

51) Review personnel policies and procedures to remove any homophobic/heterosexist references.

52) Showcase positive images of gays, lesbians, bisexuals, and other sexual minorities in company newsletters, communications, and events.

53) When interviewing candidates for jobs, let them know that your organization is all-inclusive.

54) Extend a big welcome to newly hired sexual minorities.

55) Add a domestic partnership option to the usual "married/single" choice.

56) Think before raising eyebrows over a named beneficiary, or an honest medical history.

57) Promote, sanction and even subsidize educational and training programs for all employees that promote better understanding and tolerance.

58) Be sure to specifically invite same sex partners to company events, travel, and so forth where spouses are traditionally included.

59) If you have a company matching policy for charitable contributions, let it apply to any group with IRS 501 (c) 3 standing.

60) Order and display gay publications, like *The Advocate* or *Outweek*, where other magazines are displayed.

61) Bring gay, lesbian, and bisexual speakers into the workplace to talk about workplace and/or social issues.

62) Put the word out that if people have to "hide" who they are they will be wasting valuable corporate time and personal energy that could be well spent contributing to the profitability of the company.

63) Use Gay Pride Month (June) and National Coming Out Day (October 11) to acknowledge the contributions of gays and lesbians in the workplace. Fly the gay (rainbow) flag at your place of business during these times.

64) Publicize organizations like PFLAG (Parents and Friends of Lesbians and Gays), which support people learning about gay and lesbian issues, and support upcoming gay related events like Gay Pride Day and National Coming Out Day.

65) Respond to homophobic jokes and statements by saying, "That's not okay in this organization."

66) Review, on a regular basis, employees' responsibility to be non-discriminatory.

67) Provide public as well as private recognition to employees who are contributing to making the workplace more inclusive.

68) Use the words gay, lesbian, and bisexual as part of your everyday vocabulary (you will become totally comfortable).

101 Steps on the Road to Acceptance

69) Give your gay employees time off to attend funerals of close friends.

70) Refer employees experiencing harassment or discrimination to the proper authorities within the organization. Follow up to ensure that harassment or discrimination cases are being vigorously and fairly pursued.

71) *Do not* assume that employees (or customers) are heterosexual.

72) Let openly gay, lesbian, and bisexual employees know that you're happy they are out.

73) Share with co-workers and higher management what other successful companies are doing in the area of gay, lesbian, and bisexual workplace issues.

74) Make a regular spot on your company bulletin board for information relevant to issues of sexual orientation and to announce important upcoming events.

75) Respond to criticism by referring to your desire to create and be part of an all-inclusive workplace.

76) Select openly gay, lesbian, and bisexual employees to represent the company/your organization at internal/external events.

77) Include openly gay, lesbian, and bisexual individuals on company boards and task forces.

78) Do ask openly gay, lesbian, and bisexual people to tell you about their lives.

79) Do tell about your experiences as a sexual minority or supporter.

At Church and in Spiritual Settings

80) Attend Metropolitan Community Church or other gay-affirmative congregations. More are listed at the end of the book.

81) Encourage your church to become a supporting congregation.

82) Sponsor dialogues around this issue.

83) Create an in-home visit program that brings gays and heterosexuals together talking about these issues.

84) Establish an all-inclusive membership policy in your church and live it.

85) Write to church higher-ups in support of an all-inclusive church.

86) Stand up to all forms of bigotry.

87) Reach out to new members of differing sexual orientations.

88) Extend a warm welcome to same-sex couples

89) Encourage same-sex couples to celebrate their commitment to one another in the church.

101 Steps on the Road to Acceptance

90) Support and sponsor events that raise money for AIDS organizations.

91) Establish a volunteer organization to help kids who are gay, lesbian and bisexual and who are dealing with gender issues.

92) Make your church available for religious organizations like Dignity (gay Catholics), Integrity (gay Episcopals), and others.

93) When someone uses the Bible to condemn homosexuality, point out that the Bible also condemns people for wearing jewelry, and braids and for condemning others. Refer to the vast number of references about acceptance.

94) Don't argue with the religious extremists. Focus your energies on (the much larger number of) decent people who simply lack information or have been misinformed.

95) Identify church policies that might be exclusionary. Ask your church leaders to change them.

96) Organize your church to march in the annual lesbian and gay pride parade.

97) Ask gay and straight people to speak at church events and tell about incidents in their lives related to these issues.

98) Write to the Metropolitan Community Church for information and additional resources (UFMCC 5300 Santa Monica Blvd, Suite 304, Los Angeles, CA 90029, USA Telephone (213) 464–5100).

99) Sponsor a sexual orientation and spirituality group in your church. Encourage heterosexuals to attend.

100) Extend gratitude for your acceptance.

101) Celebrate crossing the magic line. DO ASK, DO TELL!

OPENING YOUR HEART

The stories you have read in this guide and the list of 101 steps have given you a close look at the lives of a diverse community of accepting people.

When we see an individual on the street there is seldom an opportunity to develop an awareness of the depth of that person's life experience. All too often, we focus on the differences between us rather than the similarities. When we are able (and willing) to spend time reading or hearing another's story, we are struck by the depth of the emotional experience embodied in their tales of joy, pain, and daily existence. Perhaps we are most struck by the commonness of the emotional experience of all humans and the realization that the humanity that joins us is foremost rather than the categories of race, nationality, religion, sexual orientation, disability, or lifestyle that we have used to create perceptions of difference

101 Steps on the Road to Acceptance

and division. The stories you have just read can help you move beyond the categories that often divide us and move toward common ground and acceptance, as well as out of the closets that close people's hearts and divide us.

Most gays, lesbians, bisexuals, and transgender people have lived their whole lives thinking they would not live to see the majority of Americans accept them. Much of the pain they have experienced has been a direct result of lack of acceptance. Today, many gays and lesbians see glimmers of acceptance—acceptance of people for who they are rather than who society thinks they should be. For many, the possibility produces utter euphoria; for others, dread.

Not a day passes that most sexual minorities don't think about being different. Nor does a day pass that they forget that 30 to 40 percent of all teen suicides are committed by gay and lesbian youth because they feel rejected; that hate crimes against gays and lesbians in Colorado increased 275 percent after the passage of the anti-gay Amendment 2; that 64 percent of all CEO's would not put a gay or lesbian on a management committee because of fear; or that, despite the fact that almost all sexual abuse in America is committed by heterosexual males, gay men are thought of as America's sexual predators. Gays, lesbians, bisexuals, and transgender people have watched, in excruciating pain, religious, political, and military leaders define them, talk about them, and represent them to the rest of America, as if they know who they are.

They are not the child molesters Pat Buchanan portrays them to be; they are the foster parents of a runaway youth. They are not the gawking queer soldier catching glimpses of his straight peers in the shower but the ex-Marine who took a bullet to save the life of President Ford and the soldier who died in Kuwait. They are not the ones who scribble "kill queers" on brick walls; they are the queer young women trying to tear down the walls of hate. Nor are they the parents who disowned their son because he was gay; they include the man who lived with your son for many years, who loved him, who cleaned him when he was near death, and who buried him, all too often, in your absence.

There is too large a divide between gay and straight, a divide that we believe can be mended by opening our hearts and working to bridge that divide.

BRIDGING THE DIVIDE

People are sharply divided on their views of gays, lesbians, and other sexual minorities. Those who know a homosexual and/or recognize that homosexuality is a status, rather than a choice, are much more accepting than those who know no homosexuals or who view homosexuality as a choice. This split shapes attitudes on everything from homosexuals in the military to gay life in general, according to the New York Times/CBS News Poll conducted February 9–11, 1993.

In the March, 1993 issue of *The Atlantic* (see cover story on homosexuality and biology) the author states that "Today's psychiatrists and psychologists, with very few exceptions, do not try to change sexual orientation, and those aspiring to work in the fields of psychiatry and psychology are now trained not to regard homosexuality as a disease." He adds, "Five decades of psychiatric evidence demonstrates that homosexuality is immutable, and non-pathological, and a growing body of more recent evidence implicates biology in the development of sexual orientation." Further, he says, "Homosexuals have long maintained that sexual orientation, far from being a personal choice, is something neither chosen nor changeable; heterosexuals who have made their peace with homosexuals have often done so by accepting that premise." Just as there is nothing to suggest that heterosexuals can change into homosexuals, there is no scientific evidence that homosexuality can be changed. While we can't change our sexual orientation, we can change our attitudes about homosexuality.

We hope that you have learned much about gay and straight individuals as you read the moving, real-life histories presented within these pages. We have written this book to help people bridge the divide between gay and straight. We hope that as you read the stories of these ordinary and courageous human beings that you too have found the bridge—the acceptance—that brings people together rather than separates or tears them apart.

You read how it was possible to dramatically change one's attitudes when you read stories like Vince's and his encounters with "Homer the Homo Man," or Art's and his relationship with his son, or Luann's and her life as a fundamentalist. All three moved from a place of judgment or bias to a place of acceptance and love. These were just three of the many stories that can help you move along your path to acceptance and enrich your life at home, in your community, at work, and in church.

THE NEXT STEP: WRITING YOUR LIFE HISTORY

For each of our storytellers, telling or writing their life history became an important part of their road to acceptance. Each of us had the opportunity to contemplate more fully the roles that our childhood experiences, our families, and society played in the development of our attitudes and beliefs about sexual orientation and our own expressions of sexuality. Taking the time to write your own life history can be a very significant and useful approach to further progress along the path to acceptance. We encourage you to use the stories in this book as a model for writing your own life history focusing on beliefs and experiences around homosexuality. Follow these three steps:

1. **Note what you learned about homosexuality when you were young.**
2. **Tell how you came to terms with either being a homosexual or the homosexuality of others.**
3. **Write how you live your life as either an openly gay person or as someone openly accepting of the homosexuality of others.**

In writing your life history you may find it beneficial to review your comments and reactions to the various stories. In addition, the following questions may help guide you:

- *Where were you born, and how do your childhood experiences relate to your attitudes about sexuality in general (e.g., cultural and religious upbringing)?*

- *When did you first hear about homosexuality? What was said and who said it? How did it make you feel?*

- *What do you recall as your first contact with a gay person? What feelings do you remember from that experience?*

- *When was your first sexual experience and what feelings are associated with it?*

- *How do you feel about your own sexuality today?*

- *If you have friends or relatives who are lesbian, gay, bisexual, or transgender—how has your relationship developed? If you knew them before they were "out" to you how did you initially respond to their sexual orientation, and how has your relationship changed since then?*

- *How did and how does your family deal with sexuality issues?*

■ *What issues do you feel comfortable with in talking about sexuality and where do you see yourself experiencing discomfort? What do you think would help you become more comfortable?*

6

Using Resources
Tools for the Trip

This chapter provides an array of resources to help you effectively relate to and to create a supportive and inclusive community.

We encourage you to fully use the resources in this chapter. This may involve taking new risks and stretching yourself. For example, you may feel embarrassed about calling a gay group on the phone. However, by doing so, you increase the likelihood of feeling more comfortable when you next talk with a gay relative or friend. You also open yourself to the possibility of discovering new and exciting information about the world that we all share.

The resources in this section include the following lists:

■ **Family and Friends Organizations: International, national and U.S. state offices of Parents, Families, and Friends of Lesbians and Gays (PFLAG).**

■ **Community Organizations: Community service organizations and health-related organizations that provide information and help in areas related to sexual orientation.**

■ **Business Organizations: Gay, lesbian, and bisexual business organizations throughout the English-speaking world (Australia, Canada, Great Britain, and the United States).**

■ **Religious and Spiritual Organizations: Religious and spiritual organizations with a specific focus on gay and lesbian issues.**

■ **Recommended Books: Books related to the above categories**

on such topics as gay and lesbian history, physical and
mental health issues, gay and lesbian parenting, aging, and
AIDS.

These resources will help you to stay current and effectively relate to
new developments in the various issues we've touched on in this book.

FAMILY AND FRIENDS' ORGANIZATIONS

Parents, Families, and Friends of Lesbians and Gays (PFLAG)

PFLAG provides a network of individuals and chapters that offer support
and information to family members and friends of lesbians and gays. Their
mission statement is the following:

> Parents, Families and Friends of Lesbians and Gays promotes
> the health and well-being of gay, lesbian, and bisexual per-
> sons, their families, and friends through: support, to cope with
> an adverse society; education, to enlighten an ill-informed
> public; and advocacy, to end discrimination and to secure
> equal civil rights. Parents, Families and Friends of Lesbians
> and Gays provides opportunity to dialogue about sexual ori-
> entation, and acts to create a society that is healthy and
> respectful of human diversity.

International Offices

Parents, Families, and Friends
of Lesbians and Gays (PFLAG)
1101 14th Street NW, Suite 1030
Washington, D.C. 20005
Phone: (202) 638–4200
Fax: (202) 638-0243
E-mail   PFLAGNTL@AOL.COM

United States

■ **Alabama**
230 E. Samford #107
Auburn, AL 36830
(205) 826–2286

957 Church Street
Mobile, AL 36604
(205) 438–9381

■ **Alaska**
P.O. Box 203231
Anchorage, AK 99520
(907) 277–6888

3135 Forrest Drive
Fairbanks, AK 99709
(907) 479–4944

P.O. Box 2888
Fairbanks, AK 99645
(907) 746–1089

Arizona
805 Country Club
Kingman, AZ 86401
(602) 753–6493

P.O. Box 37525
Phoenix, AZ 85069
(602) 843–1404

920 E. Goodwin Street, A
Prescott, AZ 86303
(602) 445–7672

P.O. Box 36264
Tucson, AZ 85740
(602) 575–8660

Arkansas
P.O. Box 2897
Fayetteville, AR 72702
(501) 443–4159

600 North 6th, #8
Ft. Smith, AR 72901
(501) 784–9925

P.O. Box 251191
Little Rock, AR 72225
(501) 663–5233

California
2012 E. Street
Bakersfield, CA 93311
(805) 327–7010

555 Vallombrossa, #73
Chico, CA 95926
(916) 891–5718

211 West Foothill Blvd.
C/O M Church of Claremont
Claremont, CA 91711
(929) 624–6134

P.O. Box 21
Concord, CA 94522
(510) 685–6119

P.O. Box 27382
Fresno, CA 93729
(209) 292–7661

P.O. Box 3493
Hayward, CA 94544
(510) 782–5462

P.O. Box 1266
Healdsburg, CA 95448
(707) 431–8364

P.O. Box 485
Idyllwild, CA 92549
(909) 659–5110

P.O. Box 24565
Los Angeles, CA 90024
(310) 472–8952

5755 Dow's Prairie Road
McKinleyville, CA 95521
(707) 839–3984

P.O. Box 1626
Mill Valley, CA 94941
(415) 479–3535

P.O. Box 4311
Modesto, CA 95353
(209) 527–0776

P.O. Box 9052
Monterrey, CA 93942
(408) 655–3524

244 Pinyon Crest
Mt. Center, CA 92561
(619) 346–3228

100 Monte Cresta Avenue, #209
Oakland, CA 94611
(510) 547–4657

300 Cherry
Pasadena, CA 91105
(213) 225–3595

1452 Parkview Court
Pleasanton, CA 94566
(510) 846–0745

1 East Olive Avenue
Redlands, CA 92373
(909) 335–2005

3891 Ridge Road
Riverside, CA 92506
(909) 341–5755

P.O. Box 661855
Sacramento, CA 95866
(916) 722–0327

P.O. Box 82762
San Diego, CA 92138
(619) 579–7640

P.O. Box 640223
San Francisco, CA 94164
(415) 921–8850

P.O. Box 3313
San Luis Obispo, CA 93403
(805) 528–5770

P.O. Box 3315
San Ramon, CA 94583
(510) 829–8528

P.O. Box 28662
Santa Ana, CA 92799
(714) 997–8047

849 Almar, #C–222
Santa Cruz, CA 95267
(408) 662–4780

P.O. Box 77725
Stockton, CA 95267
(209) 476–1525

P.O. Box 2718
Sunnyvale, CA 94087
(408) 270–8182

25404 Via Macarena
Valencia, CA 91355
(805) 254–2177

P.O. Box 5401
Ventura, CA 93005

P.O. Box 94
Walnut Creek, CA 94597
(510) 933–4688

17801 County Road 97
Woodland, CA 95695
(916) 841–2842

Colorado

P.O. Box 1581
Alamosa, CO 81101
(719) 852–3188

P.O. Box 19696
Boulder, CO 80308
(303) 444–8164

P.O. Box 10076
Colorado Springs, CO 80917
(719) 575–8658

P.O. Box 18901
Denver, CO 80218
(303) 333–0286

P.O. Box 1350
Dillon, CO 80435
(303) 262–0609

c/o Betsy Stephens
203 West 22nd Street
Durango, CO 81301
(303) 247–7778

P.O. Box 1349
Estes Park, CO 80517
(303) 586–0941

P.O. Box 265
Evergreen, CO 80439
(303) 377–2266

P.O. Box 4904
Grand Junction, CO 81502
(303) 242–8965

P.O. Box 516
Hartsell, CO 80449
(719) 395–2544

P.O. Box 611
Longmont, CO 80502
(3030 772–1005

P.O. Box 4484
Pueblo, CO 81006
(719) 545–7426

Connecticut

P.O. Box 752
Coventry, CT 06238
(203) 742–9548

66 Bower Road
Madison, CT 06443
(203) 453–3895

600 Prospect Street, H8
New Haven, CT 06511
(203) 782–9466

49 Beechwood Lane
S. Glastonbury, CT 06073
(203) 633–7184

c/o Diane L. S. Hewat
P.O. Box 278
Salisbury, CT 06068
(203) 435–2738

P.O. Box 16703
Stamford, CT 06905
(203) 544–8724

Delaware

P.O. Box 26049
Wilmington, DE 19899
(302) 654–2995

District of Columbia
P.O. Box 28009
Washington, D.C. 20038
(301) 439–FLAG

Florida
P.O. Box 12267
Brooksville, FL 34614
(904) 796–4038

8747 SW 52nd Street
Cooper City, FL 33328
(305) 434–2993

7652 Mansfield Hollow
Delray Beach, FL 33446
(407) 272–1634

16530 Lake Tree Drive
Ft. Lauderdale, FL 33326
(305) 389–0378

5100–318 S. Cleveland Avenue,
#219
Ft. Myers, FL 33907
(813) 481–6270

P.O. Box 140176
Gainesville, FL 32606
(904) 377–8131

3820 La Vista Circle, #116
Jacksonville, FL 32217
(904) 448–6885

519 Cresap Street
Lakeland, FL 33801
(813) 683–5204

No Public Address
Miami, FL 33143
(305) 666–0770

199 N. Timberland Drive
New Smyrna Beach, FL 32168
(904) 423–9103

P.O. Box 141312
Orlando, FL 32814
(407) 236–9177

P.O. Box 34479
Pensacola, FL 32507
(904) 492–0742

1932 Woodring Road
Sanibel, FL 33957
(813) 472–5484

P.O. Box 7382
Sarasota, FL 34278
(813) 378–3536

16301 Sonsoles Drive
Tampa, FL 33613
(813) 961–6684

P.O. Box 327
Venice, FL 34284
(813) 497–1806

181 Springline Drive
Vero Beach, FL 32963
(407) 231–3675

Georgia
P.O. Box 8482
Atlanta, GA 31106
(404) 875–9440

P.O. Box 7304
Macon, GA 31209
(912) 745–2671

Hawaii

2085 Ala Wai Blvd. Twin Towers
#16–3
Honolulu, HI 96815

74–5615 Luhia Street, D–2
Kailua-Kona, HI 96740
(808) 329–1116

Idaho

3773 Cayga Place
Boise, ID 83709
(2088) 362–5316

1415 Filmore
Caldwell, ID 83605
(208) 459–9535

Route 2, Box 488
Mountain Home, ID 83647
(208) 587–5497

1434 Pole Line Road East
Twin Falls, ID 83301
(208) 733–2578

Illinois

505 Orchard Drive
Carbondale, IL 62901
(618) 457–5479

P.O. Box 11023
Chicago, IL 60611
(312) 472–3079

114 Westridge
Collinsville, IL 62234
(618) 344–7765

112 East Taylor Street
Dekalb, IL 60115
(815) 758–8512

P.O. Box 105
Downer's Grove, IL 60115
(708) 968–9060

3732 40th Street Court
Moline, IL 61265
(309) 797–7986

57 Vindale Drive
Sprngfield, IL 62703
(217) 529–4295

Indiana

P.O. Box 8152
Bloomington, IN 47407
(812) 339–7657

P.O. Box 113
Evansville, IN 47701
(812) 422–3269

5042 Stellhorn
Fort Wayne, IN 46815
(219) 486–2201

P.O. Box 441633
Indianapolis, IN 46244
(317) 644–3570

110 Windhorst Court
Seymour, IN 47274
(812) 522–9515

P.O. Box 4195
South Bend, IN 46634
(219) 277–2684

135 Aikman Place
Terre Haute, IN 47803
(812) 232–5188

Iowa

1216 Scott Avenue
Ames, IA 50010
(515) 292–2610

c/o Darlene McKee
514 West 4th Street
Cedar Falls, IA 50613
(319) 234–6531

P.O. Box 136
Garnavillo, IA 52049
(319) 964–2148

1002 South Elm Street
Shenandoah, IA 51601
(712) 246–2824

1730 Elon Drive
Waterville, IA
52170
(319) 535–7680

c/o Laren Lane
804 15th Street
West Des Moines, IA 50265
(515) 274–3809

Kansas

2910 Country Lane
Hays, KS 67602
(913) 625–6937

P.O. Box 364
Lindsborg, KS 67456
(913) 227–3276

P.O. Box 686
Wichita, KS 67201
(316) 687–4666

Kentucky

2814 North Mill Avenue
Bowling Green, KY 42104
(502) 782–0566

P.O. Box 55484
Lexington, KY 40555
(606) 272–7075

P.O. Box 5002
Louisville, KY 40255
(502) 451–3396

2942 Clay Street
Paducah, KY 42001
(502) 442–7972

Louisiana

P.O. Box 65398
Baton Rouge, LA 70896
(504) 766–8452

P.O. Box 31078
Lafayette, LA 70593
(318) 984–2216

P.O. Box 15515
New Orleans, LA 70175
(504) 895–3936

P.O. Box 8931
Shreveport, LA 71148
(318) 687–4577

Maine

124 Chruch Street
Brewer, ME 04412
(207) 989–5180

23 Winthrop Street
Holloweli, ME 04347
(207) 623–2349

6 Lemieux Street
Lewiston, ME 04347
(207) 783–9798

P.O. Box 8742
Portland, ME 04104
(207) 766–5158

P.O. Box O
Waldoboro, ME 04572
(207) 832–5859

■ **Maryland**
P.O. Box 5637
Baltimore, MD 21210
(41) 433–FLAG

7303 Swan Point Way
Columbia, MD 21045
(410) 290–8292

P.O. Box 171
Stevensville, MD 21666
(410) 643–3235

■ **Massachusetts**
P.O. Box 2025
Amherst, MA 01004
(413) 256–4928

20 School Street
Gardner, MA 01440
(508) 632–5186

510 Main Street
Hingham, MA 02043
(617) 749–7730

29 Stringer Avenue
Lee, MA 01238
(413) 243–2382

P.O. Box 1167
Orleans, MA 02653
(508) 240–2737

P.O. Box 187
Stoughton, MA 02072

P.O. Box 344
Stow, MA 01775
(508) 562–5807

P.O. Box 44–4
W. Somerville, MA 02144
(617) 547–2440

P.O. Box 625
W. Springfield, MA 01089
(413) 789–4330

22 Caroline Street
Wellesley, MA 02181
(508) 562–5807

P.O. Box 839
West Falmouth, MA 02574
(508) 540–2356

6 Institution Road
c/o United Congregational
Worcester, MA 01609
(508) 752–3705

■ **Michigan**
P.O. Box 7471
Ann Arbor, MI 48107
(313) 741–0659

P.O. Box 834
Bay City, MI 48707
(517) 893–2475

P.O. Box 90722
Burton, MI 48509
(810) 631–4910

3500 Kane Road
Carleton, MI 48117
(313) 654–6090

P.O. Box 145
Farmington, MI 48332
(810) 478–8408

P.O. Box 6226
Grand Rapids, MI 49506
(616) 285–9133

305 West B Street
Iron Mountain, MI 49801
(906) 774–1343

P.O. Box 4065
Jackson, MI 49204
(517) 787–5442

P.O. Box 272
Mt. Pleasant, MI 48804
(517) 772–1110

Box 35
Okemos, MI 48805
(517) 349–3612

P.O. Box 611866
Port Huron, MI 48601
(810) 987–7527

P.O. Box 1291
Portage, MI 49801
(616) 327–8107

1330 East Three Mile Road
Sault Ste. Marie, MI 49783
(906) 632–6339

229 1/2 W. Fifteenth Street
Traverse City, MI 49684

■ **Minnesota**
612 First Bank Place
Duluth, MN 55802
(218) 722–8633

714 Valley View Road
Faribault, MN 55021
(507) 334–6361

12556 E. Lake Miltona Dr. NE
Miltona, MN 56354
(218) 943–1431

P.O. Box 8588
Minneapolis, MN 55408
(612) 458–3240

5048 Ebel Way
Northfield, MN 55057
(507) 645–6453

2205 Elton Hills Drive NW
Rochester, MN 55901
(507) 282–0484

402 8th Avenue South
St. Cloud, MN 56302
(612) 259–4238

■ **Mississippi**
No public address
Jackson, MS 39211
(601) 956–4953

Missouri
P.O. Box 414101
Kansas City, MO 64141
(816) 765–9818

St Louis (see Collinsville, IL)

Montana
P.O. Box 4815
Butte, MT 59702
(406) 723–7251

5110 Hoblitt Lane
Florence, MT 59833
(406) 777–2526

P.O. Box 6416
Great Falls, MT 59406
(406) 453–8989

38 Sloway West
St. Regis, MT 59866
(406) 822–3352

Nebraska
P.O. Box 833
Fullerton, NE 68638
(308) 536–2521

721 North Hastings
Hastings, NE 68901
(402) 461–7372

P.O. Box 427
Hendley, NE 68946
(308) 265–7620

1320 8th Avenue
Holdrege, NE 68949
(308) 995–5490

P.O. Box 4374
Lincoln, NE 68505
(402) 467–4599

2912 Lynnwood Drive
Omaha, NE 68123
(402) 291–6781

Nevada
1190 Sharrow Way
Carson City, NV 89703
(702) 883–9221

P.O. Box 20145
Las Vegas, NV 89112
(702) 438–7838

1685 Whitewood Drive
Sparks, NV 89434
(702) 358–4874

New Hampshire
158 Liberty Hill Road
Bedford, NH 03110
(603) 623–6023

18 Hobbs Road
Kensington, NH 03833
(603) 623–6023

P.O. Box 981
Lebanon, NH 03766
(603) 623–6023

P.O. Box 386
Manchester, NH 03105
(603) 623–6023

26 Deerwood Drive
Nashua, NH 03063
(603) 623–6023

Willard Farm Road
New Ipswich, NH 03701
(603) 623–6023

■ New Jersey
P.O. Box 1542
Asbury Park, NJ 07712
(908) 905–6823

P.O. Box 244
Belleville, NJ 07109
(201) 267–8414

103 Dover Avenue
Mays Landing, NJ 08330
(609) 653–6337

44 Kira Lane
Ridgewood, NJ 07450
(201) 652–2287

■ New Mexico
1907 Buena Vista SE, #5
Albuquerque, NM 87106
(505) 842–5281

P.O. Box 16498
Santa Fe, NM 87506
(505) 988–9708

P.O. Box 3550
Taos, NM 87571
(505) 758–8133

■ New York
P.O. Box 12531
Albany, NY 12212
(518) 482–3724

P.O. Box 728
Westview Station
Binghampton, NY 13905
(607) 729–5616

7304 5th Avenue, # 307
Brooklyn, NY 11209
(718) 680–1418

P.O. Box 861
Buffalo, NY 14225
(716) 883–0384

109 Browns Road
Huntington, NY 11743
(516) 938–8913

414 Palmer Street
Jamestown, NY 14701
(716) 488–1264

3 Leatherstocking Lane
Mamaroneck, NY 10543
(914) 698–3619

P.O. Box 553
Lenox Hill Station
New York, NY 10021
(212) 463–0629

65 Lark Street
Pearl River, NY 10965
(914) 735–8968

P.O. Box 880
Pleasant Valley, NY 12569
(914) 473–1500

179 Atlantic Avenue
Rochester, NY 14607
(716) 865–0120

31 Lincoln Mall
Schenectady, NY 12309
(518) 372–1111

232 East Onondaga Street
Syracuse, NY 13202
(315) 635–9054

423 Firoe Drive
Utica, NY 13502
(315) 733–0634

P.O. Box 24
Willeysville, NY 13864
(607) 277–1843

■ **North Carolina**
All Souls Parish, Box 5978
3 Angle Street
Asheville, NC 28813
(704) 277–7815

Route 5, Box 549–A
Boone, NC 28607
(704) 264–4109

5815 Charing Place
Charlotte, NC 28211
(704) 634–1474

P.O. Box 722
Dallas, NC 28034
(704) 922–9273

Route 2, Box 105–L
Flat Rock, NC 28731
(704) 696–8250

P.O. Box 10844
Raleigh, NC 27605
(919) 380–9325

P.O. Box 15477
Winston-Salem, NC 27103
(919) 723–6345

■ **North Dakota**
P.O. Box 2491
Bismarck, ND 58502
(701) 223–7773

1709 6th Avenue
South Fargo, ND 58103
(701) 232–8631

3210 Cherry
Grand Forks, ND 58501
(701) 775–4447

■ **Ohio**
730 Park Avenue
Amherst, OH 44001
(216) 988–8215

1710 Walnut Boulevard
Ashtabula, OH 44004
(216) 964–3350

P.O. Box 19634
Cincinnati, OH 45219
(513) 721–7900

P.O. Box 340101
Columbus, OH 43234
(614) 227–9355

P.O. Box 3204
Cuyahoga Falls, OH 44223
(216) 923–1883

P.O. Box 45
Greenville, OH 45331
(513) 548–6730

40011 Carpenter Hill Road
Pomeroy, OH 45769
(614) 698–2120

11 Offnere Street
Portsmouth, OH 45662
(614) 353–1856

14260 Larchmere Boulevard
Shaker Heights, OH 44120
(216) 321–7413

1719 Greenwood
Toledo, OH 43605
(419) 691–2325

175 Park Meadows Drive
Yellow Springs, OH 45387
(513) 767–1672

2201 Goleta Avenue
Youngstown, OH 44504
(216) 742–8796

■ **Oklahoma**
2816 N. Ann Arbor Avenue
Oklahoma City, OK 73127
(405) 948–6084

P.O. Box 52800
Tulsa, OK 74152
(918) 749–4901

■ **Oregon**
P.O. Box 13
Ashland, OR 97520
(503) 482–4017

535 9th Street, #A12
Pine Valley Apartments
Bandon, OR 97411
(503) 347–9306

1937 N.W. West Hills Avenue
Bend, OR 97701
(503) 382–7947

1687 N.W. Division Street
Corvallis, OR 97330
(503) 752–6248

P.O. Box 11137
Eugene, OR 97440
(503) 689–1630

P.O. Box 655
Garibaldi, OR 97118
(503) 322–0311

P.O. Box 121
Gates, OR 97346
(503) 378–7698

P.O. Box 321
Hood River, OR 97601
(503) 386–3108

2306 Marina Drive
Klamath Falls, OR 97601
(503) 882–3309

P.O. Box 2995
La Grande, OR 97850
(503) 963–8199

P.O. Box 1156
Newport, OR 97365
(503) 265–6368

450 Bar-O Drive
Ontario, OR 97914
(503) 889–5774

1805 Southgate
Pendleton, OR 97801
(503) 276–1074

P.O. Box 8944
Portland, OR 97297
(503) 232–7676

1567 N.W. Lester Street
Roseburg, OR 97470
(503) 673–8470

P.O. Box 555
Wilderville, OR 97543
(503) 476–4155

P.O. Box 522
Yachats, OR 97498
(503) 547–3435

▓ **Pennsylvania**
3667 Mechanicsville Road
Bensalem, PA 19030
(215) 572–1833

7430 Nyesville Road
Chambersburg, PA 17201
(717) 264–8345

1191 Treasure Lake
DuBois, PA 15801
(814) 371–8962

2030 Lehigh Street, #710
Easton, PA 18042
(610) 258–4794

1106 Oregon
Erie, PA 16505
(814) 838–6020

107 Butler Street
Forty Fort, PA 18704
(717) 287–8504

3641 Brookridge Terrace, #201
Harrisburg, PA 17109
(717) 657–1712

Lutheran Social Ministeries
797 Goucher Street
Johnstown, PA 15905
(814) 255–7169

2112–13 Stone Mill Road
Lancaster, PA 17603
(717) 392–3372

P.O. Box 223
Monroeville, PA 15146
(412) 372–4059

Lutheran Social Services
1050 Pennsylvania Avenue
York, PA 17404
(717) 843–3793

▓ **Rhode Island**
No public address
Narragansett, RI 02882
(401) 789–5705

c/o Barbara Costa
85 Roseland Terrace
Tiverton, RI 02878
(401) 624–6944

▓ **South Carolina**
P.O. Box 30734
Charleston, SC 29417
(803) 856–0577

493 Hickory Hill Drive
Columbia, SC 29210
(803) 772–7396

801 Butler Springs Road
Greenville, SC 29615
(803) 244–6675

South Dakota
Route 3, Box 94
Custer, SD 57730
(605) 673–4182

300 North Duluth
Sioux Falls, SD 57104
(605) 334–5508

Tennessee
P.O. Box 17252
Chattanooga, TN 37415
(615) 875–5750

1303 Calais Road
Memphis, TN 38120
(901) 761–1444

135 Holly Forest
Nashville, TN 37221
(615) 662–0332

Texas
P.O. Box 9151
Austin, TX 78766
(512) 302–FLAG

P.O. Box 38415
Dallas, TX 75238
(214) 348–1704

P.O. Box 51096
Denton, TX 76206
(817) 387–1491

P.O. Box 1761
El Paso, TX 79949
(915) 591–4664

P.O. Box 48612
Forth Worth, TX 76148
(817) 498–5607

P.O. Box 692444
Houston, TX 77269
(713) 867–9020

2741 N. Muskigum
Odessa, TX 79762
(915) 362–4252

P.O. Box 790093
San Antonio, TX 78279
(210) 351–0395

P.O. Box 23533
Waco, TX 76702
(817) 750–7211

Utah
3363 Enchanted Hills Drive
Salt Lake City, UT 84121
(801) 942–0157

Vermont
409 Hillwinds
Brattleboro, VT 05301
(802) 257–5409

23 Birchwood Lane
Burlington, VT 05401
(802) 863–4285

15 Vine Street
Northfield, VT 05663
(802) 479–9246

11 North Street
Rutland, VT 05701
(802) 773–7601

■ **Virginia**
301 Monte Vista Avenue
Charlottesville, VA 22903
(804) 296–9240

P.O. Box 607
Dayton, VA 22821
(703) 879–9646

12 Lakeshore Terrace
Hardy, VA 24101
(703) 890–3957

3 Maple Lane
Lexington, VA 24450
(703) 463–8645

567 Wisteria Drive
Radford, VA 24141
(703) 639–5881

P.O. Box 36392
Richmond, VA 23235
(804) 744–9016

■ **Washington**
2220 2nd Avenue
Clarkston, WA 99403
(509) 758–6437

618 Monumental Road
North Star Farm
Colville, WA 99114
(509) 684–4418

1106 E. Third Avenue
Ellensburg, WA 98926
(509) 925–5594

165 D Street SW
Ephrata, WA 98823
(509) 754–4776

217 Orchard Street
Leavenworth, WA 98826
(509) 548–7911

P.O. Box 6123
Olympia, WA 98502
(206) 866–0511

648 Saint Street
Richland, WA 99352
(509) 735–4643

1202 E. Pike Street, Suite 620
Seattle, WA 98122
(206) 325–7724

2880 N.E. 72nd Street
Silverdale, WA 98383
(206) 692–7029

P.O. Box 40122
Spokane, WA 99202
(509) 489–2266

12102 N.W. 21st Avenue
Vancouver, WA 98685
(206) 693–1476

732 Summitview, #584
Yakima, WA 98902
(509) 576–9625

■ **West Virginia**
550 Second Street, #3
Huntington, WV 25701
(304) 522–3328

1610 Park Street
Parkersburg, WV 26101
(304) 422–5528

115 18th Street
Wheeling, WV 26003
(304) 232–8743

502 1/2 Columbia Avenue
Williamstown, WV 26181
(304) 375–6412

■ **Wisconsin**
Box 399
Galesville, WI 54630
(608) 582–2114

P.O. Box 75
Little Chute, WI 54140
(414) 499–7080

P.O. Box 1722
Madison, WI 53711
(608) 271–0270

50 North John Paul Road
Milton, WI 53563
(608) 868–3291

c/o Lutheran Campus Ministries
3074 North Maryland
Milwaukee, WI 53211
(414) 962–9320

831 Union Avenue
Sheboygan, WI 53801
(414) 458–4889

■ **Wyoming**
404 South McKinley
Casper, WY 82601
(307) 265–6569

P.O. Box 2704
Jackson, WY 83001
(307) 733–0584

518 9th Street
Rawlins, WY 82301
(307) 324–5488

Canada

■ **Alberta**
51 Beacon Cres.
St. Albert, Alberta T8N 0A2
(403) 462–5958

■ **British Columbia**
POB 30502, Brentwood Post
201–4567 Lougheed Highway
Burnaby, BC V5C 2A0
(604) 255–4429

P.O. Box 1477
Oliver, BC V0H 1T0
(604) 498–6520

5635 Moriarity Crescent
Prince George, BC V2N 3P7
(604) 964–6753

P.O. Box 5474 Station B
Victoria, BC V8R 6S4
(604) 642–5171

■ **Manitoba**
20 Fort Street, #541
Winnipeg, MB R3C 4L3
(204) 947–3060

New Brunswick
P.O. Box 249
Sackville, NB T8N 0A2
(506) 364–2556

Ontario
35 Willis Drive
Brampton, Ontario L6W 1B2
(905) 457–4570

P.O. Box 1751
Kingston, Ontario V5C 2A0
(604) 255–4429

3266 Yonge Street, Post Office
Box 2020
Toronto, Ontario M4S 2N4
(416) 322–0600

Quebec
12 A Radcliffe Road
Montreal West P.Q. H4X 1B9
(514) 488–4608

Australia

49 Darcey Road
Castle Hill NSW 2154
61–2–3602211

P.O. Box 354
Northbridge, W. Australia 6865
61–9–313–1484

United Kingdom

c/o V.A. Leeds, Stringer House
34 Lupton Street
Leeds, LS10 2QW
0532–577523

Israel

c/o Dvora Luz
34 Hanadiv Street 46
485 Herzlia
09–587779

COMMUNITY ORGANIZATIONS

Many community organizations throughout the United States and Canada offer resources that may be useful to you. These resources include educational and social materials and information primarily about the local gay community. In addition, these organizations generally provide referrals for psycho-social support for gays and heterosexuals dealing with this issue on a personal or professional level, and may have an organized speakers' bureau, as well as providing other forms of support and education.

The following is a list of non-profit community organizations. The list includes organizations in the United States and Canada. In areas where there is no listing, refer to your local phone directory or check to see if there is a gay, lesbian, or bisexual student organization on a nearby university campus. Many smaller communities and most universities have such organizations. In some cases, groups in certain areas of the country (for safety and other reasons) do not use the words "gay or lesbian" in their names. Instead, they use words related to the gay community such as "Lambda," "Pride" or "Triangle." These community organizations are volunteer groups and, as such, they undergo frequent changes. If you have difficulty in locating an organization in your community, check to see if there is a listing for a Gay and Lesbian Switchboard in your local phone book or call the National Gay and Lesbian Task Force (202–332–6483). They should be able to connect you to the community organization nearest to you.

United States

National

National Gay/Lesbian Task Force
2320 17th Street N.W.
Washington D.C. 20009
(202) 332–6483

Human Rights Campaign Fund
P.O. Box 1396
Washington, D.C. 20013
(202) 628–4160

The NAMES Project Foundation
310 Townsend St., Suite 310
San Francisco, CA 94107
(415) 882–5500
(*Sponsors the AIDS Memorial Quilt, a quilt composed of tens of thousands handmade panel honoring people who have died of AIDS.*)

State

Alabama
Lambda Resource Center
205 32nd Street, S.
Birmingham, AL 35255
(205) 326–8600

Alaska
Identity, Inc.
P.O. Box 200070
Anchorage, AK 99520
(907) 258–4777

Arizona
Lesbian/Gay Community Line
P.O. Box 16423
Phoenix, AZ 85011
(602) 234–2752

Arkansas
Arkansas Gay and Lesbian
Switchboard
P.O. Box 45053
Little Rock, AR 72214
(501) 375–5504
(800) 448–8305 (in AR only)

California
Gay and Lesbian Community
Services Center
1625 Schrader
Los Angeles, CA 90028
(213) 993–7430 (ask for community outreach)

Lesbian and Gay Men's
Community Center
P.O. Box 3357
3916 Normal Street

San Diego, CA 92163
(619) 692–2077 ext. 820
(Common Ground/Outreach
Services)

■ **Colorado**
Gay and Lesbian Community
Center of Colorado, Inc.
1245 E. Colfax #125
Denver, CO 80218
(303) 831–6268

■ **Connecticut**
Gay, Lesbian and Bisexual
Community Center
1841 Broad Street
Hartford, CT 06114
(203) 724–5542

■ **Delaware**
Griffin Community Center
214 Market St.
Wilmington, DE 19801
(no phone)

■ **District of Columbia**
One in Ten
1555 Connecticut Ave., NW
Suite 200
Washington, D.C. 20036
(202) 986–1119

■ **Florida**
Gay and Lesbian Community
Center
P.O. Box 4567
Ft. Lauderdale, FL 33304
(305) 563–9500

Gay and Lesbian Community
Services of Central Florida
P.O. Box 533446

Orlando, FL 32583
(407) 843–4297

■ **Georgia**
Atlanta Gay Center
63 12th Street
Atlanta, GA 30309
(404) 876–5372

■ **Hawaii**
Gay Community Center
1820 University Avenue, 2nd
Floor
Honolulu, HI 96801
(808) 951–7000

■ **Idaho**
The Community Center
P.O. Box 323
Boise, ID 83701

■ **Illinois**
Horizons Community Services,
Inc.
961 W. Montana
Chicago, IL 60614
(312) 472–6469

■ **Indiana**
Justice
P.O. Box 2387
Indianapolis, IN 46206
(317) 920–1330

■ **Iowa**
Gay and Lesbian Resource
Center
4211 Grand Avenue
Des Moines, IA 50312
(515) 281–0634

Kansas
Gay and Lesbian Services of
Kansas
Box 13 Kansas Union
University of Kansas
Lawrence, KS 55045
(913) 864–3091

Kentucky
Williams-Nichols Institute
P.O. Box 4264
Louisville, KY 40204
(502) 636–0935

Louisiana
Lesbian/Gay Community Center
816 N. Rampart
New Orleans, LA 70116
(504) 522–1103

Maine
Queer Alliance
88 Winslow Street
Portland, ME 04103
(207) 874–6596

Maryland
Gay and Lesbian Community
Center
241 W. Chase Street
Baltimore, MD 21201
(410) 837–5445

Massachusetts
Bisexual Community Resource
Services
95 Berkeley St., Suite 613
Boston, MA 02116
(617) 338–9595

Michigan
Affirmations Lesbian and Gay
Community Center
195 W. 9 Mile Road, Suite 106
Ferndale, MI 48220
(810) 398–7105

Minnesota
Gay and Lesbian Community
Action Council
310 E. 38th Street #204
Minneapolis, MN 55409
(612) 822–0127

Mississippi
G.L. Friendly, Inc. Community
Center
311 Caillavet ST.
Biloxi, MS 39530
(601) 435–2398

Missouri
Gay Services Network
P.O. Box 32592
Kansas City, MO 64111
(816) 931–4470

Challenge Metro
P.O. Box 23227
St. Louis, MO 63156
(314) 367–0084

Montana
Lambda Alliance of Bisexuals,
Lesbians and Gay Men
(406) 994–4551

Nebraska
Angle Gay/Lesbian Information
and Referral Line
P.O. Box 8343
Omaha, NE 68108
(402) 558–5303

Nevada
Gay and Lesbian Community
Center of Las Vegas
P.O. Box 60301
Las Vegas, NV 89160
(702) 733–9800

New Hampshire
26 S. Main St. Box 181
Concord, NH 03301
(603) 224–1686

New Jersey
New Jersey Lesbian and Gay
Coalition
P.O. Box 1431
New Brunswick, NJ 08903
(908) 828–6772

New Mexico
Common Bond Gay and Lesbian
Information
P.O. Box 26836
Albuquerque, NM 87125
(505) 266–8041

New York
Lesbian and Gay Community
Center
208 W. 13th Street
New York, NY 10011
(212) 620–7310

North Carolina
Our Own Place
P.O. Box 11732
Durham, NC 27703
(919) 821–0055 (Gay/Lesbian
Helpline of Wake County)

North Dakota
Praire Lesbian/Gay Community
PO Box 83
Moorhead, MN 56561
(701) 237–0556

University Gay/Lesbian
Community
Box 8055
University Station
Grand Forks, ND 58202
(701) 777–4321

Ohio
Greater Cincinnati Gay/Lesbian
Center
P.O. Box 19518
Cincinnati, OH 45219
(513) 651–0040

Stonewall Community Center
P.O. Box 10814
47 W. 5th Avenue
Columbus, OH 43201
(614) 299–7764

Lesbian and Gay Community
Center of Greater Cleveland
1418 W. 29th
Cleveland, OH 44113
(216) 522–1999

Oklahoma
Oasis Community Center
2135 N.W. 39th Street
Oklahoma City, OK 73112
(405) 525–2437

Oregon
Oregon Gay and Lesbian Cultural
Resource Center Task Force
P.O. Box 6012
Portland, OR 97228
(503) 283–1811 (NGLTF Task
Force)

Pennsylvania
Gay and Lesbian Community
Center of Pittsburgh
P.O. Box 5441
2214 E. Carson Street
Pittsburgh, PA 15206
(412) 422–0114

Rhode Island
Gay/Lesbian Hotline of Rhode
Island
P.O. Box 5671
Providence, RI 02903
(401) 751–3322

Lesbian/Gay & Bisexual Alliance
P.O. Box 1930
SAO Brown University
Providence, RI 02912
(401) 863–3062

Network of Rhode Island
P.O. Box 1474
Pawtucket, RI 02862–1474

Rhode Islande Alliance for
Lesbian, Gay and Bisexual Civil
Rights
P.O. Box 5558
Weybosset Hill Stn.
Providence, RI 02903

South Carolina
South Carolina Gay and Lesbian
Pride Movement, Inc.
1108 Woodrow St.
Columbia, SC 29211
(803) 771–7713

South Dakota
The Coalition
P.O. Box 89803
Sioux Falls, SD 89803
(605) 333–0603

Tennessee
Memphis Gay and Lesbian
Community Center
1486 Madison Avenue
Memphis, TN 38104
(901) 726–5790

Texas
Gay/Lesbian Community Alliance
2701 Reagan
Dallas, TX 75219
(214) 528–4233

Utah
Utah Stonewall Center
770 South 300 West
Salt Lake City, UT 84101
(801) 539–8800

Vermont
Vermont Coalition of Lesbians
and Gay Men
P.O. Box 1125
Montpelier, VT 05602

Virginia
Triangle Services Center
P.O. Box 11471
Norfolk, VA 23517
(no phone)
also see D.C. listing

Washington
Seattle Commission on Gays and
Lesbians
Office of Women's Rights
700 Third Ave., Suite 220
Seattle, WA 98104
(206) 684–0390

West Virginia
West Virginia Coalition for
Lesbian and Gay Rights
P.O. Box 11033
Charleston, WV 25339
(304) 965–3187

Wisconsin
The United
P.O. Box 310
Madison, WI 53701
(608) 255–4297

Wyoming
United Gays/Lesbians of
Wyoming
P.O. Box 2037
Laramie, WY 82070
(307) 632–5362

Australia

Adelaide
Gay and Lesbian Community
Library
Darling House
64 Fullarton Street
Norwood
South Australia 5067

Albury
Central Network
P.O. Box 17 38
Albury
New South Wales 2640
(060) 53–2844

Canberra
Gayline
G.P.O. Box 229
Canberra
Austrailian Capital Territory 2601
(062) 247–2726

Hobart
Tasmanian Gay and Lesbian
Rights Group
G.P.O. Bos 1773
Hobart
Tasmania 7000
(002) 243–556

Launceston
Northern Link
P.O. Box 801
Launceston
Tasmania 7000
(002) 34–3254

Melbourne

ALSO Foundation
35 Cata Street
Pahran
Victoria

Newcastle

Newcastle Gay & Lesbian
Information Service
P.O. Box 425
Newcastle
New South Wales 2300
(049) 29–3464

Perth

Gay and Lesbian Equality
P.O. Box 912
Perth
Western Australia 6005

Sandy Bay

Gay & Lesbian Community
Centre
P.O. Box 818
Sandy Bay
Tasmania 7005
297–649

Sydney

Gay and Lesbian Rights Lobby
P.O. Box 9
Darlinghurst
Sydney
New South Wales 2010
(02) 360–6650

Pride: The Sydney Lesbian & Gay
Community Centre Ltd.
P.O. Box 7
Darlinghurst
New South Wales

Sydney Gay and Lesbian
Association
P.O. Box 394
Darlinghurst
New South Wales 2010
(02) 264–6233

Canada

Alberta

Gay and Lesbian Community
Center of Edmonton
P.O. Box 1852
Edmonton, AB TJ5 2P2
(403) 488–3234

British Columbia

Gay and Lesbian Centre
1170 Bute Street
Vancouver, BC V6E 1Z6
(604) 684–6869

Manitoba

Gay and Lesbian Resource
Center
P.O. Box 1661
Winnipeg, MB R3C 2Z6
(204) 284–5208

Ontario

Coalition for Lesbian and Gay
Rights in Ontario
P.O. Box 822 Station A
Toronto, ON M5W 1G3
(416) 533–6824

Ottawa

Centre 318
318 Lisgar St.
Ottawa
(613) 233–0152

Pink Triangle Services
71 Bank Street, #203
Ottawa
(613) 563–4818

Quebec
Centre Communautaire des
Gaies et Lesbiennes Montreal
CP 476 Succ. C
Montreal, QC H2L 4K4
(514) 990–1414

Winnipeg
Gay & Lesbian Resource Centre
1–222 Osborne Street S.
Winnipeg
(204) 284–5208

Israel

Society for the Protection of
Personal Rights (SPPR)
1 Carlozorof St.
Haifa
(04) 672–665

Society for the Protection of
Personal Rights (SPPR)
28 Nahmani St.
Tel Aviv
(03) 293681

New Zealand

Auckland
Auckland Gay & Lesbian
Community Centre
44–46 Ponsonby Rd.
1st Flr
Auckland
(09) 302 0590

Christchurch
Gaylink
P.O. Box 25–165
Chirstchurch
(03) 379–9493

Napier
Gay Community Trust/Centre
Parker Chamers
Herschell Street
P.O. Box 659, 2nd Flr
Napier
(06) 835–7190

Wellington
Lesbian & Gay Archives of New
Zealand
P.O. Box 116 95
Manners Street
Wellington
(04) 474–3000

South Africa

Johannesberg
Gay and Lesbian Hotline
Johannesberg
(011) 643–2311

Pretoria
Gay Community Centre
Schoemann St
Pretoria, SA
(012) 325–6664

United Kingdom

England
Campaign for Homosexual
Equality (CHE)
38 Mount Pleasent
London WC1X OAP
(0171) 833 39 12

Stonewall Lobby Group
2 Greycoat Place
London SW1P 1SB
222 90 07

■ Ireland
Hirschfield Center
10 Fownes St
Dublin
(01) 671 09 39

NIGRA (Northern Ireland Gay
Rights Association)
P.O. Box 44
8 Long Street
Belfast BT1 1SH
66 41 11

■ Scotland
Lesbian and Gay Community
Centre
58A Broughton Street
Edinburgh EH1 3SA
(031) 558 12 79

Glasgow Lesbian & Gay Centre
Project
P.O. Box 463
Glasgow G12 8PN
221 83 72

■ Wales
CYLCH
c/o Intervol
Shand Hose
2 Fitzalan Pl.
34 01 01
Wales

BUSINESS ORGANIZATIONS

Many major urban areas have assocations for gay and lesbian business professionals such as the Golden Gate Business Association of San Francisco, the Greater Seattle Business Association, and the Greater Gotham Business Council in New York City. In addition to providing networking and social activities for their members, these assocations also provide educational activities for businesses and corporations. They, often, are willing to provide speakers. Like many gay groups, these organizations are growing rapidly. To determine if there is a business organization in your area, check the following list or contact the community organization nearest you (see the following section on community organizations).

United States

■ Arizona
Camelback Business and
Professional Association
P.O. Box 2097
Phoenix, AZ 85001
(602) 225–8444

■ California
Bay Area Career Women
55 New Montgomery Street,
Suite 60
San Francisco, CA 94105
(415) 495–5393

East Bay Business & Professional
Alliance
PO Box 20980
Oakland, CA 94620
(510) 287–2571

Central California Alliance
835 N. Van Ness
Fresno, CA 93721(209)
441–1953

Central Coast Business and
Professional Association
P.O. Box 14433
San Luis Obispo, CA 93406
(805) 546–9394

Desert Business Association
P.O. Box 773
Palm Springs, CA 92263
(619) 234–0178

Gold Coast Business and
Professional Association
P.O. Box 7336
Ventura, CA 93006
(805) 388–1545

Golden Gate Business
Association, Inc.
1550 California Street, Suite 5L
San Francisco, CA 94109
(800) 303–GGBA Fax (415)
441–1123

Greater San Diego Business
Association
P.O. Box 33848
San Diego, CA 92163
(619) 296–4543

Greater Santa Barbara
Community Association
P.O. Box 90907
Santa Barbara, CA 93190
(805) 568–3995

Los Angeles Business and
Professional Association
P.O. Box 69982
West Hollywood, CA 90069
(213) 651–0888

Orange County Business and
Professional Association
P.O. Box 698
Laguna Beach, CA 92652
(714) 240–2035

San Diego Career Women
P.O. Box 880384
San Diego, CA 92168
(619) 552–0650

Valley Business Alliance
P.O. Box 57555
Sherman Oaks, CA 91413
(808) 982–2650

Colorado
Colorado Business Council
P.O. Box 480794
Denver, CO 80248
(303) 595–8042

Georgia
Atlanta Executive Network
P.O. Box 77267
Atlanta, GA 30357–1267
(404) 814–1418

Florida

Key West Business Guild
P.O. Box 1208
Key West, FL 33041
(305) 294–4603

South Beach Business Guild
718 Lincoln Rd.
Miami Beach, FL 33139
(305) 234–7224

Tampa Bay Business Guild
1222 S. Dale Mabry, #656
Tampa, FL 33629
(813) 237–3751

Illinois

Chicago Professional Networking
Chicago, IL
(312) 935–4561

Louisiana

Gay and Lesbian Business and
Professional Association
940 Royal, #350
New Orleans, LA 70116
(504) 271–0631

Massachusetts

Greater Boston Business Council
P.O. Box 1059
Boston, MA 02117–1059
(617) 236–4222

Michigan

Motor City Business Forum
29555 N. Western Highway,
Suite 516
Southfield, MI 48244
(810) 546–9347

Missouri

St. Louis Business Guild
P.O. Box 16822
St Louis, MO 63105
(no phone)

New York

Gay and Lesbian Business and
Professional Guild
P.O. Box 8392
White Plains, NY 10602–8392

Nevada

LAMBDA Business Association
1801 E. Tropicana, #9
Las Vegas, NV 89119
(702) 593–2875

New Mexico

Duke City Business and
Professional Association
P.O. Box 27207
Albuquerque, NM 97125
(no phone)

Ohio

Queen City Careers Association
Cincinatti, OH
(513) 381–5640

The Network
Cleveland, OH
(216) 932–2813

Oregon

Portland Area Business
Association
P.O. Box 4724
Portland, OR 97208
(503) 223–2984

Pennsylvania
Greater Philadelphia Professional
Network
Philadelphia, PA
(215) 336–9676

Greater Pittsburgh Professional
Men's Society
Pittsburgh, PA
(412) 231–5530

South Carolina
South Carolina Gay and Lesbian
Business Guild
SCGLBG
P.O. Box 7913
Columbia, SC 29202–7913
(803) 771–7713

Texas
Stonewall Professional League
P.O. Box 191343
Dallas, TX 75219
(214) 526–6216

Washington
Greater Seattle Business
Association
2033 6th Avenue, #804
Seattle, WA 98121
(206) 443–4722

Wisconsin
Cream City Business Association
7200 W. Center St.
Milwaukee, WI 53210
(no phone)

Australia

Free Business Association
P.O. Box 18

Paddington
Brisbane QLD 4064

Canada

British Colombia
Greater Vancouver Business
Association
204–1810 Alberni
Vancouver, BC V6G 1B3
(604) 669–0851

Gazebo Connection
810 W Broadway, #382
Vancouver, B.C.
(604) 438–5442

New Zealand

Gay Auckland Business
Association (GABA)
PO Box 3092
Auckland
(09) 376–3329

Lesbian and Gay Rights Resource
Center
PO Box 11–695
Wellington
(04) 474–3000 x 8754

United Kingdom

Gay Business Association
BMCGBA
London, WCIN 3XX
(081) 985–9700

Northwest Gay Business
Association
PO Box 20
Manchester, M60 1Q4

COMPANY-SPONSORED GROUPS

In addition to business associations, hundreds of companies like Boeing, Levi Strauss, Lotus, US West, Time-Warner, and Digital Equipment have company-sponsored gay and lesbian employee groups that provide resources within their own organizations and often share information with other companies. Many federal government organizations like the I.R.S. and the Department of Agriculture have similar associations—often called GLOBE for Gay, Lesbian or Bisexual Employees of the Federal Government. To find out if your company has a company-sponsored gay and lesbian employee group, contact your human resource or personnel department. If you wish to start a group in your company, contact the National Gay and Lesbian Task Force (NGLTF) Workplace Project at (202) 332–6483. If you would like to speak to employees within companies who are a part of a company-sponsored group, contact one of the following. They will be pleased to help you.

Sample Employee Organizations

AT&T League
Hotline (407) 662–3515
TTD Hotline (800) 855–2880

APPLE LAMBDA
20525 Mariani Avenue
Cupertino, CA 95014

AT&T League National Co-chairs

John Klenert
8403 Colesville Rd. Rm. 12SB36
Silver Spring, MD 20910–3314
(301) 608–4594

BEAGLES (Boeing Employee
Association of Gays and
Lesbians)
The Boeing Company
P.O. Box 1733
Renton, Washington 98057

Margaret Burd
11900 N. Pecos St. Rm.
30H–0181
Denver, CO 80234–2703
(303) 538–4430

EAGLE (Omaha)
Gay and Lesbian Organization of
USWEST
1314 Douglas, 8th Floor
Omaha, NE 68102

Federal GLOBE
P.O. Box 45237
Washington, D.C. 20026–5237
Leonard Hirsch, Chair
(202) 986–1101

EAGLE (Spokane)
Gay and Lesbian Organization of
USWEST
501 W. 2nd Avenue, Room 201
Spokane, WA 99204

GALAXE (Gay and Lesbian
Association of Xerox)
P.O. Box 25382
Rochester, NY 14625–0382

Gay and Lesbian Employees of
the Red Cross
1197 N. Decatur Rd. NE
Atlanta, GA 30306–2362

Gay and Lesbian Medical
Association
2940 16th Street #105
San Francisco, CA 94103

Gay and Lesbian United Airlines
Employees Coalition
2261 Market St., Suite 293
San Francisco, CA 94103

Gay, Lesbian and Bisexual
Employees of Ameritech
P.O. Box 14308
Chicago, IL 60614

Gay Officers Action League
P.O. Box 2038
Canal Street Station
New York, NY 10013

Gay Pilots Association
P.O. Box 1291
Alexandria, VA 22313

Gays and Lesbians in Foreign
Affairs
P.O. Box 18774
Washington, D.C. 20036–8774

GLEAM (Gay, Lesbian and
Bisexual Employees at Microsoft)
One Microsoft Way, Bldg 1–1
Redmond, Washington
98052–6399

GLOBAL (Gay and Lesbian
Organizations Bridging Across
the Land)
P.O. Box 42406
Philadelphia, PA 19101–2406

IGLOBE (Intel Gay, Lesbian or
Bisexual Employees)
Intel Corporation
5200 NE Elam-Young Parkway
Mail Stop HF–273
Hillsboro, OR 98107

Northwest GLEN (Gay and
Lesbian Employee Network)
830 19th Ave. NE
Seattle, WA 98122

Walt Disney League and Alliance
500 S. Buena Vista St.
Burbank, CA 91521

RELIGIOUS AND SPIRITUAL ORGANIZATIONS

Many religious and spiritual organizations offer support organizations for their lesbian, gay and bisexual members (e.g., Unitarian Universalists). In addition, a number of support groups have developed for gay and lesbian members of religious organizations that do not accept, or even actively condemn, such individuals (e.g., Dignity for Catholics, Affirmation for Mormons). These groups provide information, emotional support and other resources to individuals who are working to integrate both their sexual orientation and spiritual and religious experiences. These groups also provide resources and information, and in many cases, support groups, for family and friends of bisexuals, lesbians and gays. One organization, Metropolitan Community Church (MCC), directly serves the lesbian, gay and bisexual community with congregations throughout the world. Call the international offices of MCC in Los Angeles to find out about the congregation nearest to your home.

Universal Fellowship of Metropolitan Community Churches
5300 Santa Monica Blvd., #304
Los Angeles, California 90029
(213) 464–5100

In addition to MCC, the following organizations offer support to gays, lesbians and bisexuals and their families and friends for specific religions/spiritual organizations. Call for the location of the nearest local chapter.

Buddhist

Gay Men's Buddhist
Group/Lesbian Zen Group
928 S. New Hampshire
Los Angeles, CA 90006

Baptist

American Baptists Concerned
872 Erie St.
Oakland, CA 94610
(510) 465–8652

Catholic

Dignity U.S.A.
1500 Massachusetts Ave. N.W.,
Suite 11
Washington, D.C. 20005
(202) 861–0017

Christian Scientists

Emergence International:
Christian Scientists Supporting
Lesbians, Gay Men, and

Bisexuals
P.O. Box 6061–423
Sherman Oaks, CA 91413
(800) 280–6653

Episcopal

Integrity
P.O. Box 19561
Washington, D.C. 20036–0561
(202) 720–3054

Lutheran

Lutherans Concerned
P.O. Box 10461
Chicago, IL 60610

Mennonite

Brethren/Mennonite Council for
Lesbian and Gay Concerns
P.O. Box 65724
Washington, D.C. 20035
(202) 462–2595

Methodist (United)

Affirmation
P.O. Box 1021
Evanston, IL 60204
(708) 475–0499

Mormon

Affirmation (same name as
United Methodist organization)
P.O. Box 46022
Los Angeles, CA 90046
(213) 255–7251

Pentecostal

National Gay Pentecostal Alliance
P.O. Box 1391
Schenectady, NY 12301
(518) 372–6001

Presbyterians

Presbyterians for Lesbian/Gay
Concerns
P.O. Box 38
New Brunswick, NJ 08903
(201) 846–1510

Seventh Day Adventists

Seventh Day Adventist Kinship
International
P.O. Box 7320
Laguna Niguel, CA 92607
(213) 876–2076

Unitarian Universalists

Office of Lesbian, Bisexual and
Gay Concerns
25 Beacon Street
Boston, MA 02108
(617) 742–2100

United Church of Christ

United Church Coalition for
Lesbian and Gay Concerns
5933 Holmes
Kansas City, MO 64110

RECOMMENDED BOOKS

Individuals who want to deepen their knowledge of the lesbian, gay, bisexual, and transgender community can do so by drawing from the following list of readings.

The general categories represented in the list are:

Family and Friends

- Gay, Lesbian, and Bisexual Relatives and Friends—the books in this category focus on the concerns of heterosexuals who have a friend or relative who is gay or lesbian and are wondering how best to respond.

Community

- Coming Out/General Issues—books on acceptance and the process of coming out are included here.

- Gay and Lesbian History—these are books on the history of the gay community.

- Gay and Lesbian Parenting—these books offer useful information to gay and lesbian parents.

- Aging Issues—these books focus on the concerns of aging gay men and lesbians.

- Legal Issues—these are primers on legal concerns and the rights of gays and lesbians.

- AIDS—these books deal with AIDS.

Workplace

- Sexual Orientation in the Workplace—a list of books providing helpful information on creating an all-inclusive workplace.

Religious and Spiritual

▓ Homosexuality and Religion—the books in this section offer thorough and careful considerations of the challenge many face in reconciling religious beliefs with homosexuality,

FAMILY AND FRIENDS

Borhek, M. V. (1979). *My Son Eric: A Mother Struggles to Accept Her Gay Son and Discover Herself.* New York: Pilgrim Press.

Borhek, M. V. (1983). *Coming Out to Parents: A Two-Way Survival Guide for Lesbians and Gay Men and Their Parents.* New York: Pilgrim Press.

Clark, D. (1987). *Loving Someone Gay.* Berkeley, Calif.: Celestial Arts.

Fairchild, B. and Hayward, N. (1979). *Now That You Know: What Every Parent Should Know About Homosexuality.* New York: Harcourt Brace Jovanovich.

Griffin, C. W., Wirth, M. J., and Wirth, A. G. (1986). *Beyond Acceptance: Parents of Lesbians and Gays Talk About Their Experiences.* Engelwood Cliffs, New Jersey: Prentice-Hall

COMMUNITY

Coming Out/General Issues

Clark, D. (1979). *Living Gay.* Millbrae, Calif.: Celestial Arts.

Duberman, M. (1993). *Stonewall.* New York: Dutton.

Isay, R. (1989). *Being Homosexual: Gay Men and Their Development.* New York: Farrar, Straus, Giroux.

McNaught, B. (1988). *On Being Gay.* New York: St. Martin's Press.

Rothblum, E. D., Cole, E. (1989). *Loving Boldly—Lesbianism: Affirming Nontraditional Roles.* New York: Haworth Press.

Troiden, R. R. (1988). *Gay and Lesbian Identity: A Sociological Analysis.* Dix Hills, New York: General Hall.

Unks, Gerald, ed. (1995). *The Gay Teen: Educational Practice and Theory for Lesbian, Gay, and Bisexual Adolescents.* New York: Routledge.

Gay and Lesbian History

Katz, J. N. (1992—revised edition). *Gay American History: Lesbians and Gay Men in the U.S.A.* New York: Meridian.

Liebman, M. (1992). *Coming Out Conservative.* San Francisco: Chronicle Books.

Marcus, E. (1992). *Making History.* New York: St Martin's Press.

Penelope, J., and Valentine, S. (1990). *Finding the Lesbians: Personal Accounts from Around the World.* Freedom, Calif.: Crossing Press.

Gay and Lesbian Parenting

Barret, R. L., and Robinson, B. E. (1990). *Gay Fathers.* Lexington, Mass.: Lexington Books.

Bozett, F. W. (1987). *Gay and Lesbian Parents.* New York: Praeger

Pollack, S., and Vaughn, J. (1987). *Politics of the Heart: A Lesbian Parenting Anthology.* Ithaca, New York: Firebrand Books.

Aging Issues

Berger, R. (1982). *Gay and Gray: The Older Homosexual Man.* Boston: Alyson Press.

Kehoe, M. (1989). *Lesbians Over 60 Speak for Themselves.* New York: Haworth Press.

Legal Issues

Hunter, N. D. et al. (1992). *The Rights of Lesbians and Gay Men: The Basic ACLU Guide to a Gay Person's Rights.* New York: New Press.

Rubenstein, W. B. (1993). *Lesbians, Gay Men, and the Law.* New York: New Press.

AIDS

Banta, W. F. (1993). *AIDS in the Workplace.* New York: Lexington.

Delaney, M. and Goldblum, P. (1987). *Strategies for Survival: A Gay Men's Health Manual for the Age of AIDS.* New York: St Martin's Press.

Hunter, N.D. and Rubenstein, W. B. (1992). *AIDS Agenda: Emerging Issues in Civil Rights.* New York: New Park Press.

Huber, J. T. (1992). *How to Find Information about AIDS.* Binghampton, NY:

Harrington Land, H. (1992). *A Complete Guide to Psychosocial Intervention.* Milwaukee: FSA Publishers.

WORKPLACE

Diamant, L. (1993). *Homosexual Issues in the Workplace.* New York: Taylor & Francis.

Ellis, A. L., and Riggle, E. D. (1996). *Sexual Identity on the Job: Issues and Services.* Binghampton, New York: Haworth Press.

McNaught, B. (1993). *Gay Issues in the Workplace.* New York: St. Martin's Press.

Powers, B., and Ellis, A. (1995). *A Manager's Guide to Sexual Orientation in the Workplace.* New York: Routledge.

Winfield L., and Spidman, S. (1995). *Straight Talk About Gays in the Workplace.* Washington D.C.: AMACOM.

Woods, J., and Lucas, J. (1993). *The Corporate Closet.* New York: The Free Press

RELGIOUS AND SPIRITUAL

Boswell, J. (1980). *Christianity, Social Tolerance, and Homosexuality.* Chicago: University of Chicago Press.

Denman, R. M. (1990). *Let My People In.* New York: William Morrow.

Hilton, B. (1992). *Can Homophobia be Cured? Wrestling with Questions that Challenge the Church.* Nashville, Tenn.: Abingdon Press.

McNeil, J. H. (1988). *The Church and the Homosexual.* Boston: Beacon Press.

Mollenkott, V., and Scanzoni, L. (1978). *Is the Homosexual My Neighbor? Another Christian View.* San Francisco: Harper & Row.